Jocoserious Joyce

The Florida James Joyce Series

Jocoserious Joyce

The Fate of Folly in *Ulysses*

by Robert H. Bell

University Press of Florida
Gainesville/Tallahassee/Tampa/Boca Raton
Pensacola/Orlando/Miami/Jacksonville

Paperback edition published 1996 by University Press of Florida
First published 1991 by Cornell University Press
Copyright 1991 by Cornell University

Printed in the United States of America on acid-free paper

01 00 99 98 97 96   6 5 4 3 2 1

Library of Congress Cataloging-in-Publication Data
Bell, Robert H. (Robert Huntley), 1946-
Jocoserious Joyce: the fate of folly in Ulysses / Robert H. Bell.
     p. cm.–(Florida James Joyce series)
   Originally published: Ithaca: Cornell University Press, 1991.
   Includes bibliographical references (p.) and index.
   ISBN 0-8130-1387-9 (alk. paper)
   1. Joyce, James, 1882-1941. Ulysses. 2. Folly in literature.
I. Title. II. Series.
PR6019.O9U6254   1996
823'.912–dc20   95-36524

Excerpt from *Winnie-the-Pooh* by A. A. Milne. Copyright 1926 by E. P.
Dutton, renewed 1954 by A. A. Milne. Reprinted by permission of the
publisher, Dutton Children's Books, a division of Penguin Books USA Inc.

The University Press of Florida is the scholarly publishing agency for the
State University System of Florida, comprised of Florida A & M University,
Florida Atlantic University, Florida International University, Florida State
University, University of Central Florida, University of Florida, University of
North Florida, University of South Florida, and University of West Florida.

University Press of Florida
15 Northwest 15th Street
Gainesville, FL 32611

For Ilona

Sole partner and sole part of all these joys,

Dearer thyself than all . . .

Contents

Foreword to the Paperback Edition

Part of the original design of Florida's James Joyce Series was to keep a few of the landmark Joyce studies in print and accessible to the growing audience for Joyce scholarship. *Jocoserious Joyce* is one of these: an informative and entertaining treatment of the dual nature of Joyce's comedy in *Ulysses,* which attempts a rectification of the "ordinary imbalance between such common dichotomies as the ridiculous and the sublime, the profane and the sacred, and the jocose and the serious." This duality of composition and design provides Robert Bell with a metaphor for Joyce's intent as well as methodology, informing subtly a whole new system of perceived meaning for *Ulysses.* The book is inevitably a consideration of the *joco* or comic against a traditional, critically overstated background of the serious. The embellishments of Bell's arguments, consisting often of a number of examples for a given point, regularly put new and delightful twists on passages that have never been examined under a comic lens. We are delighted to include in our list this lasting contribution to Joyce studies.

Zack Bowen
University of Miami

Preface to the Paperback Edition (1996)

One of the joyous consequences of spending a good part of my adult life with *Ulysses* is that is has so enriched my relationships with teachers, colleagues, friends, and students.

I discovered *Ulysses* as an undergraduate taking Professor Peter Bien's great Dartmouth course on Modern European Fiction. He challenged us to read *Ulysses* with the imaginative energy it deserves: "If you do, for the next few weeks you'll be in Dublin, June 16, 1904." By the time we had finished *Ulysses,* I had decided to become a teacher, though I wasn't yet equipped to understand my teacher's emphasis on "Joyce's ability to stand back with humor from all the pain and horror."

Thirty years after Peter Bien's inspiring lectures, he sent me a seven-page, single-spaced critique of the manuscript of *Jocoserious Joyce.* No matter what happens to this project, I remember feeling strongly, I had great fun writing it—and Professor Bien thought it was worth doing.

It is a special pleasure to murmur name upon name, to acknowledge the many people who helped me. I'm immensely fortunate to have splendid colleagues at Williams; my friends Peter Berek, Larry Graver, Suzanne Graver, and John Reichert read grant applications, wrote recommendations, sustained and encouraged me in myriad ways. With unstinting generosity, Don Gifford, author of the essential *Ulysses Annotated*, corrected my entire manuscript. I also benefitted greatly from the painstaking, probing critique of Clara Park.

Other dear friends helped me enormously. From our under-graduate days, William Dowling has never let me down, or off the hook; it was he who delivered the unwelcome news that my first draft was only a commentary which needed to be put aside and remade into an argument. Since our work together in Reuben Brower's Humanities 6 course, Philip Weinstein has profoundly enabled my projects, personal and professional. Michael Ferber gave me astute, contrary arguments about the text we so love to teach, and much else. John Gordon, who in 1969 inveigled Harry Levin to give us an independent tutorial on Joyce, read every word and set me right, or at least closer, on scores of points large and small.

Ilona Bell sacrificed huge amounts of time and energy taken from her own teaching, research, and writing, not to mention our daughters Kaitlin and Amanda—just to mention them—to critique draft after draft. A ruthless editor, she is Milton's ideal helpmate. Kaitlin and Amanda kept me laughing, reminding me not to take the jocose too seriously.

A National Endowment for the Humanities fellowship for college teachers and sabbatical leaves from Williams College gave me the time to finish this book. The research was conducted at Widener Library of Harvard and at Sawyer Library of Williams College, where I was especially aided by Lee Dalzell. My student research assistants, Anne Mallory, Rob Newman, Larry Sprung, and Meg Wildrick, were very helpful. Edith Baras and Anne Just gave me sustained and extremely able editorial assistance.

Another joy of working on Joyce has been meeting Joyceans. At my first Joyce conference, John Gordon introduced me to Zack Bowen, who was completing his own study of *Ulysses as a Comic Novel*, and who instantly welcomed me as a colleague and co-conspirator; it was the first of many expressions of kindness, demonstrating why Zack is so very warmly admired by fellow Joyceans.

I had great luck with the publication of my manuscript, thanks to the Boon of the Two Bernies. The keen support of Bernie Kendler at Cornell University Press expedited my project. I thank him and his staff at Cornell University Press for making my whole experience with them so pleasant, and for giving permission to publish *Jocoserious Joyce* in paperback.

The first reader of my manuscript for Cornell, Bernard Benstock, was someone then known to me only as a legendary Joycean, a great scholar and critic, and a renowned teacher of teachers. From the time we met, until his sudden death in 1994, I regarded Bernie not only with warm gratitude and profound respect but deep affection. I never met anyone who knew more, or knew better how to enjoy life, than Berni Benstock. Joyous himself, he was the cause of joy in other people. It gratifies me that he felt some of this about *Jocoserious Joyce*.

Acknowledgments

It is a great pleasure to acknowledge those who encouraged, corrected, and assisted me. A National Endowment for the Humanities fellowship and sabbatical leaves from Williams College gave me the time to finish the book.

Thanks to Edith Baras, Peter Berek, Lee Dalzell, Larry Graver, Suzanne Graver, John Reichert, and to my research assistants, Anne Just, Anne Mallory, Rob Newman, Larry Sprung, and Meg Wildrick.

Special thanks to those who gave me that most valuable gift, a critical reading: Ilona Bell, Peter Bien, Zack Bowen, William C. Dowling, Michael Ferber, Don Gifford, John Gordon, Clara Park, and Philip Weinstein.

I am grateful to The Society of Authors, Random House, Inc., and Bodley Head Limited for permission to quote passages of Joyce's *Ulysses*, edited by Hans Walter Gabler, copyright © 1986 by Random House, Inc., and to Peter Bien for allowing me to quote from his translation of C. P. Cavafy's "Ithaca." Portions of Chapter 1 appeared in different form in "Mercurial Malachi and Jocoserious Joyce," *Modern Language Quarterly* 48 (December 1987): 364–77.

R. H. B.

Abbreviations of Works Cited

Primary Works by James Joyce

Note: Most references to these texts are identified by parenthetical reference to page number. For *Ulysses*, episode and line numbers are given, and for *Finnegans Wake*, page and line numbers.

Ulysses   *Ulysses: The Corrected Text*, ed. Hans Walter Gabler with Wolf-
      hard Steppe and Claus Melchior (New York: Vintage Books, 1986).
FW   *Finnegans Wake* (New York: Viking Press, 1968).
P   *A Portrait of the Artist as a Young Man: Text, Criticism, and Notes*, ed.
      Chester G. Anderson (New York: Viking Press, 1975).
D   *Dubliners: Text, Criticism, Notes*, ed. Robert Scholes and A. Walton
      Litz (New York: Viking Press, 1975).
CW   *The Critical Writings*, ed. Ellsworth Mason and Richard Ellmann
      (New York: Viking Press, 1964).
L   *Letters of James Joyce*, Volume 1, ed. Stuart Gilbert (New York:
      Viking Press, 1957; reissued with corrections, 1966); Volumes 2 and
      3, ed. Richard Ellmann (New York: Viking Press, 1966).
SL   *Selected Letters of James Joyce*, ed. Richard Ellmann (New York:
      Viking Press, 1975).

Frequently Cited Secondary Materials

Budgen   Frank Budgen, *James Joyce and the Making of "Ulysses"*
      (Bloomington: Indiana University Press, 1960).
Ellmann   Richard Ellmann, *James Joyce* (Oxford: Oxford University
      Press, 1982).
Erasmus   Desiderius Erasmus, *The Praise of Folly*, trans. Clarence H.
      Miller (New Haven: Yale University Press, 1979).

Abbreviations of Works Cited

Gifford   *"Ulysses" Annotated: Notes for James Joyce's "Ulysses,"* ed. Don Gifford and Robert J. Seidman (Berkeley: University of California Press, 1988). This is the revised and expanded edition of Gifford's *Notes for Joyce* (New York: E. P. Dutton, 1974).

Hart and Hayman   *James Joyce's "Ulysses": Critical Essays,* ed. Clive Hart and David Hayman (Berkeley: University of California Press, 1974).

S. Joyce   Stanislaus Joyce, *My Brother's Keeper: James Joyce's Early Years*, ed. Richard Ellmann (New York: Viking Press, 1969).

All references to the Bible are to the King James Version and are specified by parenthetical reference to book, chapter, and verse.

All references to Shakespeare are specified by parenthetical reference to the play, act, scene, and line numbers in *The Complete Works of Shakespeare*, revised edition, ed. Hardin Craig and David Bevington (Glenview, Ill.: Scott, Foresman, 1973).

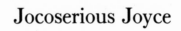

Jocoserious Joyce

"In risu veritas"

—Joyce, revising the adage

Introduction: Why Does
Virag Unscrew His Head?

"Folly. Persist"
9:42

Like Stephen Dedalus, whose "strange name seemed to him a prophecy" (*P* 168), Joyce regarded the origin of his name, from the French for "happiness," as a sign of his high calling; he once defined the purpose of literature as the revelation of eternal joy and considered joy "the emotion in comedy which makes it a higher form than tragedy" (Ellmann 379). Joyce always insisted that *Ulysses* "is fundamentally a humorous work,"[1] and he regularly complained that critics failed to see its comedy. In its range and variety of comic strategies the novel is, as in so many other ways, "a kind of encyclopedia" (*SL* 270)—so in this study of *Ulysses*, "Joyce" signifies less the originating, shaping imagination than a playground of contending comic figures: jokers, punsters, humorists, clowns, satirists, parodists, farceurs, raconteurs, fools, and quacks. In the literature of folly the word *farrago* has resonated ever since Juvenal characterized his satires as a hodgepodge or confused mixture; the word derives from the Latin for a mixed grain or fodder fed to cattle. Undoubtedly remembering Juvenal, Erasmus's erudite clown Folly also characterizes her declamation as a farrago: "you are crazy if you

---

[1]Arthur Power, *Conversations with James Joyce*, ed. Clive Hart (Chicago: University of Chicago Press, 1982), 89.

1

think I still have in mind what I have said, after pouring forth such a torrent of jumbled words" (Erasmus 138).[2] Joyceans will recall, in that other medley of discourses given to cattle, "Oxen of the Sun," the reference to "this chaffering allincluding most farraginous chronicle" (14:1412). The terms and puns aptly characterize Joyce's encyclopedic work, a receptive host to many different voices, so that its world is polyphonic, "allincluding" and "chaffering"—which picks up the farraginous implications of *chaff* and includes the old meaning of teasing, jesting, or bantering.

Ulysses is still too often read as though it were essentially a representational novel, depicting characters in realistic situations. In his emphasis upon "the permanent realities of human life," for instance, S. L. Goldberg implicitly places *Ulysses* in the line of George Eliot, Lawrence, and Conrad: "*Ulysses* is most impressive as a criticism of life . . . in its comprehensive and uncensorious vision of humanity, and its irony richest . . . when it responds to the complexity of its object, rather than in its sharp hostilities and rejections."[3] As Goldberg's brilliant analysis shows, one can contemplate and love *Ulysses* in these terms, just as one can admire the *Book of Kells* without troubling oneself very much about the marginal exfoliations. To do so exclusively, however, is to overlook or undervalue the follies (sometimes marginal, sometimes central)—the absurdity, virtuosity, and slapdash skittle-knocking—that derive not from the great tradition but from the great clowns: Cervantes, Rabelais, Fielding, and Sterne.

Generally, readers tend to value humorous material in a work of literature more highly when they can tie it to something patently substantial, such as Hal and Falstaff playing King as a rehearsal for the Prince's forthcoming interview with his father, or Hamlet's bantering with the gravediggers as evidence of tragic equanimity. Much Joycean humor, like Bloom's recovery at the end of "Hades" or Molly's hymn to nature, is in this sense conventional, serving a traditional comic vision. Nonetheless, we must always be prepared to take the comedy of *Ulysses* in two ways, not just ambiguously but

[2]The Latin, here rendered "jumbled words," is *farraginem*. In *Magnetick Lady* (I.7.19–20), Ben Jonson mentions "A farrago / Or a made dish in Court: a thing of nothing."

[3]S. L. Goldberg, *The Classical Temper: A Study of James Joyce's "Ulysses"* (New York: Barnes & Noble, 1961), 142.

also oxymoronically, as "jocoserious" (17:369). Persistently, Joyce rectifies the ordinary imbalance between such common dichotomies as the ridiculous and the sublime, the profane and the sacred, and the jocose and the serious, empowering the underprivileged term and often implying that apparent opposites must be seen simultaneously—in words from *Finnegans Wake,* "by the coincidance of their contraries reamalgamerge in that indentity of undiscernibles" (*FW* 49:36–50:1).[4]

Yet if *Ulysses* is the playful work of "Jocoserious Joyce," its jocose and serious elements are unstable, often reamalgamerged yet sometimes distinct—for in comedy, identity itself is a problematic, funny idea, things being both similar and different. Naturally *Ulysses* jokes about the distinction, because, for Joyce, categories are themselves an object of humorous assault: à propos Milly and the cat, the Ithacan narrator concludes, "their differences were similar" (17:907–8). Some Joycean humor is evidently gratuitous and profoundly disorienting, beyond or beneath "the permanent realities of human life," at least as defined by formalist or Arnoldian critics: its catalogs and lists, its in-jokes and sideswipes, its sniggers and guffaws, its manic proliferations, nonsense, and highjinks, the stuff that is rarely explicated in new critical studies or highlighted by students' yellow markers. At one point in "Circe," in what strikes me as the most intriguing stage direction since "Exit, pursued by a bear," Virag "*unscrews his head in a trice and holds it under his arm*" (15:2636). Not to be silenced by a mere technicality, Virag, or rather his head, quacks. *Ulysses* devotes at least as much loving attention to such antics—clowning that is an end in itself, or a homage to folly—as it does to the "eternal affirmation of the spirit of man in literature" (17:30).

When *Ulysses* gives free rein or fool's licence to the discourse, readers may try to pierce through the clowning to a central core, a process that the text sometimes resists and occasionally repudiates utterly. Even critics as highly attuned to Joycean comedy as Richard Ellmann, Karen Lawrence, Marilyn French, and James Maddox remain most comfortable with Joycean folly in the service of the

---

[4]Cf. Joyce citing Coleridge's gloss of Bruno: "Every power in nature or in spirit must evolve an opposite as the sole condition and means of its manifestation; and every opposition is, therefore, a tendency to reunion" (*CW* 134).

serious, what Maddox terms "the structures of personality which make ethics possible and operative in the world."[5] Though many whimsical interpolations—such as the Cyclopsean seance or the botched type in Dignam's obituary—have broad or ingenious implications, in other riffing sequences, like the catalog of tree-names, the sense of proportion is manifestly out of whack; caprice, free play, and absurdity run rampant, only tenuously related to plot, character, and design. Especially in the second half of *Ulysses,* as everybody has noticed and many have deplored, the virtuoso manner competes with the "novelistic" matter. If our conception of the vital matter is the development of character, we will naturally be frustrated and disappointed, and we may judge Joyce guilty of self-indulgence or "irresponsible (and nasty) trifling."[6] Robert M. Adams's *Surface and Symbol: The Consistency of James Joyce's "Ulysses"* (1967) makes a provocative critique of precisely these extraneous antics, and does so with uncommon erudition and insight. Yet a great many of the deficiencies upon which Adams elaborates could be regarded, topsy-turvy, as ludic triumphs. Adams approaches the text with essentially new critical premises that prize formal patterning, selection and discrimination, controlled connotation and implication, ultimate unity of tone, and a coherent standard of comprehension and evaluation. For Adams, as for Goldberg, "the proper novelistic qualities" of *Ulysses* should be "the moving and complex confrontation of Bloom, Stephen, Molly, and the icy void";[7] that is, the drama of character and fate, rather than the "proliferent continuance" (14:15) of language.

But if we regard *Ulysses* as a book in praise of folly, an encyclopedia of comedy, as intent on humorous performance as on conventional fictive representation, its excesses become splendidly inventive pirouettes, a dazzling and daring performance. In Lockean terms, comic associations are often made by wit rather than by judgment. To characterize this antic strain in *Ulysses,* one might adapt T. S. Eliot's description of the modern poet's use of rhyme and meter:

[5]James H. Maddox, Jr., *Joyce's "Ulysses" and the Assault upon Character* (New Brunswick, N.J.: Rutgers University Press, 1978), 203–4.

[6]F. R. Leavis's famous dismissal of *Tristram Shandy,* in *The Great Tradition: George Eliot, Henry James, Joseph Conrad* (London: Chatto and Windus, 1955), 2. The importance of Leavis to Goldberg is obvious.

[7]Robert M. Adams, *Surface and Symbol: The Consistency of James Joyce's "Ulysses"* (New York: Oxford University Press, 1967), 248.

sometimes plotting and characterization are bits of meat that the burglar throws to the watchdog while he goes about his business. With surprising consistency, folly provides a means of comprehending and discussing many of the book's least appreciated and most baffling elements. "A catchword is enough to set me off" (*L* 1, 147), Joyce remarked, moving with increasing self-consciousness, boldly, righteously, even recklessly, toward a gospel of folly. When *Finnegans Wake* provoked widespread disbelief, even from patrons, family, and admirers, Joyce took comfort in Blake's proverb of hell: "If the fool would persist in his folly he would become wise." From the time this conviction bolsters Stephen for his Shakespeare lecture, *Ulysses* embraces that Blakean credo: folly becomes a principle and a technique, a means of defying conventions and authority, and very often an organizing principle of the novel.

Elevating rather than regretting or excusing folly stimulates us to view seemingly excessive or extraneous material as part of a consistent comic enterprise. A blatant fool like D. B. Murphy may deserve more respect than critics usually give him, as when Ellmann succumbs to seriousness by judging him in misleadingly earnest, Bloomian terms: "What Murphy purveys is a fiction within a fiction, based on an unspoken aesthetic theory, rival to Stephen's, that the novel is a Munchausen performance. With falsimilitude Murphy would ambush the verisimilitude that is claimed in *Ulysses,* and turn Aristotle's imitation of nature into mere fakery. The sailor is spokesman for false art, for art as *gamesmanship.*"[8] But "Sirens," "Oxen," "Cyclops," "Circe," and "Eumaeus" might all be characterized as Munchausen performances, and a good deal of Joyce's art as gamesmanship. Ellmann posits precisely the false dichotomies that *Ulysses* dissolves: "the sailor would change the impulse of art to create into the pseudo-artistic impulse to gull." The rejection of Murphy attests that *Ulysses* is "not a confidence trick" but "sincerity." The opposite seems to me more nearly true: Antic Joyce cherishes confidence tricks, games, gulling, concealment, impostures, and horseplay, even inviting an excreting horse to make a comic point. Creating and gulling, and sincerity and fooling, are not always distinct in this work so "carried away by a wave of folly"

[8]Richard Ellmann, *Ulysses on the Liffey,* 2d. ed. (New York: Oxford University Press, 1973), 155.

(16:1387–88), so frequently following "the *fools rush in where angels* principle" (16:1867–68).

It would be ungenerous, not to mention foolish, to pretend that my book represents the first time *Ulysses* has been read jocoseriously.[9] Like Milton or Shakespeare studies, Joyce criticism is always a collaborative enterprise. If I stress the ways Joyce's funny, perplexing book has been and is often interpreted in unsatisfying terms, too solemnly or sentimentally, I am also mindful that my own project is made possible by many other critics. Frank Budgen's *James Joyce and the Making of "Ulysses"* (1934) saw the novel as, first and last, a great human comedy. Hugh Kenner's *Dublin's Joyce* (1956) argued powerfully for an ironic separation between Joyce and Stephen Dedalus, for the "double vision" of *Ulysses,* its simultaneous vision and parodic revision of Dublin, and for the vitality of its Irish humor. Richard Ellmann's *James Joyce* (1959) never underestimates the importance of the author's "favorite disposition, comedy," and depicts him working "in humanity's name and comedy's method" (Ellmann 127, 379). More recently, several critics have commented acutely on aspects of Joycean comedy. David Hayman's article "Forms of Folly in Joyce: A Study of Clowning in *Ulysses*" and his book *"Ulysses": The Mechanics of Meaning* (1970) demonstrate Joyce's "growing reliance on . . . clowns and farce"[10] and provide the fruitful conception of "a behind-the-scenes persona like the shaper of pantomimes"[11] whom Hayman terms "the arranger." Among the many other critics whose thinking, though not principally concerned with comedy, has stimulated me are Karen Lawrence, Fritz Senn, and James Maddox. The current construction of "Post-Structuralist Joyce," with its love of free play, infinite supplement, and sliding signifiers in some ways advances the cause of

---

[9]Cf. Harvey Window's tribute to "the pioneering works of Ogle, Smythe, Bunker, and Wart. No subsequent treatment of *Pooh*, including the present one, can afford to pass by the profound discoveries of these scholars. It is, then, with a sense of my own temerity—if not, indeed, of outright rashness—that I assert that Ogle, Smythe, Bunker, and Wart have completely missed the point of *Pooh*." See Frederick C. Crews, *The Pooh Perplex* (New York: E. P. Dutton, 1963), 3–4.

[10]David Hayman, "Forms of Folly in Joyce: A Study of Clowning in *Ulysses*," *ELH* 34 (1967): 260.

[11]Hayman, *"Ulysses": The Mechanics of Meaning*, rev. ed. (Madison: University of Wisconsin Press, 1982), 123.

comedy, but also, as I will explain, threatens to throw out the baby with the bath water. Several writers energetically contend that *Ulysses* is, after all, a book and only a book, and that it knows it. What seems to me still debatable is the attitude *Ulysses* exhibits toward its status as artifice; I see *Ulysses* neither languishing in the prison house of language, nor dismayed by the anxiety of influence, but instead reveling in contrariety and insufficiency, sporting in a fun house, enjoying a "high grade ha" (4:69–70).

Himself one of our most heroic literary figures, Joyce persisted in folly and survived the miseries of neglect, poverty, imbecilic publishers, eye ailments, Lucia's illness, and world conflict. Nora once complained that she couldn't sleep nights because "Jim is writing at his book. . . . I go to bed and then that man sits in the next room and continues laughing about his own writing. And then I knock at the door, and I say, 'Now, Jim, stop writing or stop laughing.'"[12] When *Ulysses* appeared, Joyce put on his long face to lament, "The pity is the public will demand and find a moral in my book, or worse they may take it in some serious way, and on the honor of a gentleman, there is not one single serious line in it" (Ellmann 523–24). Here we have the jocoserious assertion that refuses to settle the hash: both the authoritative guarantee of what is and is not "in my book," and the playful, almost self-defeating renunciation—vowing solemnly by the thing he values least, "the honor of a gentleman." Though most happy moving shuttlewise, Joyce was genuinely exasperated by the inability of his readers to enjoy what he'd written. Of Jung, he said, "He seems to have read *Ulysses* from first to last without one smile. The only thing to do in such a case is to change one's drink" (Ellmann 628). Having originally characterized himself as the oppressively grim Stephen Dedalus, even once publishing under the pseudonym "Stephen Daedalus" (*sic*), he later styled himself "Jeems Jokes" (*SL* 316) and reveled in his role as "the masterbilker here" (*FW* 111:21).

Such pendulations and revaluations, doubling back to reconsider one's earlier perspectives, are crucial to the process of reading *Ulysses*. I confess that originally, and for many years, my native optimism produced a satisfyingly life-affirming interpretation, which I now

---

[12]"An Interview with Carola Giedion-Welcker and Maria Jolas," ed. Richard M. Kain, *James Joyce Quarterly* 11 (1974): 96.

view as insufficiently responsive to the novel's fiercer, more hectic energies.[13] Like Samuel Johnson's old schoolmate, "I tried to be philosophical, but cheerfulness kept breaking in." My more unsettled but, I think, more accurate argument makes Joycean comedy less homogenous and coherent, more volatile and antic. Both the variety and the primacy of Joycean comedy are suggested by the Sterne voice in "Oxen of the Sun": "How mingled and imperfect are all our sublunary joys!" (14:770–71). Even without knowing how much Joyce admired Sterne,[14] we might underline this utterance as one that characterizes the world of *Ulysses:* a self-reference in which the author crows his own name, a fair name, in the pun that insists on being heard at the end of the sentence.

I hope the tenor, method, and direction of my argument, elaborated in the following four chapters, are evident from these prefatory observations. Chapter 1, "Types of Folly," delineates the configuration of major characters, seen as humorous figures and evaluated on folly's terms. I challenge the assumption that Buck is a foil for the author's surrogate. Instead, I treat Buck as a brilliant clown in the Shakespearean tradition, as a source of harsh truths and a lover of folly. He provides a valid satiric critique of Stephen, and it is his spirit, not Stephen's, that seems closer to the brash voices of the book's middle and late episodes. Conversely, I view Stephen less as a privileged protagonist than as a displaced Malvolio or Jaques, often at odds with the novel's prevailing comic ethos: in other words, a kind of fool, a proper object of mockery, who might do well to heed his adversary Buck more attentively. I construe Bloom as another kind of fool and the jocoserious hero. Generally Bloom articulates the comic (as opposed to Buck's satiric) perspective, especially in his resilience, tolerance, corporeality, petty follies, and splendid magnanimity. In ways I both trace and query, Bloom becomes the novel's center of value, progressing from a simple fool to a holy one. Molly I depict as a comic heroine, a sublimely ridiculous figure, and I consider her episode a fitting closure for what we felicitously call

[13]The most compelling "optimistic" argument I have read is Zack Bowen, *"Ulysses" as a Comic Novel* (Syracuse: Syracuse University Press, 1989)— especially the introduction.

[14]"Did you ever read Laurence Sterne?" Joyce asked Gillet (Ellmann 534). Budgen tells us that Joyce "always held that [Swift and Sterne] ought to change names" and compares Joyce's humor to "the bright mocking laughter of Sterne" (Budgen 214, 72).

"the body" of the text. She is crucial to Joyce's comic project because her body is the ultimate ground of being, and because her amusing contradictions represent the ultimate ascent of folly.

Variously manifest in the characters, the novel's powerfully comic energies are always contradictory. Chapter 2, "The Generic Conditions," focuses on several paradoxical patterns of Joycean comedy, consistent tensions that provide both persistent humor and continual flux. Generally, but not without contending claims, we regard Dear Dirty Dublin with comic "plenitude of sufferance" (14:863). Inhabitants of this comic world have powerful vitality, capacity for recuperation, and means of connection, in each case threatened or balanced by opposing proclivities. A loosely scientific term, what Bloom calls "magnetic influence" (13:984–85), is the jocoserious analog of conventional comic confluence, drawing characters together in strange and risible ways. Another insistent comic rhythm is the pattern of revival, visible most obviously in Bloom's temperament, and more subtly in the structure of episodes and in jokes, allusions, and signs. Yet these tendencies toward connection and revival are balanced by equally potent comic laws: descent—"Up like a rocket, down like a stick" (13:895)—and frustration—"Incomplete" (8:743). I contend that hopes and signs of impending reunion and regeneration are stoked in the early chapters, only to be severely qualified and mocked. In this sense, too, readers of the novel are deliberately fooled, continually tempted to magnify a throwaway or scant a "visible luminous sign" (17:1171).

"Carried Away by a Wave of Folly," my third chapter, gives particular and sympathetic treatment to those puzzling, objectionable, often slighted elements of folly. It is these antics that complicate and sometimes threaten the more stable comic values represented by Bloom and Molly. As the novel progresses, narration is often entrusted to a flamboyant trickster, or showoff, close kin to Buck. "Sirens," for instance, is told by a manic maestro, whose echoing, mocking manner seems more concerned with his own performance than with Bloom's plight or the reader's struggle. "Cyclops" splits into two dominant voices, which I identify as that of the Satirist and the Parodist; while they seem to collaborate on the mockery of Bloom, and most readers perceive ironic praise of the hero, I stress how the episode's sympathies with folly make perception and evaluation extremely mercurial. "Oxen of the Sun" is in some ways an epitome of the novel in its mélange of competing, contrary voices and its satire of authorial authority: its motto is "proliferent continuance" (14:15) not because it endorses procreation but because it disseminates meanings so antically. "Circe" is the apex or nadir of folly, a saturnalian festival or absurd farce where anything might pop up, in some familiar comic and satiric patterns, both enriching and confounding our understanding. To an extent in "Circe," and especially in "Sirens" and "Eumaeus," Joyce tests the limits of folly by impersonating fools so thoroughly that he provokes the opprobrium heaped on all great fools, though such inspired fatuity is as crucial to the novel as its initially more conventional kinds of comedy.

The fourth chapter, "Follies of 'Indentity,'" addresses personal identity as both a traditional comic conundrum and a particularly central jocoserious subject. I investigate the comic demolition of Bloom's identity and contest the recent tendency to regard it as a definitive philosophic argument. The annihilation of selfhood in *Ulysses* is never conclusive and always comical, for it is carried out by a series of madcap and disreputable, though alluring and compelling, narrators. My conclusion is an extended exploration of the disorienting yet reassuring presence of the implied author as an illustration of comic "indentity" (*FW* 49:36), like the neologism itself, simultaneously negated and affirmed. The antic principles I have delineated also apply, emphatically, to the author and reader of the text, so that we are all inextricably, joyously bound in a web of folly.

Post-Script: "Strolling through the street one day, Joyce laughed and said to me: 'Some people were up at our flat last night and we were talking about Irish wit and humour. And this morning my wife said to me, 'What is all this about Irish wit and humour? Have we any book in the house with any of it in? I'd like to read a page or two'" (Budgen 37).

1

Types of Folly

Mercurial Malachi

Most readers of *Ulysses*, even many of those who emphasize its comedy, are extremely wary of Buck Mulligan.[1] Entering the novel via *A Portrait of the Artist as a Young Man*, one naturally assumes Stephen's perspective, implicitly privileging his values and denigrating Buck's. Since we never enter Buck's consciousness and he remains a static, flat character, always spouting quips like "Redheaded women buck like goats" (1:706), it is understandable that he is often regarded as a one-dimensional foil for Stephen. This narrow conception of his role seems to have been given authorial sanction by Joyce's remark to Budgen that Buck "should begin to pall on the reader as the day goes on" (Budgen 116). It is my contention that Buck is far more complicated and important to the novel than Joyce acknowledged or is generally recognized. Buck's

---

[1]Frank Budgen hears a rare "note of condemnation" in Joyce's treatment of Buck (Budgen 72). Richard Ellmann seems to accept Stephen's view of Buck as "brutal and cruel," a "spirit of denial" (Ellmann 379 and 265). A third powerful advocate of Joyce's comic vision is David Hayman, whose *"Ulysses": The Mechanics of Meaning* argues that Buck "has earned the fool's privileges and his license goes unpunished" (58). Robert M. Adams, in *Surface and Symbol* (46), says that Joyce wants to show Buck as "No Good" and Stephen as "All Right." James H. Maddox, in *Joyce's "Ulysses" and the Assault upon Character* (21), characterizes Mulligan as "the false hero . . . just as the light-heartedly blasphemous Mass he celebrates is a false version of the book's celebration of life."

spirit has surprising affinities with the humor, satire, and playfulness of *Ulysses;* as the novel progresses, the spirit of folly appears increasingly persistent, pervasive, and Buck-like, so much so that Buck himself eventually becomes dispensable.

Buck is felt initially as a potent force, providing the impetus and most of the energy in the opening chapter. If the style of "Telemachus" is "Narrative: Young," as Joyce suggested to Stuart Gilbert,[2] Buck is its *élan vital,* its court jester. He is a gifted clown. Indeed, with his "blithe broadly smiling face" and "eyes, from which he had suddenly withdrawn all shrewd sense, blinking with mad gaiety," Buck is happy to play the fool: "He moved a doll's head to and fro . . . and began to chant in a quiet happy foolish voice" (1:579–83).[3] Like all great clowns, he takes his performance utterly seriously—to the extent that in his curtain raiser, an elaborate parody of the Mass, he does not even need an audience; so meticulous and solemn is his performance that it has the aura of genuine ritual. Using his lather, mirror, and razor as props, he extemporizes brilliantly, like a latter-day Autolycus, that engaging, unreliable "snapper-up of unconsidered trifles . . . littered under Mercury" (*WT:* IV.iii.25–26). Buck is extremely skillful at mockery through imitation; it is he and not Stephen who deserves the epithet "lovely mummer" (1:97).[4] As with Shakespeare, "all events [bring] grist to his mill" (9:748), and as with the clowning of Touchstone, Mercutio, or Feste, a bit of Buck's wit goes a long way.

Still, Buck occupies pride of place, the honor of beginning the book, a strategy no one could suspect Joyce of taking lightly. Twice in the opening episode Buck addresses Stephen as "bard" (1:134, 475). What are the bard's first words? "Tell me, Mulligan" (1:47). Joyce's modern epic echoes the apostrophe of the conventional invocation, with Mulligan replacing the muse of yore; perhaps Buck should be regarded as a sort of muse. Another reading of Buck's position might be that he stands for Joyce, delivering the invocation

[2]Stuart Gilbert, *James Joyce's "Ulysses": A Study,* 2d ed., rev. (New York: Vintage, 1952), 41.

[3]For the time being, I use the terms "clown" and "fool" synonymously, as Shakespeare did.

[4]Later repeated as "peerless mummer" (9:554) and "mournful mummer" (9:1155).

to the work—"*Introibo ad altare Dei*"—and conjuring the hero—
"Come up . . . Come up" (1:8); from his first entrance Buck laugh-
ingly introduces several of the principal themes of the novel. The
subjects that concern Joyce and preoccupy Stephen—Ireland, religion, sex, paternity, and creativity—are mocked by Buck, when he
says, for example, that Stephen "proves by algebra . . . that he himself is the ghost of his own father" (1:555–57) or when he addresses
Stephen as "Japhet in search of a father" (1:561). Even puerile
offerings like the "ballad of joking Jesus" (1:608) and "*A Honey-
moon in the Hand*" (9:1173) burlesque Joycean themes of redemption and communion. Beginning the novel with Buck signals the
significance of folly in *Ulysses*.

Buck's elaborate antics are clearly contrasted to Stephen's "medieval abstrusiosities" (3:320), "morose delectation" (3:385), and
"moody brooding" (1:235–36).[5] One is plump, playful, always in
motley; the other is gaunt, "displeased" (1:13), still in mourning.
Buck seems unshaped by history and free of responsibility, the very
incarnation of play; Stephen is obsessed by the past and burdened
by destiny. One sings "the ballad of joking Jesus"; the other "love's
bitter mystery" (1:253). Much less clear is Joyce's evaluation of
Buck's clowning and Stephen's seriousness. Buck, "laughing with
delight" (1:44), may seem harmless, even appealing—a call to life,
to the here and now, "sunshine merrying over the sea" (1:306). Yet
Joyce's clown, like many of Shakespeare's (including Falstaff), is
also sinister. Buck's curtain raiser, the parody of the Mass, almost
seems to be assisted by supernatural forces; his "ungirdled" dressing
gown "sustained gently behind him on the mild morning air" (1:3–
4) suggests a diabolic tail, and when he whistles, "Two strong shrill
whistles answered" (1:26). Whence the mysterious whistles? As
Buck continues his almost uncanny show for Stephen's benefit, it
becomes more explicitly a black Mass, the diabolic priest citing
Scripture—"body and soul and blood and ouns" (1:21–22)—and
mocking Christ's words to his disciples at the Last Supper. Practically his first word, and one often on his tongue, is "mockery."
Stephen aptly views Buck as one of the "brood of mockers" (9:492);
possibly he remembers Saint John Chrysostom's insistence, in a

---

[5]The first two phrases are bits of Stephen's self-characterization from "Proteus," while "moody brooding" is what Buck tells Stephen to give up.

sermon on Ephesians 4:32–5:1–2, that "great evils do dwell in a soul that is given over to jesting."[6]

We begin to fear and distrust Buck more markedly just when he calls for Stephen's trust. In response, Stephen recalls overhearing Mulligan say, almost a year ago, "*O, it's only Dedalus whose mother is beastly dead*" (1:198–99). Temporarily shaken, Buck delivers (with the exception of his memorized performances) his longest and most revealing speech in the novel, thereby demonstrating why an aspiring artist might dread him like poison. "To me," declares Buck, "it's all a mockery and beastly." A dying mother is not a suffering soul but a rotting dogsbody one should merely "humour . . . till it's over" (1:210–12). Insisting, like Touchstone or Falstaff, that we are all mere body, Buck is a fiendish gargoyle, jeering at spiritual possibility. Buck the scoffer reduces life to its lowest common denominator.

Although Buck is difficult to pin down, his medical student's view has a familiar satiric bias. Buck persistently burlesques everything abstract, ethereal, or idealistic. Nothing is left unchallenged; everything is open to travesty, parody, mockery. The tug downward is insistent in *Ulysses,* and Buck Mulligan is the apostle of gravity (Newtonian, not temperamental). Like Panurge, Touchstone, and Lear's Fool, he sees humanity in its animal aspect—masturbating, defecating, copulating. The satiric emphasis is always pertinent, necessary if not sufficient. To be a clown is not only to arouse disgust but also to court danger and to bring chaos. Because the clown is associated with evil, he is often feared and despised as well as indulged and enjoyed. The fool is usually blasphemous; according to Lydgate, "Chyffe of folys . . . Ys he that nowther god lovethe nor dredethe."[7] The fool is often unaware of the danger and infamy he represents. Since "fool" and "knave" are so often synonymous, his fate is commonly to become an outcast or perpetual exile. Both

---

[6]*An Exposition upon the Epistle of S. Paul the Apostle to the Ephesians* (London, 1581), 224. "Chrysostomos" (1:26) seems to be an interpolated bit of Stephen's consciousness. Baudelaire, in *The Essence of Laughter and Other Essays, Journals, and Letters,* ed. Peter Quennell (New York: Meridian Books, 1956), 117, also connects the comic and the diabolic: "Laughter is satanic, and, therefore, profoundly human."

[7]Quoted by Sandra Billington, " 'Suffer Fools Gladly': The Fool in Medieval England and the Play *Mankind,*" in *The Fool and the Trickster: Studies in Honor of Enid Welsford,* ed. Paul V. A. Williams (Totowa, N.J.: Rowman and Littlefield, 1979), 45.

devils and clowns habitually jeer. In Ben Jonson's *Every Man Out of His Humour*, for instance, the character of Carlo Buffone—described in the dramatis personae as a "publick, scurrilous, and prophane jester" whose "absurd similes will transform any person into deformity" and whose "religion is railing, and . . . discourse ribaldry"—is a stock figure.

Buck Mulligan cannot propose anything positive, like Stephen's "eternal affirmation of the spirit of man in literature" (17:30), because he does not believe in anything—his project is always mockery. Buck's antic spirit subverts everything on reflex. No sooner has the old milkmaid said, "Glory be to God" than he replies, "To whom? . . . Ah, to be sure" and jokes over her head about "the collector of prepuces" (1:390–94). We sense the systematic fervor of his blasphemy when he undresses for a swim and depicts himself on the stations of the cross—"Mulligan is stripped of his garments" (1:510) and "going forth he met Butterly" (1:527)—and in his diabolic revision of Scripture: "He who stealeth from the poor lendeth to the Lord" (1:727) for "he that hath pity upon the poor lendeth unto the Lord" (Proverbs 19:17). Even Buck's pervasive intensifiers express the urgency of his blasphemy: "To tell you the God's truth. . . . Damn all else. . . . To hell with them all" (1:505–6).

Yet to see Buck as a devil figure is to accept too quickly Stephen's demonology. For one thing, Mulligan's Christian name is Malachi, Hebrew for "my messenger." In the last book of the Old Testament, Malachi foretells the second coming of "Elijah the prophet before the coming of the great and dreadful day of the Lord" (Malachi 4:5).[8] The name also has prophetic connotations in Irish history and lore, associated with Malachy, a twelfth-century saint believed to have had prophetic powers. Willeford notes that fools, despite their unrelenting grossness and hyperbolic sexuality, are often regarded as sharing "magical and religious functions with priests and medicine men."[9] It is almost too apt that Buck is a medical student who opens the book with a mock Mass. So we had best pause before accepting Stephen's story in which the profane jester tries to strangle the priest of eternal imagination. There is at least as much truth to Buck's version, in which Stephen is "the jejune jesuit," "you

---

[8] There is also a sacred text called *The Prophecies of Malachias*.

[9] William Willeford, *The Fool and His Sceptre: A Study in Clowns and Jesters and Their Audience* (Evanston, Ill.: Northwestern University Press, 1969), 4.

fearful jesuit," "Thomas Aquinas," "in a funk," "an impossible person" (1:45, 8, 546–47, 59, 222). An example of Buck's vision—
both its scope and its limits—is his treatment of Bloom at the
library, in "Scylla and Charybdis." Bloom is immediately reduced
by Buck to "the sheeny!" (9:605). But Buck's next sally reverses the
process: "What's his name? Ikey Moses? Bloom" (9:607).[10] The
comic name suggests both a stereotype and an archetype, Moses
being one of many mythic figures and historical personages to
whom Bloom corresponds. Like Lear's Fool, this jester rattles on
astutely and irrelevantly: "He knows you. He knows your old fellow.
O, I fear me, he is Greeker than the Greeks. His pale Galilean eyes
were upon her mesial groove" (9:614–15). Buck's inextricable
blend of supernatural insight and prattle is disorienting. Bloom does
"know" Stephen through some mystical connection, evidenced by
the bits of consciousness common to them. Buck's powers of perception are extraordinary, as though he were endowed with some divine
or authorial knowledge. How does *he* know that Bloom knows Simon Dedalus, that Bloom will be Stephen's surrogate "old fellow,"
and that Bloom is associated with the Messiah? "Greeker than the
Greeks" is a homosexual insinuation, but it also suggests that Buck
has discussed the novel's schema with Joyce. He is remarkably pre-
scient; who else, spying Bloom in back of a statue, would intuit that
he was looking specifically for her "mesial groove," or would just
happen to boom out the same song Stephen sang to his dying
mother and murmurs again at the climax of "Circe" (1:239–41 and
15:4932–33, 4942–43)? One is given pause by Buck's facetious
assertion, "The Lord has spoken to Malachi" (9:1056).

Like Shakespearean fools, then, Buck is more important than his
hour upon the stage suggests. He stands apart from the main action
and acts, to some extent, as a privileged commentator upon the
action; if not consistently prophetic, Buck is surely a cogent commentator, like those Shakespearean fools who, blending sense and
nonsense, question the hero's abstractions, speculations, and ideal-
izations. For instance, such observations as "he kills his mother but
he can't wear grey trousers" (1:122) or "the unclean bard makes a
point of washing once a month" (1:475) wittily express an under-

[10]"Ikey," diminutive of Isaac or the derogatory term "kike," is slang for
"Jew." A London illustrated weekly depicted a character named "Ikey Moses"
in a satiric or anti-Semitic fashion (Gifford 227–28).

standable impatience with Stephen's rigid, obsessive behavior. Even more shocking attacks—diagnosing Stephen's "general paralysis of the insane" (1:128–29), for example—have some validity. Relentlessly vulgar, Buck's wit can also be casually learned. Familiar with Swinburne, Homer, and Nietzsche,[11] he makes fun of Stephen's ignorance of Greek: "Ah, Dedalus, the Greeks! I must teach you. You must read them in the original" (1:79–80). When Buck disappears, leaving us alone with Stephen, it is not long before we remember his simple exhortation: "Chuck Loyola, Kinch, and come on down" (1:231–32).

Like Lear's Fool (who is sometimes sentimentalized), Buck overflows with hostility, although he would deny it as he denies everything. To Buck, all his banter is "friendly jest," meant "gaily" and "tripping and sunny like the buck himself" (1:35, 34, 42). In fact most of his remarks to and about Stephen mix frivolous play, serious concern, and a good deal of unmistakable cruelty. When he notes "something sinister" in Stephen (1:94) he is holding a mirror up to nature—and in front of himself. In a manner reminiscent of Lear's Fool, Buck veers from gaiety to fury, tenderness to viciousness, reveling to reviling; Buck's railing may sometimes be playful and gay, at other times harsh and cruel. Split between innocence and malice, he alternates cold blasts of irony with warm gushes of sentiment.

Small wonder that Stephen, Haines, and we respond so uncertainly to Buck's mixed signals. He terms Stephen "poor dogsbody," but utters the phrase "in a kind voice" (1:112). Suddenly linking arms with Stephen, he says, "it's not fair to tease you like that, Kinch, is it? . . . God knows you have more spirit than any of them" (1:150–51) as though he truly values Stephen's spirit. Buck believes, or pretends to believe, that they could "work together" to "do something for the island" (1:157–58). "Why don't you trust me more?" he demands of Stephen. "What have you up your nose against me?" (1:161–62). The effect of such overtures is to rob

---

[11]Mulligan may have learned the part of the Fool King from his favorite philosopher, Nietzsche. In *Thus Spoke Zarathustra,* introduced by Mulligan (1:728) and subsequently mentioned twice (14:363, 1431), appears a blasphemous parody of the mass, called "The Ass Festival." See Friedrich Nietzsche, *Thus Spoke Zarathustra,* trans. R. J. Hollingdale (Baltimore: Penguin Books, 1964), 322–26.

Stephen of any easy defense and to break down any oversimplified notions of Buck's character. "Parried again" (1:152) is Stephen's response to Buck's "kind" word and gesture, for Buck's attacks cannot be attributed to mere jesting or diabolic iniquity. Buck is not just inconsistent, he is inherently ambiguous, as he knows. "Do I contradict myself?" he asks, quoting *Song of Myself*, "Very well then, I contradict myself. Mercurial Malachi" (1:517–18). As usual, his epithets are wonderfully appropriate. "Mercurial" suggests both the ever-shifting trickster and the divine messenger. Mercury or Hermes is an archetypal trickster, as C. G. Jung notes, because of "his fondness for sly jokes and malicious pranks, his powers as a shape-shifter, his dual nature, half animal, half divine, . . . and— last but not least—his approximation to the figure of a savior."[12]

In a sense Buck has no identity, only a series of masks. To Buck nothing, including himself, has a meaningful, enduring identity; he is all the poses, attitudes, and masks he momentarily assumes. He is a grand mimic who hears and impersonates many voices; the result is an indiscriminate, equivocal, and cacophonous din. His tone can perhaps best be captured, if one can contain mercury, by an oxymoron—that favored rhetorical trope of Jocoserious Joyce— "honeying malice" (9:1087). Honeying malice, Mercurial Malachi voices memorable insights, pithy half-truths, and reductive or irrelevant nonsense. The scathing remark quoted earlier, "The unclean bard makes a point of washing once a month" (1:475), indicates how demanding the job of untangling can be. Buck draws our attention to Stephen's abhorrence of water,[13] which is metaphorically associated with baptism, women, sexuality, our mighty mother, the stream of life, and artistic creativity. Yet Buck himself would consider these symbolic connotations wildly silly. In plunging naked into the ocean he may be expressing gusto and accepting life, immersing himself in meaningless flux, or merely taking a swim. Insofar as he believes in anything, Buck stands for the multiplicity that Stephen adamantly resists. He fulfills the classic role of the clown, to threaten our assumption that identity is anything

[12]"On the Psychology of the Trickster-Figure," *Four Archetypes: Mother/Rebirth/Spirit/Trickster,* trans. R. F. C. Hull (Princeton: Princeton University Press, 1970), 135.

[13]Worse than Buck knows: Stephen hasn't bathed since October, 1903; see 17:238–39.

substantial or reliable. Stephen's analytical mode is fission: split the subject into ever smaller units in quest of the absolute, essential, and irreducible. Buck's witty mode is that of *Ulysses*, the fusion of disparate things, joked by violence together. "One or two?" (9:297) wonders Stephen, whose univocal mind prefers Aristotelian and Thomistic ordered unity.

Judging fools like Buck is ultimately impossible since they are thoroughly amoral and systematically disorienting. "Every clown is two beings—never one."[14] Buck plays to his mirror or himself, and is amalgamized in "Circe" as Father Malachi O'Flynn (15:4698).[15] Buck is an incarnate oxymoron, both static and protean. In "Scylla and Charybdis" his name itself undergoes permutations: Buck Mulligan gives way to "pseudo Malachi" (9:492), "Monk Mulligan" (9:773), "Cuck Mulligan" (9:1025), and "Puck Mulligan" (9:1142). Before Buck slips away entirely, we might ask who christens him "Buck" in the first place?[16] He is called "Malachi Mulligan" or "Mulligan" by everybody except the evanescent impersonator who narrates the fictions. This giddy name-game suggests that the personal identity implicit in names is provisional and dubious. His very appearance is Scylla-like, "head wagging" (9:546) or "lolling a to and fro head" (9:1190) like a many-headed creature, or one of those untrustworthy characters described by Erasmus's Stultitia as two-tongued or double-men. So, too, is it difficult to separate Buck's discourse into true and false or prophetic and silly; such confusion is central to the fool, who perpetually delights in ambiguities of language and identity. Because the clown is an enemy of order and an advocate of anarchy, he is reviled and feared. Welsford says that "one of the perennial functions of the fool [is] the power of melting the solidity of the world."[17] Buck, like many clowns before him, serves as Master of the Revels and Lord of Misrule, celebrating confusion.

[14]Adriane L. Despot, "Some Principles of Clowning," *Massachusetts Review* 22 (1981): 661.

[15]He appears with another "twinned" priest, the Reverend Mr. Haines Love, whose name, "Hate Love," is another oxymoron.

[16]The word "buck" is slang for "to falsify, to chatter; talk with egotistical superabundance" (Eric Partridge, *Dictionary of Slang and Unconventional English*).

[17]Enid Welsford, *The Fool: His Social and Literary History* (London: Faber & Faber, 1935), 221.

In a persistently paradoxical way, perhaps dramatizing the fool's self-division, Buck suggests both Eros and Thanatos, life and death, the elemental processes of the body. Recalling the origins of the word "comedy," Buck struts about like a mummer in a fertility festival, as "Ballocky Mulligan" (9:1176) and "Le Fécondateur" (14:778). He loves to present himself as a pagan force of life, an adversary of death like so many clowns,[18] yet he is equally associated with death. Like the devil, Buck has an evil eye; not only Stephen but Bloom and Simon Dedalus recoil from him as from demise and decay—which helps to explain Simon's furious denunciation of Buck as a "contaminated bloody doubledyed ruffian" whose "name stinks all over Dublin" (6:64–65). Intimacy with both life and death is another perennial feature of the fool in both high and low art. Shakespeare's Richard II imagines that "within the hollow crown / That rounds the mortal temples of a king / Keeps Death his court, and there the antic sits" (III.ii.160–62). And in medieval and Renaissance depictions of the dance of death, the figure of death often wears the cap and bells. It is interesting to note that Joyce, while writing *Ulysses,* felt that he himself possessed a power of blight. As he wrote to Harriet Shaw Weaver on 20 July 1919: "The word *scorching* . . . has a peculiar significance for my superstitious mind . . . for the fact that the progress of the book is in fact like the progress of some sandblast. As soon as I mention or include any person in it I hear of his or her death or departure or misfortune: and each successive episode, dealing with some province of artistic culture (rhetoric or music or dialectic), leaves behind it a burnt up field" (*SL* 241).

With an abundance of both positive and negative powers, Buck the Fool naturally elicits strong and confused reactions. Unable to be anything without playing at being it, Mulligan, like Joycean humor, is elusive and disorienting. As Haines nervously says, "We oughtn't to laugh, I suppose. He's rather blasphemous. . . . Still his gaiety takes the harm out of it somehow, doesn't it?" (1:605–7). Like the rest of us, Haines does not know quite how to take Buck; in a novel

---

[18]The coat of arms of Dan Rice, American frontier clown, depicted Rice "in his clown suit, using a birch branch to chase away the skeleton spectre of death." See Ron Jenkins, "Vita: Dan Rice," in *Harvard Magazine,* May–June 1981, 51. Laurence Sterne devotes Book 7 of *Tristram Shandy* to the same theme.

that challenges stable systems of belief, including many of its own initial assertions or implications, Buck is the first powerful destabilizer. Like the Abbot of Unreason at a Feast of Fools, Buck brings to the novel what Bakhtin notes in Rabelais: a "sense of the gay relativity of prevailing truths and authorities . . . a characteristic logic, the peculiar logic of the 'inside out', of the turnabout, of a continuing shift from top to bottom, from front to rear, of numerous parodies and travesties, humiliations, profanations, comic crownings and uncrownings."[19] Nothing is sacred, although Joyce would not agree with its Buckish corollary, that all is profane.

In "Oxen of the Sun" Buck holds the stage for one last vivid appearance, staying very much in character, then suddenly, mysteriously disappearing. He can disappear, like Lear's Fool, because the lessons of folly have been absorbed—not by the hero as in *King Lear,* but by the book itself. In vanishing, Buck fulfills another of the fool's classic roles: he becomes a scapegoat who somehow manages to "elude the sacrifice."[20] Although he mocks the possibility of resurrection, the fool defies death and makes eternal revivals. There is a prominent law of comedy to which Joyce subscribes: nothing is final, not even death. In *Finnegans Wake,* the title of which is a triple pun on the theme, this decree is promulgated early: "Phall if you but will, rise you must" (*FW* 4:15–16). In *Ulysses,* too, everything obeys the "law of falling bodies" (5:44–45) but nothing stays down for long, not a mood, a word, or a corpse; things don't merely continue to flow like the sea—they recuperate, return, rise. As in *Finnegans Wake,* death in *Ulysses* becomes a *"funferal"* (*FW* 120:10).

Although much remains beyond Buck's ken, a good deal is illuminated by his light. More suprisingly, even in this book of many turns, the text eventually approaches Buck's view, wherein facts seem less reliable, truths less important, possibilities more proliferent, and fooling more predominant. Buck is not, like Jaques in *As You Like It,* a discordant note left out of the ultimate harmony. From about halfway through his eighteen chapters, with several anticipations in opening episodes, *Ulysses* is flamboyantly analogical, antic, foolish. Thus one important result of focusing upon Buck is to perceive the connection between the clown and the author.

[19]Mikhail Bakhtin, *Rabelais and His World,* trans. Hélène Iswolsky (Bloomington: Indiana University Press, 1984), 11.
[20]The phrase is from Willeford, *The Fool and His Sceptre,* 101.

That Buck performs "joyfully," a word repeated (9:549, 556), is one small hint of the larger association, for Joyce shares with Shakespeare pleasure in play with his own name.[21] Buck's influence clearly affects the narrator of "Scylla and Charybdis," for example, who responds to Buck's arrival on the scene with musical notation, bizarre typography, "Sirens"-like wordplay, a scene in dialogue, and other jester's high-jinks.

For Joyce, narrative fun is verbal antics, pure exuberance—the kind of wordplay that amuses Joyceans and annoys sensible people. Like clowning, it is deliberately preposterous and frequently pertinent. Joyce's encyclopedic lists or epic catalogs, for instance, express the spirit of free play and the possibility of infinite supplement; the phrase "proliferent continuance" (14:15) in "Oxen of the Sun" defines not only the sacred procreative instinct but the writer's comic fecundity. The novel, like Buck, becomes a great picker-up of unconsidered trifles, refusing to let pass any throwaway. An admirer of the Book of Kells in the Trinity College library, Joyce gives us verbal equivalents for the visual profusion in medieval illuminated manuscripts, including "free designs not connected with the story" that represent "chimeras . . . comic devils . . . that is, purely grotesque, carnivalesque themes."[22]

Buck's role of comic devil is also relished by Joyce. One irresistible bit of biographical evidence is Stanislaus's first memory of his brother in a household skit as the devil, "wriggling across the floor with a long tail probably made of a rolled-up sheet or towel" (S. Joyce 1). Thus young James Joyce makes his appearance in *My Brother's Keeper* much as Buck Mulligan seizes the stage in *Ulysses*. Like Buck, Joyce had a devilish talent for clowning, exhibited in amateur theatricals, and a love for popular entertainment; he once declared that "the music hall, not poetry, was a criticism of life" (S. Joyce 96). He was clearly a man who loved and studied his Pierrots, Harlequins, Grocks, and Chaplins.[23] Playing charades, he could

---

[21]Stephen says Shakespeare bestows "his own name . . . [on] a clown there" (9:921–22).

[22]I borrow Bakhtin's characterization of illuminated manuscripts, in *Rabelais and His World*, 95.

[23]In "Chaplin and Joyce," a paper delivered at the 1989 Joyce Conference in Philadelphia, Austin Briggs notes several connections between Chaplin and

provoke roars of laughter with his clowning, imitating a look of blank imbecility, weeping, blowing his nose loudly.

Joyce shares many other important traits and inclinations with Mercurial Malachi, such as a "strong weakness" (7:594) for oxymoronic attitudes and formulations. A principal "seriocomic" (15:447) technique, introduced by Mulligan and increasingly evident in the novel, is what Bakhtin calls "polyglossia," or a multiplicity of voices. Both Buck and his maker are splendid mimics, with a wide repertory and dubious attachment to anything uttered. In a brilliant article, "Mockery in *Ulysses,*" James Maddox characterizes Buck as "capable of mastering so many discourses . . . the destabilized play of voices,"[24] and persuasively argues that the novel's intitial style is the discourse to which Stephen aspires. But I disagree with Maddox that "the multiple styles of the second half of the book are extrapolations from Joyce's discovery of the character of Leopold Bloom."[25] I think, rather, that Stephen is correct to consider Buck a "Usurper" (1:744), for the novel is "carried away by a wave of folly" (16:1387–88), a tendency set in motion by the dominant figure of the first episode.

With his irrepressible energy and unceasing vitality, Buck Mulligan is central to Joycean comedy—yet not in the sentimental sense of some commentators who find *Ulysses* comic in vaguely "life-affirming" ways. To listen to Buck and to hear his voice more prominently in Joyce's chorus is not to deny the possibility of stable and jocoserious comedy, but rather to insist upon the frightening force of the fool's antics, his power of melting solidity, including the meaning of his own discourse. *Ulysses* is never simply optimistic and joyful; it is also skeptical, even suspicious, especially of uncritical optimism and reassuring conventions. Mercurial Malachi is a figure as volatile, elusive, unstable, gifted, and dangerous as any fool. As "Ballocky Mulligan" (9:1176), or, in another of his self-

---

Joyce, including the comedian's appearances in *Finnegans Wake,* and the fact that Lucia Joyce, with Valery Larbaud's help, published an essay on Chaplin in the February 1924 issue of *Le Disque Vert.*

[24]James H. Maddox, "Mockery in *Ulysses,*" in *Joyce's "Ulysses": The Larger Perspective,* ed. Robert D. Newman and Weldon Thornton (Newark: University of Delaware Press, 1987), 143.

[25]Maddox, 148.

styled titles, "Le Fécondateur" (14:778), he is the novel's father of folly, its fertile source of clowning and fooling, spawning several of Joyce's later narrators. Joyce does more than create a great fool in Buck: investing a substantial portion of himself in Buck Mulligan, Joyce ultimately plays the fool himself, a Foolosopher King, who proclaimed himself "nothing but an Irish clown, a great joker at the universe."[26]

Poor Dogsbody

Though Oliver St. John Gogarty made a small reputation publishing relatively fond memories of Joyce and quotably harsh opinions of *Ulysses,* he rarely objected to the character of Malachi Mulligan. No fool, he. Gogarty was perceptive enough to recognize that Buck is far more than a caricature, and *Ulysses* far from special pleading for Stephen Dedalus. Listening to Buck more attentively encourages us to query Stephen's privileged view of himself. Though Stephen may not have changed appreciably since *A Portrait of the Artist,* his world has, for in *Ulysses* he is assessed more comically and rigorously by the presence of just such mocking gargoyles as Buck Mulligan. A reader like Gogarty might well construe the relationship between Buck and Stephen this way: a gifted Swiftian satirist tries vainly to prod his saturnine roommate toward a healthy ironic vision of himself and life. The world indulges the latter's pseudo-artistic pretensions but treats the brilliant jester with the usual trepidation and hostility—as when Bloom urges Stephen "to sever his connection with a certain budding practictioner who, he noticed, was prone to disparage and even to a slight extent with some hilarious pretext when not present, deprecate him" (16:1868–71).

Gogarty would doubtless agree with the horse at the end of "Eumaeus," who comments on the wisdom and appropriateness of Bloom's counsel by dropping three smoking globes of turds. Buck Mulligan is indeed a classic clown, "prone to disparage," but Stephen Dedalus is in many ways a fool, and we should "to a slight extent with an hilarious pretext . . . deprecate him." Discussing

[26]Jaques Mercanton, "The Hours of James Joyce," trans. Lloyd C. Parks, *Kenyon Review* 24 (1962): 728.

Stephen with Haines, presumably with whatever sincerity the old mummer's word is worth, Mulligan regards Stephen with a characteristic blend of cruelty, prattle, and insight: "They drove his wits astray, he said, by visions of hell. He will never capture the Attic note . . . That is his tragedy. He can never be a poet" (10:1072–74). Most readers continue to assume that the existence of the book in their hands repudiates Buck's assessment, and eagerly underline Buck's sarcastic conclusion: "Ten years . . . He is going to write something in ten years" (10:1089–90). Knowing that 1914 is the year Joyce completed *A Portrait of the Artist as a Young Man* and began *Ulysses* suggests the kind of self-reflexive (or self-serving) joke Joyce sometimes favored, but like most Joycean jokes, this one explodes in fragments, not in any one trajectory. The irony does not simply rebound upon Buck, who, after all, establishes himself as someone well worth heeding, a voice conveying some of the power and value of folly in *Ulysses,* but also upon Stephen, who indeed gives as much evidence of stray wits as of poetic genius.

Stephen's grandiose self-image is based on lamentably little achievement. So far he has produced several inflated "epiphanies," like God is "a shout in the street" (2:386) and "Ireland must be important because it belongs to me" (16:1164–65), and a few verses that the world might willingly let die. Granted, he is an extraordinarily sensitive youth whose reflections are often subtle and lyrical, but Buck Mulligan hasn't seen that, and the world is clogged with literary lads. Moreover, while our privileged access to Stephen's consciousness brings occasional pleasure in his meditations and formulations, and awareness of his potential, it also divulges several objectionable and some disturbing things as well.

To call Stephen "derivative" would be too kind: almost nothing he says or thinks all day long is original, which may be why he is always "feeling one behind" (9:1197). When Stephen says that Shakespeare's speech "is always turned elsewhere, backward" (9:472), he reveals something telling about himself, for his own reliance upon the ideas and language of others expresses the need, despite his rebellious postures, for patriarchal sanction, as we might expect from someone who prayed for guidance from "Old father" (*P* 253) and conceives Shakespeare as "the father of all his race" (9:868–69). His conception of the author, though in one sense comically impudent, is remarkably authoritarian, verifying the first thing Buck says about Stephen—that he is still a "fearful jesuit"

(1:8). Deference to authority and a tendency to voice other people's ideas and words is a long-standing problem with Stephen, one that Joyce seems more eager to expose in *Ulysses* than in *Portrait*. Denis Donoghue[27] has recently drawn attention, in *Portrait,* to a remarkable instance of Stephen practicing what professors call "allusion" when we do it and "plagiarism" when students try it. In a crucial location, moving toward his climactic self-revelation on the beach, "he drew forth a phrase from his treasure and spoke it softly to himself.—A day of dappled seaborne clouds" (*P* 166). That this is a sentence Stephen has collected from a book by Hugh Miller, rather than created himself, is certainly not obvious: "drew forth from his treasure" is meticulously ambiguous, in keeping with the novel's shifting, wary, but protective attitude toward the hero.

Subsequent dips into his treasure, which Stephen would just as soon conduct secretly, *Ulysses* reveals. That Stephen's *bon mots,* regarded as quotably clever by the fatuous Haines, are usually warmed-over Wilde is only mildly disconcerting, for few of us bother to document our witty banter. More problematic are Stephen's compositions like the vampire quatrain. It is not only notable but curious that Stephen's lines bear close resemblance to Douglas Hyde's poem—for, had he wished, the author of *Chamber Music* could surely have provided his hero with an original piece. Even more intriguing is the way *Ulysses* slyly and smugly acknowledges Stephen's borrowing—"stolentelling" is the splendid neologism in *Finnegans Wake* (424:35)—by providing two references to Stephen's source. At the library, Mr. Best mentions that Haines is "quite enthusiastic . . . about Hyde's *Lovesongs of Connacht* . . . [and] has gone to buy it" (9:93–94). No sooner has Hyde been mentioned than Stephen thinks of Haines: "We feel in England. Penitent thief" (9:101). To the extent to which James Joyce is, or ever was, Stephen Dedalus, he is now the "Penitent thief," revealing the stolen goods.[28] My sense that the text, "Sherlockholmesing"

[27]Denis Donoghue, *We Irish: Essays on Irish Literature and Society* (New York: Alfred A. Knopf, 1986), 89–90. Though Donoghue neglects to say so, Stephen's allusion to Hugh Miller was noted by Don Gifford in *Joyce Annotated: Notes for "Dubliners" and "A Portrait of the Artist as a Young Man"* (Berkeley: University of California Press, 1982), 219.

[28]Cf. Shem's "pelagiarist pen" (*FW* 182:3) and the "epical forged cheque" (*FW* 181:16).

(16:831) like a triumphant detective, provides the evidence to nab Stephen is reinforced by another gratuitous reference to the anthology: just when Buck appears, Best says, "Haines missed you . . . He's gone to Gill's to buy Hyde's *Lovesongs of Connacht*" (9:513–14). Mentioning the book to Buck is ominous, for if Stephen ever makes the mistake of showing Haines his quatrain, Buck and the boys will have laughter for a month and a good jest forever. This little drollery is perfectly typical of jesting Joyce, playing his merry game of Hyde-and-seek with his readers.

A second illustration of Joyce's cunningly revealing Stephen's sources is stronger evidence still that Stephen's folly exists to be exposed. Everyone will recall Stephen's telegram, celebrated by Buck as a "wonderful inspiration!" (9:548): "*The sentimentalist is he who would enjoy without incurring the immense debtorship for a thing done*. Signed: Dedalus" (9:550–51). Cryptic as it is, the telegram compactly conveys Stephen's pompous aversion to pleasure. (I don't rule out a pun on *debt* and *dead,* culminating in "Signed Dead alas.") Whatever Stephen means, it is he and not Buck who bears debts, both financial and literary, for once again the text encourages us to discover what Buck seems not to realize—that this wonderful inspiration was lifted verbatim from *The Ordeal of Richard Feverel.* A few minutes after Buck's entrance, John Eglinton comments that we "should not now combine a Norse saga with an excerpt from a novel by George Meredith" (9:993–94), and if that isn't enough of a hint, the inspired fool whose slangy patter concludes "Oxen of the Sun" declares, "Mummer's wire. Cribbed out of Meredith" (14:1486). Such simultaneous use and exposure of folly is quintessentially jocoserious—that is, apparently irrelevant, yet finely pertinent—and, in its part playful, part malicious treatment of Stephen, is another link between Antic Joyce and Mercurial Malachi.[29]

Stephen's folly seems more serious than juvenile pilfering because it is so pervasive and touches so intimately on his vocation: "No voice. I am a most finished artist" (15:2508), he frets. Indeed, he is constrained to lie to his comrades by misrepresenting his salary from Deasy as payment "for a song which he writ" (14:287), then bombastically quoting Blake, of course without attribution. If literary

[29]Stanislaus Joyce reports that he brought Joyce's attention to Meredith's epigram; Stephen is thus borrowing a phrase that Stanislaus had, along with so much else, lent to his brother.

achievement is so crucial to his self-esteem, one might fairly ask why Stephen spends his half-holiday drinking, carousing, and wasting time.

It is telling that young James Joyce worked busily and successfully in 1903 and 1904, not only completing his stories and poems, but beginning *Stephen Hero*. Stephen Dedalus has no such productivity, nor any apparent project. Given an opportunity to think and write, he spends a few moments musing on the beach, composes or plagiarizes four lines, and soon starts drinking, which he continues to do all day and into the night. Rabelais's Panurge says he never saw a fool who didn't gladly drink enormous quantities, and he has seen a lot of fools. Often Stephen is the prime mover to pubs such as Mooney's, and generally he seems less devoted to the muse than to those three traditional companions of folly: wine, wenches, and song. Though we know that drinking is a good man's failing and not necessarily fatal to a writer's hopes, Stephen's wilful neglect makes it unlikely that he will be in any shape to work the next morning, and one wonders whether he is capable of concerted effort in the foreseeable future.

Of course, evaluation of Stephen is a vexed issue, more complex than Buck could acknowledge. What keeps us from dismissing Stephen as "an impossible person" (1:222), in Buck's words, is uncertainty about Buck himself, and dim but discernible evidence of Stephen's potential. Another large factor is our sympathy for his pain. To what extent Buck is right to say that Stephen's wits are astray is another complicated subject. Melancholy, Freud tells us, expresses itself in guilt, as when Stephen remembers walking about Paris carrying punched tickets "to prove an alibi if they arrested you for murder somewhere" (3:180). And self-loathing also surfaces as hostility: "Shoot him to bloody bits with a bang shotgun" (3:187–88). Presently he thinks of the terrible telegram from his father, which called him home. Yet even its message, "Nother dying come home father" (3:199), suggests the difference between tragic Stephen, for whom everything is painfully particular, and the more detached sense that "Nother dying" is part of the eternal cycle. Stephen is naturally grieved by his loss, but he is persistently and melodramatically depressed. Claudius urged Hamlet to "throw to earth / This unprevailing woe" (*H:* I.ii.106–7) as most people eventually do, including James Joyce, after the death of his mother.

Stephen's self-destructive dissipation and paralysis, punctuated by that burst of frenzied energy at the library, resemble manic depression; someone observing Stephen in Nighttown might well regard him as suffering from what "Herr Docktor" Mulligan diagnoses as "general paralysis of the insane" (1:128–29). Just as it remains impossible to distinguish Buck's jocose and serious assertions, though, it is hard to separate Stephen's anguished heart from his antic disposition, for he relishes the stock role of *poet maudite/young Werther/Hamlet*. Perhaps he is exaggerating grief the way he postured in Paris: "God, we simply must dress the character" (3:174). At least since Terence, "the self-tormenter" has been a stock comic type. Although it has been nearly a year since May Dedalus died, Stephen is still mourning in inky black; possibly he is suffering more acutely as the first anniversary nears, but one suspects that he wants to play Monsieur Remorse in any event. "If I fell over a cliff that beetles o'er his base" (3:14), Stephen muses, alluding to *Hamlet*—and, later in "Proteus," he again imitates his favorite tragic hero: "I pace the path above the rocks, in sable silvered, hearing Elsinore's tempting flood" (3:280–81). Before we conclude that Stephen is in suicidal despair, we would do well to remember his explanation to Buck: what really torments him is not his mother's suffering but the offense to himself. That Stephen carries on preposterously seems to be one of the points of "Circe," which burlesques his operatic egocentricity.

Instead of succumbing to Stephen's solemnity, let us sustain the spirit of Buck Mulligan by considering another way in which Dedalus is ridiculous. For all his drunken carousing, Stephen's jollity is forced, enacted rather than experienced, for he embodies that "mechanical inelasticity of spirit" defined by Bergson as the essence of the ludicrous. Adamantly opposed to "joyicity," Stephen has progressed very little, on this Joycean scale, since his youth. Trained in Aristotelian and Thomistic logic, he suffers from hardening of the categories. In *Stephen Hero,* the protagonist, however satirical toward the world, is virtually humorless about his role in it; he could always suck melancholy from an egg. For a good part of *A Portrait of the Artist as a Young Man,* laughter is threatening—"mirthless," "scornful," or "jeering" in tone. Almost always it is others who laugh, and almost invariably Stephen ponders, "O how could they laugh about it that way?" (*P* 45). Though Stephen occasionally "tried to share their merriment, he felt himself a gloomy figure" (*P* 68). He can only gambol in strictly defined situations, such as the school drama, in which he is cast as the farcical pedagogue. Much too rigidly, Stephen conceives heroism and folly as distinct categories. After being pandied, for example, deliberating an appeal to higher authority, he imagines mutually exclusive possibilities: either he will become a hero, or the boys will "make fun" of him (*P* 55). As a teacher himself at Mr Deasy's school, Stephen still cannot imagine any middle ground between authority and folly, or any place for "strong weakness" (7:594). When the boys laugh at Armstrong's silly confusion between Pyrrhus and a pier, Stephen regards it as "mirthless high malicious laughter" and immediately worries that they will "laugh more loudly, aware of my lack of rule" (2:28–29). Even with schoolboys Stephen remains afraid of laughter, fearful of being "a jester at the court of his master, indulged and disesteemed" (2:43–44). He still does not understand the rigidity of his false dichotomy between authority and folly; as we have seen in Buck Mulligan's discourse (to repeat a word I vowed to suppress), authority and folly are hard to sort out, and sometimes identical. Folly per se may indicate damnation or grace, as Stephen, that young man on whom nothing is lost, might have noticed as far back as the hellraising sermon on the retreat, where he heard of devils who "mock and jeer at the lost souls" (*P* 123) but also of Christ "mocked at as a fool" (*P* 119).

Though Buck is a marvelous Gospeller in the mouth, devilishly citing Scripture for his own purposes, he would gleefully say in his own offense that, on the great question of folly, Scripture is wonderfully mercurial. One of the crucial ways the New Testament reverses the Old is by redefining folly. The Preacher in Ecclesiastes, who believed that the number of fools is infinite, had no difficulty recognizing folly: fools are those who fail or refuse to accept divine injunctions, as interpreted and promulgated by sages like himself. He assails folly and valorizes sorrow, sadness, and mourning: "It is better," he says flatly, "to go to the house of mourning, than to go to the house of feasting . . . Sorrow is better than laughter. . . . The heart of the wise *is* in the house of mourning; but the heart of fools *is* in the house of mirth" (Eccles. 7:2–4). Singers of folly like Buck Mulligan, always happiest in the house of mirth (assuming more exotic houses are fully booked), naturally prefer the higher authority of St. Paul, who asks, "hath not God made foolish the wisdom of this world" and insists that "we *are* fools for Christ's sake" (1 Cor. 1:20 and 4:10). Paul's reversal forcibly strikes Erasmus's Stultitia, who argues that "the Christian religion taken all together has a certain affinity with some sort of folly and has little or nothing to do with wisdom" (Erasmus 132).

Stephen's first model of folly before he meets Buck Mulligan is, of course, his father, from whom he shrinks. Life, so grim and mortifying to Stephen, is usually amusing to Simon—as when he recounts Stephen's vindication by the rector as a joke, or deftly contrives a punch line to Bloom's account of Dodd's son. Simon Dedalus is "the comic Irishman" (*P* 193), the "storyteller" (*P* 241), the archetypal humorist, "a born *raconteur* if ever there was one" (16:261). Stephen stubbornly resents and distrusts Simon's garrulous, glib wit, mostly borrowed from John Joyce, whose importance, in contrast, James Joyce frankly and generously acknowledged: "Hundreds of pages and scores of characters in my books came from him. His dry (or rather wet) wit and his expression of face convulsed me often with laughter" (*L* 1:312). There is no shame or duplicity, notice, about "borrowed words," nor any high falutin' nonsense about being made, not begotten. In fact, Joyce moved as far as possible from *Portrait's* apparent endorsement of Stephen for resisting "the constant voices of his father and of his masters" (*P* 83)—praise that in *Ulysses* turns out to be both premature and inappropriate.

Stephen's "easily embittered heart" (*P* 190), inordinately aggravated by any hint of mockery, gradually opens itself to the ubiquity of folly. When it does, though, Stephen's mordant wit and acute sense of irony are directed at everything except himself; he is quick to size people down. Later in *Portrait,* he begins to view himself less solemnly; his diary conveys more amusement, even at his own expense. Although there are intermittent hints of Stephen's growth in folly throughout *Portrait* and *Ulysses,* by the time he became a character in *Ulysses,* Joyce said of him, "Stephen no longer interests me. . . . He has a shape that can't be changed" (Budgen 105). As the author became increasingly playful and tolerant, he must have seen in his younger *alter ego* the "tragic jester" he mocks in *Finnegans Wake:* "O! the lowness of him was beneath all up to that sunk to! . . . Instead the tragic jester sobbed himself wheywhingingly sick of life" (*FW* 171:15–16). It is my argument that the Stephen of *Ulysses* is no longer, even in the ambiguous manner of *Portrait,* the primary source of value; in *Ulysses,* folly itself has become a glorious standard. Joyce measures Stephen, in part, by his receptivity to the human comedy, including his own role in it—and, on this scale, he is weighed and found wanting. The metamorphosis from Stephen Hero to "tragic jester" is an illuminating way to track Joyce's development toward the comic vision he regarded since his youth as "the perfect manner in art" in that it "excites in us the feeling of joy" (*CW* 144).

Stephen's humor, conspicuously absent until the end of *Portrait,* is usually defensive, hostile, tortured, self-loathing. In physics class he whispers to a classmate, "Ask him . . . if he wants a subject for electrocution. He can have me" (*P* 193). As a teacher himself, his lame-witted definition of a "pier" as a "disappointed bridge" expresses his own pervasive frustration or impotence: sexually isolated, he has also failed his mission to the continent from that bridge. Halfhearted and discombobulated in the classroom, Stephen makes a feeble effort to end the lesson on a humorous note, with the riddle about "the fox burying his grandmother" (2:115), which baffles the boys, since this is a riddle at the expense of riddles, to which one must already know the answer. As is so often the case in *Ulysses,* even unamusing humor is telling, for Stephen's riddle conveys his "agenbite of inwit," indicated by his itching throat and nervous laughter. We soon learn that his internal censor has substituted "grandmother" for "mother," that he is the "fox": "A poor soul gone to heaven: and on a heath beneath winking stars a fox, red reek of rapine in his fur, with merciless bright eyes scraped in the earth, listened, scraped up the earth, listened, scraped and scraped" (2:147–50). The riddle evades sense in an interesting way: for the moment Stephen seems to be trying out the style of Lear's Fool, with his scathing, cryptic puzzles, an association that is strengthened by the image of "a poor soul gone to heaven: and on a heath. . . . " In its gratifying release of inhibiting pressure, Stephen's "riddle" is a textbook illustration of Freud's *Jokes and their Relation to the Unconscious.*

When Stephen finally shows signs of appreciating the ridiculous at the end of "Circe," he insists on imposing it on the least receptive audience, Privates Carr and Compton. His priggish idea of humor is to lecture soldiers on niceties of grammar, allude to mythology, proffer elegant puns and insults—"Noble art of selfpretense. Personally, I detest action" (15:4413–14)—and make a stagey, provocative declaration: "But in here it is I must kill the priest and the king" (15:4436–37). Small wonder, then, that Stephen strikes Buck as a ridiculous figure whose company, despite his forced

jollity, is intolerable; one can understand why he is pointedly excluded from A. E.'s literary party and abandoned by his put-upon
pals. A few paragraphs of "Proteus," that gloomy cavern, should be
enough to persuade most people that Buck's impatient mockery is
apt. Most people, of course, are not as patient, magnanimous, and
solicitous as Leopold Bloom, who rescues and comforts Stephen,
but is treated with minimal civility for his pains. Stephen yawns in
Bloom's face and hardly says a word in the shelter; when he does
speak, it is to sing an anti-Semitic ballad, or to talk allusively and
abstractly over his host's head, or to renew his patent on the egotistical sublime.

The failure of Stephen to connect with Bloom may disappoint,
but it should not surprise us. Imagining his Uncle Richie's home, he
thinks, "Houses of decay, mine, his and all . . . Beauty is not there"
(3:105–7), a snobbish ethereality belied by *Ulysses* itself. Predictably, Stephen doesn't perceive Leopold Bloom, with his petit-
bourgeois taste, as worth artistic consideration or even polite behavior. Though their experiences together in Nighttown might have
given them something to laugh about, Stephen's appreciation of
folly, especially when he is the proper object of ridicule, is minimal
by any standard, and invisible compared to that of Bloom.

Bloom carries that *moly,* characterized by Joyce as "the gift of
Hermes [bestowing] power of recuperation . . . [such as] a sense of
the ridiculous" (Ellmann 497). In this way, Bloom approaches his
maker, while Stephen's morbidly egocentric humor is the opposite
of Joyce's antic energy, delight in role-playing, and capacity for
amusement. These qualities in James Joyce, though well-documen-
ted, are too rarely remembered in connection with Stephen Dedalus. Gogarty recalls Joyce's "ways of mocking outrageous fortune"; the young man he knew was "a carefree student . . . the very
susceptible stage of adolescence was not really a period of gloom for
him."[30] Stanislaus Joyce repeatedly stresses that "in temperament
[my brother] was as unlike [Stephen], mourning under the incubus
of remorse, as he could well be" (S. Joyce 187). James was "of such
a cheerful and amiable disposition that in the family circle he was
given the nickname . . . of 'Sunny Jim.'" Stanislaus constantly recounts how Jim's "good humour and gaiety" were evident in his

[30]Oliver St. John Gogarty, *Intimations* (New York: Abelard Press, 1950), 3,
69.

interests and pleasures. After hours of studying upstairs, Jim would descend "in high good humour," sustained by a "joyous certainty" in his ability. Such confidence and "frank hilarity" endured through university, where "his loud laugh was characteristic and occasionally disconcerting" (S. Joyce 23, 59, 76, 109, 147). So often do we hear about Jim's gay pranks that Stanislaus runs out of synonyms for good cheer, amusement, and laughter.

Accounts of James Joyce's schooldays depict a Sunny Jim happy as a horse in clover.[31] On this point the contrast between biography and fiction is starkly clear. For instance, in *A Portrait,* Stephen, like the actual Joyce, has the lead in the Whitsuntide play, the part of "a farcical pedagogue. He had been cast for it on account of his stature and grave manners" (*P* 73). Scrupulously omitted from the story of Stephen Dedalus is what James Joyce did in the role, a turn worthy of Kingsley Amis's Lucky Jim: according to Eugene Sheehy, Joyce ignored his part and impersonated the Rector of Belvedere College, sustaining his parody "often for five minutes at a time, with the pet sayings of the Rector, imitating his gestures and his mannerisms. The other members of the cast collapsed with laughter on the stage—completely missing their cues and forgetting their parts— and the schoolboy audience received the performance with hysterical glee."[32]

All such playfulness the author withholds from Stephen Dedalus, a figure conspicuously deficient in the ability to play anything, even riddles, except in "Circe," where his capering enacts a kind of comic justice that requires foes of fun like Stephen and Malvolio to play the fool. It is hard to imagine Stephen Dedalus insisting that his writing was "meant to make you laugh" (Ellmann 703) or speaking, as Joyce did when he was Stephen's age, of "my foolishness which is now to be reckoned one of my permanent assets" (*SL* 69). In his attempt to stay life, to repudiate the flesh, to impose artificial, rigid, ideal, and immutable categories upon the flux of experience, Stephen is the implacable adversary of folly. In *A Portrait,* Stephen

---

[31]See Bruce Bradley, S. J., *James Joyce's Schooldays* (New York: St. Martin's Press, 1982).

[32]Eugene Sheehy, *May It Please the Court* (Dublin, 1951), 8–10. Cited by Don Gifford in *Joyce Annotated,* 166. A trace of this incident survives in Heron's exhortation to Stephen: "what a lark it would be tonight if you took off the rector" (*P* 75).

participates so rarely in ordinary fun that the very impulse to play is remarkable, and rendered as carnivalesque upheaval: "His fellowstudents' rude humour ran like a gust through the cloister of Stephen's mind, shaking into gay life limp priestly vestments that hung upon the walls, setting them to sway and caper in a sabbath of misrule" (*P* 192). Consequently, in *Ulysses,* Buck's clowning steals the show, while Stephen's moody brooding appears to be the posturing of a conventional humorous character, whose very name suggests he is moribund. Mired in gloom, nearly paralyzed, self-consciously tragic, suspicious of humor, he resembles Shakespeare's Jaques and Malvolio as much as the Hamlet he emulates. Understandably apprehensive of Buck's "honeying malice," Stephen is willfully full of "grim displeasure" (1:625). Poor Haines tries to engage Stephen on the subjects that most concern him, but is met with stiff-necked conversation-stoppers like, "I am the servant of two masters . . . an English and an Italian" (1:638). Making such pronouncements, mostly of grandiose self-definition, with "his colour rising" (1:643), he seems as priggish as that very young man in *Portrait,* though he has redeeming flashes of self-irony, usually kept to himself. To Joyce, the epitomal *homo ludens,* self-irony is an indispensible condition, not simply of joining the human community (which Stephen might abjure), but of writing about it. "Any individual," Bergson reminds us, "is comic who automatically goes his own way without troubling himself about getting into touch with the rest of his fellow-beings. It is the part of laughter to reprove his absent-mindedness and wake him out of his dream."[33]

Stephen violates a traditional value of folly, "leading [our] lives according to the dictates of nature," as Erasmus's Stultitia advocates (Erasmus 130) and Buck enacts. If Buck is a *body,* constantly stressing the intractably physical nature of our lives, with all its joys and woes, Stephen seeks to be pure spirit: "His soul was soaring in an air beyond the world and the body he knew was purified . . . and delivered of incertitude and made radiant and commingled with the element of the spirit" (*P* 169). However lyrically compelling, Stephen's epiphany on the beach is a false dichotomy between body and soul, and an aspiration that in Joyce's comic world demands mortification. That is why "Telemachus" has nearly as many references

[33]Henri Bergson, "Laughter," in *Comedy,* ed. Wylie Sypher (Garden City, N.Y.: Doubleday Anchor, 1956), 147.

to bodily parts and functions as that encyclopedia of human anatomy, "Penelope." [34] The opening line of the episode notes that Buck
is "plump," an observation worth repeating three times (1:31, 125,
729) because it implies that Buck, like Falstaff and Sancho Panza, is
a creature of the flesh, and a formidable adversary of anyone whose
body would be purified and delivered of incertitude. Even Buck's
voice is "wellfed" (1:107). Buck's mock Mass celebrates "body and
soul and blood and ouns" (1:21–22) and he flaunts physicality in
every gesture: shaving, wiping his razor, feeling his "smooth skin"
(1:124), linking arms with Stephen, plunging into the sea. Seen in
this context, Buck's relentless vulgarity is thematically crucial, part
of Joyce's larger comic project. When Buck jokes about prepuces,
making water, or "rotten teeth and rotten guts" (1:412), "that's all
done with a purpose" (6:735): his jibes incessantly link the sublime
and the bodily, as when he coins his own Homeric epithets: "The
snotgreen sea. The scrotumtightening sea" (1:78). Most important,
it is Mulligan who dubs Stephen "poor dogsbody" (1:112). This
characteristically blasphemous inversion sticks in Stephen's mind,
as well it should, for it summarizes the part of himself that disgusts
and appalls him.

Since Stephen's aversion to his own body and the way of all flesh
transgresses a fundamental comic law, it is both humorous and
pathetic: "As he and others see me. Who chose this face for me. This
dogsbody to rid of vermin" (1:136–37). His allegiance to spirit and
repulsion from flesh helps account for the terror inspired by his
mother's ghost, always appearing with a "wasted body" (1:103,
270). It is not simply the pain of her loss but the fact of her rot that
horrifies Stephen. One's mother is preeminently a body, the source
of comfort and nourishment; for that primal flesh to decay is a kind
of betrayal, an "offense to me," Stephen specifies, undermining any
faith in flesh: God's piece of work is finally a tattered coat upon a
stick. Even Buck's phrase for handkerchief, "noserags" (1:113),
implies deterioration. This antipathy to mortality is why Stephen so
vividly remembers his mother squashing "lice from the children's

[34]Among the bodily parts specified (I cite only line numbers here) in "Telemachus" are skin (124), arm (159), nose (162), ribs (166), omphalos (176),
face (185), hair (186), eyes (187), pulses (225), prepuces (394), shoulder
(679), legs (681), face (688), pate (689), chest and paunch (690), thumbnail
(693), "brow and lips and chestbone" (693–94), hand (742), and head (742).

shirts" (1:269), protecting them from harm, and why he so heatedly and oddly expresses his resentment toward Mulligan for saying that Mrs. Dedalus is "beastly dead." The child of a beast must be mortal, eventually "dead alas." He would rather be "the boy / that can enjoy / invisibility" (1:260–62) to escape the bodily prison, to become the "ghost of his own father" (1:556–57), as Buck aptly banters, to transcend the carnality that engendered him. Another sign of Stephen's estrangement from "the stream of life" (5:563, etc.) is his fear of women, with their "womb[s] of sin" (3:44). In this sense the error in his father's telegram is apt, for a woman is a-Nother. Stephen is alienated from his body and from carnal processes, deliberately so, as suggested by his odd phrase "made not begotten" (3:45) to describe his own conception. His rejection of the Church is fueled by his abhorrent fear that God is after all a "chewer of corpses!" (1:278), a particularly appropriate bogeyman. In this light, Stephen's rejection of Mulligan, which he seems to imagine as some kind of heroic refusal to capitulate, could be another false flight; he might be better off living in the omphalos and joining Buck in those waters of our "great sweet mother" (1:77–78).[35]

Though *Ulysses* refuses to sanction humor in any categorical way, as illustrated by the complexity of Buck's portrait, certainly Stephen would benefit from greater comic flexibility; he needs to learn to expect a world of flux, incongruity, and confusion, and to see how often he wears motley. Stephen dimly intuits the "joyous" association between Buck and free play. One of the few heartening moments in "Proteus" is this fanciful vision: "Gaze in your *omphalos*. Hello. Kinch here. Put me on to Edenville. Aleph, alpha: nought, nought, one" (3:38–40). Here Stephen is gaily inventive: calling himself by Buck's nickname for him, substituting "nought" for God's "omega," and using the word "omphalos" implicitly acknowledging the value of dwelling with Buck in the house of mirth. I would state this even more sharply: the closest Stephen comes in *Ulysses* to resembling his author is precisely when he is most dra-

[35]I disagree with Bernard Benstock's interpretation of "Telemachus" on this important point. He views Buck as "the perverse tempter" who "lures the sleepy, displeased Stephen toward the precipice" and "points Stephen toward the menacing sea" (Hart and Hayman 9). In my view, this tempter is not simply perverse, nor is the sea merely menacing; Bloom's reiterated phrase, "stream of life" is one contrary suggestion.

matically touched by Buck's spirit of folly. Buck's clowning, always implicit as jester's antics, becomes explicit in "Scylla and Charybdis": he is "blithe in motley" (9:486), has a "happy patch's [clown or fool] smirk" (9:1177), whispers "with clown's awe" (9:1209), and carries the fool's bells (9:501). Yet Buck in "Scylla and Charybdis" has an effect upon Stephen that is strikingly different from the one he had in the opening episode. Upstaged, Stephen accepts the interruption, radically shifts his ground, and moves toward free play. It is notable that Joyce twice presents his supposed surrogate Stephen in pivotal sequences, episodes 1 and 9, "usurped" by Buck. In "Scylla and Charybdis" Buck remains as witty as ever, and is now the cause of wit in Stephen. To put the case bluntly: Buck influences Stephen for the better.

Evidently provoked by Buck, Stephen shares in the fun. The telegram Stephen sent to Buck that morning, with whatever cryptic intent, suggests the solemn pretensions of its author. But what happens when Stephen finds himself mocked by "mine enemy" (9:483)? "Stephen laughed" (9:567). Jesus wept! Stephen is actually enjoying himself! Even more important, his delight is therapeutic, salutary: "He laughed to free his mind from his mind's bondage" (9:1016). Or, in another sign that he perceives the process of serious play: "Jest on. Know thyself" (9:1153). In this frame of mind, he is asking himself the right questions: "What have I learned? Of them? Of me?" (9:1113).

In apparent response to the sharp challenge posed by Buck Mulligan, Stephen seems less pathetic and more acute in the second half of "Scylla and Charybdis." Although he continues to allude and crib fairly heavily, both in words and thought, he is far less dependent on authorities than he was before Buck arrived. Once he weathers Buck's attack on his telegram, he seems more spirited, confident, and fluent. He laughs, trades banter with Buck, and recovers the floor with an undeniably virtuoso performance. Its theatrical gusto is notable in a young man who seemed paralyzed by glum thoughts only hours earlier. Like Buck, Stephen now appears moved by the conviction that "the play's the thing" (9:876–77)—as he indicates when Eglinton asks, "Do you believe your own theory?" (9:1065–66) and he promptly answers no.

Stephen appears more relaxed, playful, almost jovial. His auditors want to hear more—a monologuist's fantasy!—and the spirit of ludic allusion burgeons. The tone both of Stephen's meditations and of the discussion is now entertaining, almost gay, as in this sequence: "As for fay Elizabeth, otherwise carrotty Bess, the gross virgin who inspired the *Merry Wives of Windsor,* let some meinherr from Almany grope his life long for deephid meanings in the depths of the buckbasket." To himself he adds, "I think you're getting on very nicely. Just mix up a mixture of theolologicophilolological. *Mingo, minxi, mictum, mingere*" (9:757–62). When John Eglinton catches the spirit and dares Stephen to prove that Shakespeare was a Jew, Stephen happily obliges, in what is becoming more and more of an intellectual romp, not regarded seriously even by that most austere of self-critics, Kinch the Knife-Blade.

Joyce signals Stephen's general upturn or recovery with numerous signs. The word *"Entr'acte"* (9:484), marking Buck's entrance, comes near the midpoint of the chapter. Stephen thinks, "Read the skies," and in response to Lyster's sarcastic question, "Was it a celestial phenomenon?" he replies, "A star by night . . . a pillar of the cloud by day" (9:944). As Buck and Stephen are about to leave the library, Bloom passes between them, a cleavage that to Stephen suggests more than a momentary "parting": "Part. The moment is now" (9:1199). Readers usually take this reflection to suggest Stephen's parting from Buck and consider it a necessary and important step in Stephen's development toward the artist who creates *Ulysses.* I submit that the opposite is equally true: Stephen's separation from Buck Mulligan is significant but lamentable, evidence that he could never create the book we are reading. If we realize that Stephen is a drowning man, and remember that Buck "saved men from drowning" (1:62), the conclusion is inescapable that Stephen forsakes not only a prophet of folly but a potential savior. Perhaps "Part. The moment is now" refers to Joyce's separation from the youth who, because his character is fixed, ceased to interest his creator: the older Joyce comprehended the need to part, to become double, like Buck and all fools. In any event, the rest of *Ulysses* is far less seriously concerned with Stephen's development and much more profoundly, profanely moved by (although not limited to) the spirit of the fool. If Stephen is influenced by the proximity of Bloom, as the standard interpretation of the novel maintains, he is also *and should be* stimulated by the spirit of folly, embodied in Mercurial Malachi. If only Stephen would and could "take a fool's advice" (15:2515).

I Am a Fool Perhaps

Folly persists and rises in incongruous places. The beginning of "Eumaeus" specifically echoes the opening of the novel, as suggested by the phrase "preparatory to anything else" (16:1). We cannot help thinking of Buck Mulligan as we read, "Mr Bloom *brushed* off the greater bulk of the *shavings* and handed Stephen the hat and ashplant and *bucked* him up" (16:1–3, my emphases).[36] Moreover, and quite surprisingly, the first and last advice Bloom gives Stephen in "Eumaeus" is to banish Buck; one of the small mysteries of the book is the urgency with which the normally tolerant Bloom urges the break. He has hardly taken Stephen under his wing when he stresses, "I wouldn't personally repose much trust in that boon companion of yours who contributes the humorous element, Dr Mulligan, as a guide, philosopher and friend if I were in your shoes" (16:279–81). Though Bloom hardly knows either youth or the nature of their relationship—for one thing, Stephen is literally in Buck's shoes—Bloom considers Buck an obstacle to his own influence. Buck and Bloom represent contending discourses, jostling for supremacy in the novel, for "earnestly Mr Leopold Bloom" (11:1262) himself wishes to be Stephen's guide, philosopher, and friend in an entirely different spirit—that of practicality and solemnity. The importance of the conflict between folly and earnestness is underscored at the end of the episode, when Bloom reiterates his counsel to abandon Buck and Folly—advice that, as I've noted, prompts an apt reaction from the horse.

Comic justice insists we record what the much-maligned jester thinks of Bloom. Given his genius for satiric diminution, Mulligan's immediate impressions of Leopold Bloom are predictably unfavorable, as he makes clear to Stephen when he notices Bloom's remarkably intense gaze: "The wandering jew, Buck Mulligan whispered with clown's awe. Did you see his eye? He looked upon you to lust after you. I fear thee, ancient mariner. O, Kinch, thou art in peril. Get thee a breechpad" (9:1209–11). As usual, Buck's clowning blends prattle and acumen, mistakenly attributing homosexual

[36]Fritz Senn makes this point, in *Joyce's Dislocutions: Essays on Reading as Translation,* ed. John Paul Riquelme (Baltimore: Johns Hopkins University Press, 1984), 135, as does Hugh Kenner, *Joyce's Voices* (Berkeley: University of California Press, 1978), 35–36.

designs to Bloom but correctly intuiting the wandering Jew's special interest in Stephen. In some versions, the Wandering Jew's repentance is rewarded with the gift of prophecy, which suggests a very good reason for Buck to distrust and fear Bloom: he is the holy fool, whom the jester must discredit to maintain his own supremacy.

It is the usual fate of holy fools to be regarded as mere fools. Buck, like most Dubliners, considers Bloom foolish in the simplest sense: a natural butt of humor, a stock figure of fun. Bloom is Dublin's Insignificant Other, who never gets to complete the anecdote, who inspires street urchins to mimic him (as Lenehan notices and dramatizes for the amusement of the company), who gets caught peeping at the goddess's rectum, who is mistakenly understood to have won a big bet and scorned for not standing drinks. In many such moments Bloom is a Chaplinesque figure,[37] a shlemiel or Pierrot le Fou, comically henpecked and cuckolded, a combination bound to inspire mockery. "The deceived husband," says Folly, "is a standing joke" (Erasmus 33). Details or rumors of Bloom's private life are bandied about the town. Lenehan gleefully recalls a scene, straight out of a music hall farce, in which he bumped Molly's bosom while Bloom described the constellation. The notion of Bloom as a fool is so deeply rooted that not even marriage to such a "gamey mare and no mistake" (10:566–67) raises the possibility that he might have redeeming attributes: "In God's name," declares John Henry Menton, "what did she marry a coon like that for?" (6: 704–5). So prevalent is the mockery of Bloom that even his wife has noticed people "making fun of him . . . behind his back" (18:1276–77). The very label on his hat laughs at him, with a "high grade ha" (4:69–70).

Bloom sometimes aggravates his "image problem" by preaching to his cohorts, in his "Herr Professor Luitpold Blumenduft" (12:468) mode, claiming the moral or informed position. He prefers tennis to boxing, deplores violence, pities women, children, and animals, and remains maddeningly sober: not, in short, a real Irish man. More insufferable to most people than Bloom's foolish pedantry and pontification is his hopeless effort to put a lid on gaiety and revelry, thus becoming another stock comic butt, a killjoy or party

[37]According to Austin Briggs, in "Chaplin and Joyce," Louis Zukofsky suggested Chaplin for the part of Bloom in his proposed screenplay of *Ulysses*.
[38]This is a variation on Frye's "blocking force," and a figure alive and merrily

pooper.[38] As Erasmus's Stultitia observes, "Just as nothing is more foolish than misplaced wisdom, so too, nothing is more imprudent than perverse prudence" (Erasmus 44). No wonder his fellow Dubliners see Bloom as the conventional fool, all in motley, for Bloom is indeed pathetic and ridiculous.

In the classic comic tradition, Bloom is frequently stymied, as though taunted by an annoyed minor deity. He remembers the inane advertisement for Plumtree's Potted Meat because it summarizes so much of his life: "Incomplete." Bloom is frustrated all day long by failures of connection large and small. When he wants to ogle a lady's legs, a tram intervenes. In a series of potential recognition scenes in "Circe," instead of receiving the comfort and insight enabling epic and tragic heroes of yore, he is chastized by his father, castigated by his grandfather, and ignored by his son. Bloom's homage to his wife's bottom, his topsy-turvy sleeping posture, and his "10 years, 5 months, and eighteen days during which carnal intercourse had been incomplete" (17:2282–83), bespeak a life of folly and provoke (in most common readers, if my students are representative) incredulity and hilarity.

Of course we evaluate Bloom much more sympathetically than "base minds [and] rash judgers" (14:864). One of the many ways Bloom transcends ordinary folly lies in his astonishing ability to see himself as others see him. By contrast, Buck Mulligan can brilliantly play the fool but can never *know* the fool. In a sublimely comic self-recognition near the end of "Nausicaa," Bloom hints that he has discovered his essential identity. He picks up a stick and etches "I," then loses heart, realizing it will be tramped or washed away by the tide. "Useless" (13:1259), Bloom thinks, with Joyce's pun on the title of the novel suggesting that the hero is approaching authorial awareness. "AM. A." he continues, then "efface[s] the letters with his slow boot" (13:1264–66). Like so many cryptic signs and ambiguous indicators in the novel, Bloom's message is a wonderful Rorschach test, or a fool's glass for the reader: "Bend, see my face there, dark mirror . . . " (13:1260).[39]

---

abused in contemporary movies. Every "youth" flick has to have the stuffy character who orders the kids to turn down that awful music. See, if you must have evidence, *Beach Blanket Bingo, Footloose,* and *Good Morning Vietnam!*

[39]Cf. Stephen's vision of "dark men . . . flashing in their mocking mirrors the obscure soul of the world" (2:159–60).

What Bloom intended to write is a critical crux. Speculations include ALPHA, the first and the last; the sign of the fish, traditional icon of Jesus; MARRIED MAN; NAUGHTY BOY; and ALONE. As one of Joyce's best readers notes, AMA suggests *ama-*, the Latin root for love, the word known to all men.[40] Maybe Bloom was thinking, "CUCKOLD," which brings to his consciousness the sounds of the cuckoo-clock at the end of "Nausicaa." Most likely, though, Bloom is simply and aptly inscribing what he had thought only moments earlier: "I am a fool perhaps" (13:1098). Reinforcing this possibility is the near reiteration earlier in "Nausicaa," "Might have made a worse fool of myself however" (13:942–43), and a subsequent variation in "Circe," "Absurd I am" (15:658).

To define himself as a fool makes sense in terms of both Bloom's immediate dramatic situation and his larger symbolic role. Standing on a deserted beach, feeling considerably less serious about himself, his pressing needs satisfied and his pants sticky, he has played the fool and now recognizes his folly. In this implicit affirmation of his fundamental identity, Bloom is the comic hero, infinite and "Useless" (13:1259), as Odysseus is both *outis*, "no-man" and *Zeus*, godlike. Joyce's foolish hero, simultaneously "nobody" and "godlike," becomes both a source and an object of humor—not merely the figure of fun in Buck's burlesque, but a definer of Joycean comedy. (Joyce knew, and enjoyed the fact, that his name stemmed from the French for "happiness, sexual climax"; hence in coming, Bloom becomes Joyce). To argue that Bloom is both the object of comic exposure and the source of comic values, simultaneously all too human and yet somehow heroic, is to perceive him as a conventional fool and a holy fool, descended from venerable ancestors like Don Quixote, Uncle Toby, and Myshkin, whose follies demonstrate such profound comic values.

These values are expressed in Bloom's simple, sometimes silly fashion, not as grand epiphanies about history and nightmares or God and a shout in the street, but in casual rumination. Wondering why you "couldn't sink if you tried" (5:39) in the Dead Sea, Bloom roughly remembers from school physics the definition of weight: "Law of falling bodies: per second, per second. They all fall to the ground. The earth. It's the force of gravity of the earth is the weight" (5:44–46). To Bloom the law of falling bodies governs mortal crea-

[40]Fritz Senn, *Joyce's Dislocutions,* 163.

tures metaphorically as well as physically: falls are universal, natural, and incessant, but not irreparable, as they might be in satire or tragedy. Bloom's comic perspective calculates the "force of gravity" in ways that root or ground without burying us: "Couldn't sink if you tried." "The earth" is our habitat, our natural home, from which we come and to which we return; movement up is possible but limited, a fact of our earthbound condition. To a satirist like Buck Mulligan, our corporeal nature is the fundamental and pervasive fact of life, "all a mockery and beastly" (1:210); to Stephen, the self-styled tragic hero, this fact constitutes an insuperable barrier between dogsbody and godsbody. Bloom, the comic hero, is apparently at ease with this condition: the law of falling bodies is inevitable but not debilitating.

"My fireworks," Bloom thinks, after masturbating. "Up like a rocket, down like a stick" (13:894–95). No truer words appear in this encyclopedic novel. In the Foolosopher's theology, we are all fools perpetually falling, but no fall is fatal or irremediable, for we may always recover and rise again. Another law of folly that apparently prevails in the novel (and in Erasmus's *The Praise of Folly*) is that if something is true, so is its opposite: the coincidence of opposites is an emphasis of Bruno and a tenet of folly. In Joycean terms, we are also down like a stick, up like a rocket, which is why Bloom so often remembers Breen's postcard, "U.p: up" (13:1239). Down and up, up and down, like all other opposites, attract each other and become one. So that when Bloom, tired and down at the end of "Nausicaa," asks himself "Will I get up?" (13:1101), we can guess the answer because we are familiar with the comic rhythm of "Handy-dandy," as Lear's Fool calls it. Topsy-turvy is the way of folly, always countering with an opposite, always reversing up and down. The fool is thus elusive, defined by his momentary stance rather than his settled position. Bloom next to the Citizen looks romantic, idealistic, high-minded; after Gerty's section, he sounds realistic, skeptical, occasionally cynical. Folly prefers associations to syllogisms, analogies to nuances, existence to essence, process to product.

"The number of fools is infinite" in part because folly is marvelously resilient: Bloom endures indignities, disappointments, misfortunes, and frustrations, yet his setbacks are almost invariably followed by a marked revival. This capacity for survival and revival makes Bloom quintessentially foolish, kin to all the comic figures who are constantly undone but never finished. Falstaff, always a tough clown to keep down, bounces back from any insult. "By the Lord, I knew ye as well as he that made ye," he replies to Hal's exposure of his cowardice at Gadshill (*1H4:* II.iv.296–97), and plays dead only to make a mock-resurrection in comedy's third most memorable stage direction: "Falstaff riseth up" (V.iv.111). Constantly knocked from his saddle and abused, Don Quixote is carried forward by his dauntless spirit, which ultimately converts that stubborn realist Sancho Panza and the whole skeptical world. Odysseus, much buffeted by fortune and malign gods, returns home disguised as a beggar and provokes scorn from the suitors, degradation being a condition of his great triumph. If one law of comedy is "Pride goeth . . . before a fall" (Prov. 16:18), another is also scriptural: "he that shall humble himself shall be exalted" (Matt. 23:12).

Bloom's kinship with these heroic fools is most evident in his elastic vitality and powers of recuperation: the comic rhythm is a perpetual series of ups and downs. Picking up what is probably a Zionist tract selling land in Palestine prompts a precise and energetic daydream of Eastern fecundity,[41] but—with the fool's insistent realism—he entertains and rejects fantasy: "No, not like that. A barren land, bare waste" (4:219). Bloom's detailed evocation of "desolation" (4:229) matches in gloomy horror Stephen's morbid sensations; the crucial difference is how fully and by what means Bloom recovers. Typically, he consciously combats his "grey horror" (4:230) and settles for skeptical equanimity, as he does when he thinks of his father's suicide or his son's death. In this recuperative and stabilizing capacity, Bloom is a worthy if shrunken successor to Odysseus, exhorting himself ("Down, my heart!") to persevere. "Well, I am here now," muses Bloom. "Got up wrong side of the bed. Must begin again those Sandow's exercises" (4:232–34). Even the pushups rehearse the down-up, down-up pattern. Bloom's recuperations illustrate Susanne K. Langer's conception of comic action, "the upset and recovery of the protagonist's equilibrium, his contest with the world, and his triumph by wit, luck, personal power, or even humorous, or ironical, or philosophical acceptance of mischance."[42]

---

[41]The "melonfields" (4:194) he envisions connect him to the dream Stephen was "almosting" (3:366) on the beach.

[42]Susanne K. Langer, *Feeling and Form: A Theory of Art* (New York: Charles Scribner's Sons, 1953), 331.

Acceptance is paradoxically associated with both wisdom and folly. In *Hamlet,* for example, the hero moves closer toward equanimity in graveyard banter with a wise fool. It is characteristic of folly, Hamlet's progress and the gravedigger's philosophy being prime examples, to maintain a foolish faith in nature, as opposed to custom, ceremony, or conventional wisdom. Erasmus's Folly cites Christ, who "carefully prescribed folly, warning . . . against wisdom, when he set before [us] the example of children, lilies, mustard seed, and sparrows—stupid creatures lacking all intelligence, *leading their lives according to the dictates of nature,* artless, and carefree" (Erasmus 130, my emphasis). So powerful is the association between folly and nature, that the word "natural" came to signify "a fool," a connotation that still clings to the word.[43] Bloom's recoveries are enabled by just such foolish faith in the benevolent dictates of nature: "Poisons the only cures," he thinks at the pharmacy. "Remedy where you least expect it. Clever of nature" (5:483–84). When Bloom generalizes about life, he thinks in tropes of cycles or "the stream," ongoing like comedy, not truncated like tragedy or static like satire. The jocoserious rhythm is evidenced by an almost oxymoronic fusion of down and up, death and regeneration, fall and revival, poisons and cures. When Bloom remembers Molly saying, "Give us a touch, Poldy. God I'm dying for it," he instinctively adds, "How life begins" (6:80–81) to link death and life.

A striking disparity signifying the gap between the community's view of Bloom as a conventional fool and our sense of him as Joyce's holy fool is that this pathetic outsider is so little alienated and so thoroughly at home in his world. Bloom feels part of humanity and the community, no matter how stintingly society reciprocates; we are, he thinks, "in the same boat" (5:185–86), "all in the same swim" (5:363), "No roses without thorns" (5:277–78). He feels this way because he is of the kindly race of men, naturally related to everyone. Life does not oppress him as he basks "in happy warmth" (4:81). He does not imagine himself ("Circe" being the exception that proves the rule) enslaved or exiled, which is another reason why he is only temporarily inspired by the Zionist pamphlet. Odysseus-like, Bloom radiates a fundamental comic equanimity, unlike Ste-

---

[43]For instance, in the lyrics of a James Taylor song, "Country Road": "I'd have to be some kind of natural-born fool / To want to pass that way again. . . . "

phen, who struggles melodramatically with his fate. Contemplating separation from his daughter, for example, and wondering if she is destined to become like Molly, whose liaison is being planned under his very eyes, he thinks, "A soft qualm, regret, flowed down his backbone, increasing. Will happen, yes. Prevent. Useless: can't move. Girl's sweet light lips. Will happen too. He felt the flowing qualm spread over him. Useless to move now. Lips kissed, kissing, kissed . . . " (4:447–50). Bloom is nearly overwhelmed by his nostalgia and deprivation, until, through a muscular effort of will, he again controls his feelings and rests upon that fundamental folly, acquiescence. Again, the reiteration of "Useless" puns on the title of the novel and slyly reinforces the connection between Bloom and his Homeric model.

Bloom is at home in another important sense that reveals his strong, natural affinity with fools: he is comfortable in his flesh. Many fools enjoy sensual pleasures and come to be identified almost emblematically by their bodies: one thinks fondly of Falstaff's fat guts, Sancho's belly, and Bottom's bottom, all of which locate the fool's identity not in the soul, with its abstractions (honor, chivalry, romance) but in the body, with its imperious needs. Here, in man's "second nature" or "the lower bodily stratum," Bakhtin locates the origins of laughter that simultaneously degrades and regenerates.[44] The first thing we hear about Bloom the Fool is that he "ate with relish the inner organs of beasts and fowls" (4:1). Like Odysseus, Falstaff, Sancho, and Tom Jones, men of flamboyant corporeality,[45] Bloom is a man with a stomach and a hearty appetite, not a man of the spirit or of ascetic self-denial. Sensual and appetitive, with "all kinds of crazy longings" (13:779), such as masturbating in public[46] or smelling his toenail, Bloom takes what humble pleasures his body affords him, unlike Stephen, so wary of "morose delectation" (3:385) and demeaned by bodily necessities. Like many comic characters, Bloom regards the limits of mortality and the functions of the body with neither satiric contempt nor tragic anguish, but with

[44]Bakhtin, *Rabelais,* 75.

[45]Fielding fondly speaks of "that eating poem of *The Odyssey*" (*Tom Jones,* 9:5).

[46]Joyce's self-characterization as "masterbilker" (*FW* 111:21), cited earlier, also puns on the activity Rousseau charmingly termed "cheating nature by the vice."

acceptance and joy. "Enjoying nature now" (13:1055), whatever creaturely pleasures might be, if you will, at hand: "what harm?" (13:885).[47]

A particularly Joycean corollary of folly's traditional emphasis upon the body is Bloom's preoccupation with waste. He sees defecation as nature's way to "reclaim the whole place" (4:482). Lots of waste, apparently meaningless, sometimes execrable, might also be seen as the stuff of life and art; Bloom shares his maker's interest in life's "flotsam, jetsam" (17:1686). Heading for the jakes, Bloom muses of dung and the cycle of fertilization, "dirty cleans" (4:481), an oxymoronic conjunction of opposites summarizing another whole attitude or law of folly. While earlier works such as *Gargantua and Pantagruel, Gulliver's Travels, Tom Jones,* and *Tristram Shandy* refer to defecation, no hero before Bloom has so thoroughly enjoyed a bowel movement or found in it so comforting a philosophy. Bodily functions in *Ulysses* have the important metaphoric value peculiar to folly: Bloom begins his first episode savoring the tang of urine and ends it wiping his bum, as though to underscore that *Inter urinas et faeces nascimur.* Bloom is not so much erotic as polymorphously perverse, taking infantile delight in his body; it is only in the special case of "Circe" that he seems haunted or troubled by his appetitive self. Otherwise animal functions feel utterly natural: "Hope it's not too big bring on piles again. No, just right. So. Ah! . . . Life might be so" (4:509–11). Bloom regards excretion as a kind of creativity: in accepting this irreducible, essential condition of humanity, comic figures may rise above themselves. In folly, the way down is the way up.

The virtues of Bloom's folly are richly conveyed at the end of "Lotos-Eaters": "Heavenly weather really. If life was always like that. . . . Heatwave. Won't last. Always passing, the stream of life, which in the stream of life we trace is dearer thaaan them all. Enjoy a bath now: clean trough of water, cool enamel, the gentle tepid stream. This is my body" (5: 558–66). Then in his mind's eye, he "foresaw his pale body reclined in it at full, naked, in a womb of warmth, oiled by scented melting soap, softly laved. He saw his trunk and limbs riprippled over and sustained, buoyed lightly upward, lemonyellow: his navel, bud of flesh: and saw the dark tangled curls of his bush floating, floating hair of the stream around the limp father of thousands, a languid floating flower" (5:567–72).

[47]Compare Molly (18:1517–18).

In such a moment, folly appears enormously appealing. A break in the clouds is enthusiastically greeted ("Heavenly weather really") although Bloom knows it too is passing. Here is the fool's faith in the natural cycle, with its yearly decline and regeneration: "Always passing, the stream of life. . . . " Continuity, not curtailment, is the dominant emphasis. Always content to take what small pleasure life affords, with special tenderness toward man's second nature, the bodily lower stratum, Bloom's casually blasphemous "my body" is folly central to *Ulysses,* organized in part as an epic of the body. Bloom's foolish, tender regard for the simply human associates him with Jesus ("This is my body").

This passage, in moving from "falling bodies" to "rising bodies," reflects in miniature the fool's progress toward comic consecration. Like Tristram Shandy, Bloom is much more than a humour character; he is also the reader of a comic work, alert to incongruities and correspondences but not always sure how to distinguish the two. When a throwaway is placed in his hands, Bloom illustrates the folly and value of reading both jocosely and seriously.

> Heart to heart talks.
> Bloo . . . Me? No.
> Blood of the Lamb. (8:7–9)

For this instant, Bloom is Stanley Fish's ideal reader, reacting to a phoneme by devising a full-blown meaning that is both ridiculous and relevant. Bloom is a holy fool, the perpetual alien and possible scapegoat who somehow eludes sacrifice, endures, and attains a measure of triumph. Endowed with a dollop of prophetic power, he obliviously predicts the winner of the Gold Cup race and the 1907 Dublin mayorality. Many small details reinforce this sense of Bloom as prophetic. At the newspaper office, for example, as the company takes to the pub, Bloom wonders, "is that young Dedalus the moving spirit" (7:984–85). Although not present to have seen or heard it, Bloom somehow intuits Stephen's "motion": "As the next motion on the agenda paper," Stephen had said, "may I suggest that the house do now adjourn" (7:885–86). (His phrase for Stephen, "the moving spirit," also implies the connection between Stephen and the author of *Ulysses*). Literally unable to transcend his lot—his body, mortality, history—Bloom carries with him some magic, the fool's equivalent to the "Blood of the Lamb," a power to transmute the mundane, redeem the inert, and see into the life of things. Just as Bloom dreams of vast wealth acquired by "the reclamation of dunams of waste" (17:1699), so Joyce gathers throwaways and transmutes "the daily bread of experience into the radiant body of everliving life" (*P* 221).

Even when nothing special is happening to him, Bloom's inner life seems full, rich, and bustling precisely because he is foolishly playful, constantly entertaining himself with perceptions, curiosity, and speculations. His very consciousness is polyphonic, the clash and din of myriad voices; here too the fool sacrifices integrity for possibility, unity for multiplicity. Though Bloom roughly resembles Buck in this regard, he differs in his freedom from the need for mastery: Bloom is happy "yielding but resisting" (4:506–7). Instead of tragic integrity (Achilles, Hamlet, Stephen), the "yielding" of this heroic fool represents the flexibility of folly, which is why Bloom cannot "fix" himself in a formulated phrase. Perhaps I AM A also implies I AM ANYTHING, the man of many turns, who refuses to be limited to a merely humorous inelasticity of spirit (Malvolio, Jaques).

Most of the stuff of Bloom's consciousness is foolishly mundane; Bloom has the fool's solicitude toward trivia, an affinity he shares with his maker, who once agreed his work was trivial, and added that it was also quadrivial.[48] Has any character perceived banality with more beauty and dignity? Bloom achieves this transformation by selfless immersion in the stream of life and a kind of sympathetic imagination: "Wonder what I look like to [the cat]. Height of a tower? No, she can jump me" (4:28–29). Thus we are introduced to our mock-heroic protagonist's cherished belief in multiplicity of viewpoint, summarized by his worrying over the concept of "parallax." Usually his explorations of other points of observation evince a powerful compassion, like his concern for Mrs. Purefoy's hard labor. In one of his more endearing moments of empathy, he wonders "Do fish ever get seasick?" (13:1162).[49] At times, his change of position is purely humorous, as when (Keats-like, or Keats via Charlie Chaplin) he assumes the view of a flock of pigeons: "Who will we do

[48]Frank Budgen, "James Joyce," in *James Joyce: Two Decades of Criticism,* ed. Seon Givens (New York: Vanguard Press, 1948), 24.

[49]Hugh Kenner, often as engagingly responsive to titbits as Bloom, has found an answer: according to a newspaper account of recent research, fish can get seasick. See *Joyce's Voices,* 57.

it on? I pick the fellow in black. Here goes" (8:402–3). Even when he imagines himself the hapless victim, Bloom enjoys the free play of imagination: "Must be thrilling from the air" (8:403). We see a similar leap to otherness when Bloom admires Simon's ability to cap his own story, or when he speculates that the Citizen probably didn't mean harm: "Look at it other way round. Not so bad then. Perhaps not to hurt he meant" (13:1219–20). Such sentiments, especially the foolish reversal, "other way around," lift Bloom beyond mere decency toward comic wisdom; certainly his ultimate assessment of his adversaries conveys the Christian charity of a holy fool: "Ought to go home and laugh at themselves" (13:1217–18).

Bloom progresses from the simple fool, "he who gets slapped," to one of Paul's "fools for the sake of Christ" (1 Cor. 4:10), a development that is most marked in "Cyclops." (Since I will later "look at it other way round," let me temporarily defer qualifications to this line of argument). Playing the part of the holy fool with stubborn persistence, Bloom resembles exactly what the Citizen furiously scorns: "That's the new Messiah for Ireland" (12:1642). "Some people," says Bloom, paraphrasing the Sermon on the Mount, "can see the mote in others' eyes but they can't see the beam in their own" (12:1237–38). Goaded, baited, and mocked, Bloom delivers what one might take as the gospel of *Ulysses:* "But it's no use, says he. Force, hatred, history, all that. That's not life for men and women, insult and hatred. And everybody knows that it's the very opposite of that that is really life" (12:1481–83). We forgive the awkwardness of the language because Bloom is under attack, passionately sincere, and obviously right. "Love, says Bloom. I mean the opposite of hatred" (12:1485). Having delivered the word, Bloom, Christ-like, abruptly departs—"I must go now" (12:1485)—scorned by the Citizen as "a new apostle to the gentiles" (12:1489). Bloom's middle name, Paula, incidentally, recalls the apostle who was a great advocate of folly. The nasty narrator of "Cyclops" describes Bloom's exit, "off he pops like greased lightning" (12:1488), which puns on the pronunciation of "greased/graced," suggesting another truth out of the mouths of babes and fools. Ultimately the enraged Citizen vows, "By Jesus, I'll crucify him so I will" (12:1812).

Throughout "Cyclops," Bloom is continually identified by "his cod's eye" (12:214, 410, etc.). Probably this refers literally to the phenomenon, as it were, that a fish's eye always appears open, like Bloom's probing gaze. By the time A DEADHAND in "Circe" writes on the wall, with prophetic theatricality and inscrutability, "Bloom is a cod" (15:1871), it conveys several jocoserious implications. *Cod* is slang for joker or fool, scrotum or penis—and, as such, the subject of Panurge's loving tribute.[50] But *cod* also suggests the traditional Christian icon, a fish,[51] and puns on God. Bloom's childhood nickname reinforces this cluster of associations. He was called "Mackerel" (15:3331) which, like "Cod," has both sacred and mundane connotations.[52] The suggestion that Bloom is a Holy Fool is reinforced when Bloom is termed one of those "bloody . . . Jerusalem . . . cuckoos" (12:1571–72). Like the servant of the Lord in *Isaiah* (53:3), Bloom "is despised and rejected of men, a man of sorrows and acquainted with grief." Bloom is certainly a buffoon, as when he ludicrously cites several apostates as Jews or describes God as Christ's father or uncle. Yet the wandering Jew and Jerusalem cuckoo is just as surely the truest Christian in Dublin. "Hath not God made foolish the wisdom of this world?" asks Paul, "God hath chosen the foolish things of the world to confound the wise" (1 Cor. 1:20, 27).

The implication that Bloom is a veritable "fool in Christ" is acted out, with a variation, in "Circe," where whatever was heretofore implicit becomes "actual." Previously Bloom might inadvertently make the sign of the cross, to illustrate the ad for Keyes (7:132); now he begins to speak and act, at least intermittently, as though he conceives himself as a holy fool. Looking aimlessly for Stephen as the episode opens, he mutters words John the Baptist spoke about Jesus: "Wash off his sins of the world" (15:235–36); to Mrs. Bellingham's vindictive fury he replies, "Forget, forgive" (15:1108) and offers the other cheek. To the question, "Bloom, are you the Messiah ben Joseph or ben David," Bloom answers like Christ, "You have said it" (15:1834). Having been stoned and defiled, he again quotes Christ: "Weep not for me" (15:1936). Indeed, one way to describe

[50]Rabelais, *Gargantua and Pantagruel,* Book 3, chap. 26.

[51]*The Concise Oxford Dictionary of the Christian Church* notes, "In modern times some Church of England associations willing to help those in need have adopted the symbol of a fish" (174), which was the sign of the early Church. "Fish" is connected with Christ because the Greek word for fish, ichthys, consists of the first letters of the Greek phrase, "Jesus Christ God Son Savior."

[52]Directly after Bloom is addressed as "Mackerel" (15:3331), THE ECHO calls him "Fool!" (15:3338). According to Enid Welsford, "mackerel" was also a common nickname for a court fool (*The Fool,* 4).

"Circe" is as a comic gospel: Bloom descends, declares the new Bloomusalem, raises many dead souls, endures mockery and sacrificial death, and rises from the dead.

In one extended sequence—between Zoe's "Go on. Make a stump speech of it" (15:1353) and "Talk away till you're black in the face" (15:1958)—Bloom is clearly cast as the holy fool, crowned and uncrowned at a feast of fools. Here Bloom metamorphoses from Lord Mayor of Dublin to "the world's greatest reformer" (15:1459) to Leopold the First (15:1475) to the Messiah Himself; then dissent mounts, rebellion ensues, and degradation begins. Christ preached that "he that shall humble himself shall be exalted" (Matt. 23:12), to which "Circe" adds, and "*Vice Versa*" (15:3010–11). Ultimately Bloom is mocked—"with asses' ears seats himself in the pillory" (15:1884)—desecrated, sacrificed, and "carbonised" (15:1956),— only to rise again "with a smile in his eye" (15:1962), both recapitulating and parodying his comic capacity for revival. Indeed, this Circean sequence is a textbook illustration of the "popular-festive form" that Bakhtin analyzes in *Gargantua and Pantagruel*.[53] With that smile, Bloom tells us he comprehends and enjoys his great role in Joyce's human comedy. Bloom seems to recognize his identity with folly as a source of dignity and amusement, and in that acceptance he is truly a fool and yet "not altogether fool, my lord" (*KL*.I.iv.165).

The Way a Body Can Understand

Joyce conceived *Ulysses* so that, in several senses, "the first shall be last and the last shall be first" (Matt. 19:30). One means of affirming Christ's great precept is to begin and end the novel with an ancillary yet magisterial figure of folly. "You all know," says Stul-

---

[53]"The king," writes Bakhtin, "is the clown. He is elected by all the people and is mocked by all the people. He is abused and beaten when the time of his reign is over, just as the carnival dummy of winter or of the dying year is mocked, beaten, torn to pieces, burned, or drowned. . . . The clown was first disguised as a king, but once his reign had come to an end his costume was changed, 'travestied,' to turn him once more into a clown. The abuse and thrashing are equivalent to a change of costume, to a metamorphosis." Bakhtin, *Rabelais,* 197. Literary variations on this carnival form include Dryden's "Mac-Flecknoe," Pope's *The Dunciad,* and some of Fielding's early farces.

titia, "that the ecclesiastical order of precedence places the highest dignitary at the end of the procession" (Erasmus 121). Like Erasmus's Stultitia, Molly is sublimely ridiculous, grandly trivial, and greater than the sum of her parts. Certainly Joyce's human comedy has no more passionate and eloquent advocate than Molly Bloom, especially in her conception of soul and body, sacred and profane. Out of her wonderfully amusing confusion emerges a virtual comic credo, worthy of Folly herself: "that word met something with hoses in it and he came out with some jawbreakers about the incarnation he never can explain a thing simply the way a body can understand" (18:565–67). Comedy has always been indulgent of the physical, mundane, and vulgar, and suspicious of the high-minded, abstract, and ideal.[54] Molly is impatient with "that old Bishop that spoke off the altar his long preach about womans higher functions" (18:837–38), because for her, as for most comic figures, the primary truths are not higher functions but carnal needs, the perpetual abasement of intellectual, romantic, or spiritual exaltation. The appetites of the body are no more sinful than the phases of the moon or the tides of the sea: "it didnt make me blush why should it either its only nature" (18:1386). Molly is preeminently a *body*, the essential condition of our being, who becomes The Body, a metamorphosis she suggests in recalling Bloom's love letters: "my Precious one everything connected with your glorious Body everything underlined that comes from it is a thing of beauty and of joy for ever" (18:1176–78). She is not only, in Joyce's often-quoted phrase, "the indispensable countersign to Bloom's passport to eternity" (Budgen 264), she is also the apostle of Joyce's comic gospel, "a thing of beauty" to which he affixes his own encoded signature, "of joy forever." Throughout her monologue she expresses more directly than anyone the novel's comic equanimity: "if thats all the harm ever we did in this vale of tears God knows its not much" (18:1517–18). Typically she appropriates God's name and sacred language to affirm a natural religion.

Appropriate to a chapter of incarnation in this "epic of the body,"

---

[54]Which is one reason why it is often patronized, as in Virginia Woolf's diary entry on *Ulysses:* "It is brackish. . . . It is underbred, not only in the obvious sense but in the literary sense." See Virginia Woolf, *A Writer's Diary: Being Extracts from the Diary of Virginia Woolf,* ed. Leonard Woolf (New York: New American Library, 1953), 56.

Molly's organ is "fat," or fleshiness—but her episode is also a synthesis, in that flesh contains and connects the whole body: "Penelope" is a sort of *Gray's Anatomy*. Demonstrating some of her maker's encyclopedic inclusiveness, she mentions practically all the human anatomy and characterizes almost everyone in terms of bodily parts: Boylan's "tremendous big red brute of a thing" (18:144), "big hipbones" and "hairy chest" (18:415–16), Bloom's "sly eye" (18:206), "his heart" (18:234), Bartell D'Arcy's "splendid set of teeth" (18:307), the Lord Mayor's "dirty eyes" (18:429), Mrs. Galbraith's "magnificent head of hair on her down to her waist" (18:478), the Blessed Virgin's "arms" (18:497), Mulvey's "tongue in my mouth" (18:771), his "moustache" (18:820) and "his hands over my eyes" (18:824–25), Milly's "skin . . . her lips so red" (18:1064–66), little Stephen's "curly hair" (18:1312), the "lovely young cock" on the Narcissus statue she imagines "taking . . . in my mouth" (18:1352–53), and many more.

Even more frequent are the self-delighting descriptions of her own "glorious Body." A page doesn't pass without reference to "my bottom" (18:53), "me behind" (18:122), the "big hole in the middle of us" (18:151–52), "my neck" (18:173), "my ring hand" (18:313), "my eyelids," "my heart" (18:321, 330), "my teeth . . . fingers . . . throat . . . belly" (18:430–50), "my piss . . . the skin underneath . . . my finger" (18:462–65), "my head . . . my chest" (18:522–29), "titties" (18:536), "nipple . . . breast . . . behind . . . legs . . . eyes . . . tongue . . . lips" (18:569–94), and so on. We hear about "every bit of myself" (18:904). Molly is very much the exhibitionist cavorting for "that fellow opposite" (18:921),[55] who represents the author and reader as well as her original audience: "and I in my skin hopping around I used to love myself then stripped at the washstand . . . " (18:922–23).

We have seen that bodily functions figure centrally in Joyce's comic vision; characters are depicted and distinguished in part by their attitudes toward their bodies.[56] Stephen resists and resents the body that imprisons his immortal spirit, while Bloom accepts his physical nature and can take pleasure in it. When a satirist like Swift

[55]Gerty uses the same expression to signify Bloom and imply her author.
[56]For an analysis of Joyce's "epic of the body" to which I am indebted, see Philip M. Weinstein, *The Semantics of Desire: Changing Models of Identity from Dickens to Joyce* (Princeton: Princeton University Press, 1984), 260–68.

or Buck Mulligan discusses the body and its necessities, he usually does so to expose the intractably animal aspects of self-deluded man. I take this to be the burden of masterworks like Buck's "ballad of joking Jesus" and of "The Lady's Dressing Room," where Swift's Strephon is appalled by the lady's soiled undergarments: "Thus finishing his grand Survey, / Disgusted Strephon stole away / Repeating in his amorous Fits, / Oh! *Celia, Celia, Celia* shits!" Molly's conception of this bare, forked creature is more amused and tolerant; she recognizes the creatureliness of all God's creatures, but she views it without Buck's satiric sneer. Molly's monologue is a narcissistic celebration; for her, the body and its processes are a beginning and an end in themselves, grounding or ballasting any aspiration. In the vision embodied and articulated by Molly, and shared with her husband, the body and its animal needs are conceived not as satirically mortifying but comically fundamental and potentially fructifying—the basis of being.

Comic writers like Aristophanes, Rabelais, and Joyce give so much prominence to excretion because, as the clinical Ithacan voice makes clear, there is always plenty of "human excrement" (17:1702) to remind us of our lower bodily element, or to stress that people are "traduced by their comedy nominator to the loaferst terms" (*FW* 283:6–8). Between *Paradise Lost* and *Ulysses* we come full cycle, from Adam's first movement, looking skyward to praise God,[57] to Bloom and Molly, squatting to do what no one else can do for you. Always imagining the rhythm of "life's upsomdowns" (*FW* 49:24) or the cycle of exaltation and abasement, Joyce also suggests an association between excretion and creativity, as when Stephen composes verse and passes water or when Bloom moves his bowels and enjoys "Matcham's Masterpiece," or when that excreting goat appears during the oft-recalled love scene atop Howth Hill. Our lowest function is universal and potentially positive, linking characters like Bloom and Stephen in that figuratively consecrated urination under the heavens.[58] Passing water is one of Molly's contributions to the

---

[57]*Paradise Lost* (8:257–61): "Strait toward Heav'n my wondering Eyes I turnd, / And gaz'd a while the ample Skie, till rais'd / By quick instinctive motion up I sprung, / As thitherward endeavoring, and upright / Stood on my feet, . . ."

[58]During his Shakespeare lecture, Stephen puns on the Latin for "urinate": "Just mix up a mixture . . . *Mingo*" (9:761–62).

"stream of life" and associates her with both the peeing heroes and the punning author in a "comedy nominator," her "chamber music" (11:979–80) also being the title of Joyce's book of poems.

Molly is the "indispensable" center of Joyce's comic project because her body is the ultimate ground of being. It is puzzling that Bakhtin was not more interested in *Ulysses* generally and in Molly specifically, for he could scarcely have found a richer embodiment of the "grotesque body," which he defines as open, secreting, incomplete, unformed, ever creating, becoming: "an incarnation of this world at the absolute lower stratum, as the swallowing up and generating principle, as the bodily grave and bosom, as a field which has been sown and in which new shoots are preparing to sprout . . . It stresses elements common to the entire cosmos: earth, water, fire, air; it is directly related to the sun, to the stars," as Molly is daughter of the moon, Lunita, and lover of the sun, Blazes. "This body," continues Bakhtin, "can merge with various natural phenomena, with mountains, rivers, seas, islands, and continents. It can fill the entire universe."[59]

Such terms, stressing her symbolic status at the expense of her flesh-and-blood immediacy, though apposite, Molly would regard as ridiculously high falutin'. In a compelling way, Molly is a great comic figure because she chooses to see herself and life humorously rather than as anything "O tragic" (18:24). Blessed with only a little wit, Molly certainly has a ready, broad, and deep sense of humor.[60] In this regard she is more like Aphrodite, the laughter-loving goddess, than beleaguered Penelope. Molly likes to laugh and enjoys the memory of laughter: "I was in fits of laughing with the giggles I couldnt stop . . . youre always in great humour [Josie] said" (18:211–13). One of the most enduring bonds between Molly and her husband is that they amuse each other. She cites many instances of his silliness and clowning: "O I laughed myself sick at him that day" (18:1195). So powerfully does Bloom strike her as funny that one of her few "literary" impulses—in this book of narrators—is to write about him: "if only I could remember the 1 half of the things

[59]Bakhtin, *Rabelais*, 27, 318.

[60]Although I generally admire Marilyn French's sense of Joycean comedy, I am puzzled by her notion that Molly "has little sense of humor, humor being a response to and way of handling the absurdities of the masculine, built world," in *The Book as World: James Joyce's "Ulysses"* (Cambridge: Harvard University Press, 1976), 247.

and write a book out of it the works of Master Poldy" (18:579–80). Although she regards Bloom as foolish, it is not in the cruel, dismissive tone of his adversaries in "Cyclops"; on the contrary, that each continues to find the other amusing and intriguing is significantly positive.[61] In another articulation of folly's credo, she muses, "theres many a true word spoken in jest there is a flower that bloometh" (18:775). Here, she remembers telling her first suitor that she was engaged to the son of a Spanish nobleman named Don Miguel de la Flora (18:772–74), and finds that play on her imaginary fiancé's name funny and prophetic.

Molly shares many comic traits with the Wife of Bath and Moll Flanders, whose story she once tried to read (18:658). She delights in lewdly flouting conventional morality: "small blame to me if I am a harumscarum I know I am a bit" (18:1469–70); in a letter to Frank Budgen, Joyce defined her as "amoral" (Budgen 266). Yet she also exhibits or betrays a conventional, even prudish, streak; she can sound as dainty as a convent girl. Like Moll Flanders, she is constantly casting up accounts and taking inventory, defining herself through what she wears and eats. Both utter conventional pieties and refer regularly to God, the soul, religion, and spirituality, in relentlessly prosaic and unconvincing language. On spirituality, as on everything else, Molly is inconsistent. Typical of her jaunty ungodliness is her first chatty reference, when Molly thinks of Mrs. Riordan and her talk of "politics and earthquakes and the end of the world let us have a bit of fun first" (18:8–9). But the Last Judgment, so frequently mentioned in *Ulysses,* and incidentally a stock object of mirth at the feast of fools, soon returns to her mind and seems to awaken an instinctive, deeper piety: "I popped straight into bed till that thunder woke me up God be merciful to us I thought the heavens were coming down about us to punish us . . . as if the world was coming to an end" (18:133–37).

Molly's creed is anything but philosophic; she is the bane of logic.[62] Yet her perpetual contradictions make her a source of value

[61]Bloom has a parallel impulse to record her comments (4:519–20; 8:119).

[62]For a comprehensive elaboration on Molly's inconsistency, see James van Dyck Card, "'Contradicting': The Word for 'Penelope,'" *James Joyce Quarterly* 11 (1973): 17–25, incorporated in his book *An Anatomy of "Penelope"* (Cranbury, N.J.: Associated University Presses: 1984), chap. 2. Marilyn French also approaches the last chapter as "a mass of contradictions," in *The Book as World,* 244.

as well as an object of humor. Like the sea, like the novel, she moves up and down, in and out, back and forth; if something is true, then its opposite might also be true. Molly is the very spirit of folly, the world turned upside down. It is characteristic of folly to discountenance the absolute and to urge a kind of absolute relativism, insisting that what you believe depends upon where you stand at a particular moment. This roughly defines that law of parallax, mulled over by Bloom several times during the day, that prevails throughout *Ulysses* and dominates "Penelope." On almost any subject, especially those most dear to her, Molly is like the sea, "a great sweet mother" (1:77–78), impossible to pin down: here I stand—and here, and here, and here. The voice of the last episode is as "mercurial" (1:518) as the dominant voice of Buck in the first episode. What one critic says of Stultitia applies equally well to Molly: "many of her most outrageous remarks can stand on their own feet, as well as their heads, and mean exactly what they say, as well as the opposite."[63]

On every intimate topic Molly expresses the whole cycle of attitudes, as she must, because she *is* the cycle of life's upsomedowns. About her sexual encounter with Blazes, for instance, she feels irritation—"I didnt like his slapping me behind going away so familiarly in the hall though I laughed Im not a horse or an ass am I" (18:122–24), awe—"I never in all my life felt anyone had one the size of that to make you feel full up" (18:149–50), anticipation—"I hope hell come on Monday as he said at the same time four" (18:332–33), mild disgust—"scrooching down on me like that all the time with his big hipbones hes heavy too with his hairy chest" (18:415–16), gratitude—"God I got somebody to give me what I badly wanted to put some heart up into me" (18:732–33), coyness—"he was so busy where he oughtnt to be" (18:1139–40), strong disgust—"has he no manners nor no refinement nor no nothing in his nature slapping us behind like that on my bottom. . . . Hugh the ignoramus that doesnt know poetry from a cabbage" (18:1368–71), and defiant pride—"fucked yes and damn well fucked too up to my neck nearly" (18:1511).

Another central motif that conveys folly's fundamental ambiguity is the Homeric correspondence, stressed more emphatically in the

---

[63]Walter Kaiser, *Praisers of Folly: Erasmus, Rabelais, Shakespeare* (Cambridge: Harvard University Press, 1963), 92.

final chapters.[64] Many bits imbedded in Molly's perfectly natural discourse resonate Homerically, establishing both the epic parallels and the comic incongruities between Bloom and Odysseus, such as her account of how our shrunken Odysseus nearly capsized a rowboat (18:954–60), and her revelation that the returning hero doesn't know the real origin of his marriage bed (18:1212–15). She complains that "I suppose well have him sitting up like the king of the country" (18:931) and muses, "youd never know what old beggar at the door for a crust with his long story might be a tramp" (18:989–91). Yet several of Molly's irritated assaults upon her husband have the cross-eyed insight of folly, reminding us that Odysseus was also an eminently fallible flimflam man: "he made up a pack of lies to hide it . . . what a Deceiver . . . the way he plots and plans everything out . . . hes such a born liar" (18:37, 318, 1008–9, 1253). One is persuaded by Molly's authoritative assertion, "I know every turn in him" (18:1530). Like Falstaff to Hal, she might almost say, "I know ye as well as he that made ye" (*1H4:* II.iv.296–97).

Molly's exasperating, ridiculous inconsistency, undifferentiated flow, vague referents, and ambiguous signifiers represent the ultimate ascent of unruly folly. Like the cycle of nature, Molly embraces loss and recovery, falling bodies and perennial return. Although she sometimes thinks of herself as vacancy or absence, "with a big hole in the middle of us" (18:151–52) in need of a romance that "fills up your whole day and life" (18:738), she is experienced by most readers, including those utterly unsympathetic, as a colossal presence. Even her splendid malapropism for vaginal secretions, "frequent omissions" (18:1169–70), conveys a paradoxical sense of mortal absence and enduring presence. One moment she is Mrs. Malaprop, the next she is Mother Nature: "O patience above its pouring out of me like the sea" (18:1122–23).

Molly's comic vision continually juxtaposes and ultimately balances the sublime and the ridiculous. For instance, worrying about the effect of menstruation on her next assignation, she uses the wonderfully zigzagging expression, "wouldnt that pester the soul out of a body" (18:1107–8). It is typical of the disparate responses she arouses that Molly's conclusion can be described as both a mag-

[64]I disagree with Richard M. Kain that in "Molly Bloom's long soliloquy, Homer is entirely forgotten." Kain, *Fabulous Voyager: A Study of James Joyce's "Ulysses"* (New York: Viking Press, 1947), 45.

nificent hymn and an autoerotic climax. Her tendency to veer from pole to pole encourages readers to see her as either larger than life or all too human, another false dichotomy. By the end of the episode, the common antithesis between soul and body, sacred and profane, seems to be resolved in a compelling, comic synthesis. Molly's comedy of Eros has focused on the body; now, as a sign of metaphoric benediction, she sees flowers everywhere. Molly's conclusion, simple but urgent and climactic, brings back that seminal day on Howth Hill, redeeming the time in a final and massive instance of comic salvation: "the sun shines for you he said" (18:1571–72). Then as now, the seedcake is fructifying, as she connects past and present in a tone of wondrous discovery: "it was leapyear like now yes 16 years ago my God" (18:1575). She remembers his lovetalk, as the novel wishes us to regard it, not as blabbering but as prophecy: "he said I was a flower of the mountain yes so we are flowers all a womans body yes that was one true thing he said in his life and the sun shines for you today" (18:1576–78). Through the power of love Bloom achieved the miracle of communion, entering her not only physically but spiritually, knowing her as she knows herself: "that was why I liked him because I saw he understood or felt what a woman is" (18:1578–79).

"God of heaven," she nearly sings, "theres nothing like nature" (18:1558–59), then names the glories "that would do your heart good to see" (18:1561). Having confronted the things that "dishearten" her spirit, she ends with a vision that will do her heart good. Now her carnality appears not in opposition to spirituality but in ecstatic union with it, as though "the law of falling bodies" (5:44–45) were suspended. She plainly repudiates atheists, "saying theres no God . . . why dont they go and create something" (18:1564–65). In the middle of the long dark night, at the end of her sustained narrative, she expresses homey wisdom: "might as well try to stop the sun rising tomorrow" (18:1571). Darkness is balanced, more than balanced, by the cyclical return of daylight.

Yet Molly's blooming is an apt resolution not because it seems to solidify ultimate yea-saying, often interpreted as "life-affirming," whatever that means.[65] In accepting Bloom, Molly affirms human ridiculousness, which is the first and last purpose of comedy. If

[65]Told that Margaret Fuller, the American transcendentalist, now "accepted the universe," Carlyle grunted, "Gad! She'd better."

Molly bears the burden of the novel's final wisdom, that vision is not onerous but humorous, for the Blooms' transport to eternity is also a comic diminution, even in Molly's memory of their day on Howth head, which becomes a recollection of what she was remembering when "he asked me to say yes" (18:1580–81): "I was thinking of so many things he didnt know of" (18:1582). At the same instant she acquiesces to Bloom, without any romantic illusions—"and I thought well as well him as another" (18:1604–5),—she was thinking of how "he [Mulvey] kissed me under the Moorish wall" (18:1604). It is typical of Molly to use the indefinite pronoun, blurring Mulvey and Bloom, so that the confused reader might echo Bloom: "who is in your mind now tell me who are you thinking of who is it tell me his name who tell me who" (18:94–95). Molly, like the world, is so full of turns—"I know every turn in him . . . my turn is coming" (18:1530–33)—that this last return to her husband seems as provisional and contingent, as gloriously bursting with folly, as everything else she, and this great comic novel, have affirmed.

2

The Generic Conditions

No one can live for long with *Ulysses* without discovering that its "proliferent continuance" not only provokes an astonishing variety of fruitful critical approaches, but requires any one interpreter to look around anxiously, backtrack, and swerve in opposite directions. My conception of *Ulysses* as a comic text, full of folly, is only partially true, as I recognize from the very great deal of the novel that remains outside my ken, and from the limited usefulness of comic theory. Though one can apply piecemeal the insights of Freud, Frye, Bergson, Meredith, Bakhtin, Langer, Jameson, and Barthes, among others, *Ulysses* refuses to yield itself to any single theory of comedy. It does not, to mention only some of comedy's most familiar earmarks, celebrate a happy ending, privilege plot over character, "cause a new society to crystallize around the hero," sustain "a toxic mood of cheerfulness," reinforce "the absence of feeling . . . [of] a disinterested spectator," render "destiny in the guise of fortune," or expose its rogues and fools to "thoughtful laughter,"[1] though it intermittently carries out and parodies most of these comic projects.

Eagerness to generalize about *Ulysses* as comedy must be tempered by realization that both the book and the genre have been, in

[1]Northrop Frye, *Anatomy of Criticism: Four Essays* (Princeton: Princeton University Press, 1957), 163; Sigmund Freud, *Jokes and Their Relation to the Unconscious,* ed. and trans. James Strachey (New York: W. W. Norton, 1963), 219; Henri Bergson, in *Comedy,* ed. Wylie Sypher (Garden City, N.Y.:Doubleday Anchor, 1956), 63; Susanne K. Langer, *Feeling and Form,* 331; and George Meredith, "An Essay on Comedy," in *Comedy,* 47, respectively.

Samuel Johnson's felicitous phrase about comedy, "particularly un-propitious to definers." One might say that comedy shares with *Ulysses* a stubborn refusal to yield itself to any single theory. If comedy isn't exactly a genre, *Ulysses* isn't simply a comedy, or even a novel, for that matter. Yet while aspects of the book complicate and elude such categories, as I will discuss in my last two chapters, *Ulysses* plentifully rewards consideration as a conventional novel, rendering in compelling, remarkable detail characters in a particular time and place. To a considerable extent, though not entirely, Joyce conceives these characters and their world in traditionally comic "generic conditions" (17:995). Of these, I focus on four: comic acceptance, recovery, confluence, and contingency.

That Plenitude of Sufferance

Highlighting the role of Buck Mulligan as one of four points of folly should not be understood to reinforce the mistaken perception that the book's satiric voices predominate. Carl and Mark van Doren, for instance, characterized the novel as "savagely satiric . . . the savage cynicism of the *Portrait of the Artist as a Young Man* . . . magnified a hundredfold."[2] Erich Auerbach deplored "its blatant and painful cynicism, and . . . impression of hopelessness . . . a turning away from the practical will to live, or delight in portraying it under its most brutal forms."[3] Buck himself is blameless, for he hardly gives the impression of hopelessness; his attitude conveys no coherent values, not even cynical nullification, and his insouciant gusto is anything but a turning away from the practical will to live. To explore Buck, Stephen, Bloom, and Molly as sources of folly is to hear polyphonic play and to perceive that *Ulysses* suffers fools gladly.

Keenly sympathetic to mischief and nonsense, responsive to competing imperatives, and skeptical of arbitrary authority, *Ulysses* mimics, mocks, and cherishes its characters with a measure of admiration and affection for all of "DEAR DIRTY DUBLIN" (7:921). *Ulysses*

---

[2]Carl van Doren and Mark van Doren, *American and British Literature since 1890* (Chautauqua, N.Y.: Chautauqua Press, 1926), 303.

[3]Erich Auerbach, *Mimesis: The Representation of Reality in Western Literature* (Garden City, N.Y.: Doubleday Anchor, 1957), 487.

cannot be said to scourge the wicked and lash every knave. Though it exposes folly everywhere, not only in Bloomsday Dublin but in the author and reader, it does not excoriate it: rarely do we detect Swiftian savage indignation or Juvenalian cold contempt. Often *Ulysses* is closer to Sterne or Erasmus in assimilating everything to folly, through endless improvisation. This antic spirit favors multiple rather than focused perspectives, "parallax" being a method as well as a motif. The absence of an authoritative center, and the proliferation of legitimate voices, make *Ulysses* a comic medley and a safe haven for folly.

Bloom, prophet of "the new Bloomusalem" (15:1544) and dispenser of "general amnesty" (15:1690), is indisputably the apostle of charity. Once we step back from Bloom's "plenitude of sufferance" (14:863), widely appreciated by humane readers if not by the "base minds" and "rash judges" (14:864) at the hospital, the comic tolerance of *Ulysses* is more problematical. Some of Joyce's most distinguished critics do not find much of it in "Wandering Rocks," which is often viewed as *Dubliners Revisited,* further episodes in the history of moral paralysis: "This labyrinth . . . epiphanizes communal death . . . [it is] a bleak world, grim, contemptible, cruel, constricting, pathetic, and helpless . . . The mind of this city is both mechanical and maliciously ironic."[4] Such views are too despairing, though it is true that "Wandering Rocks," like the whole book, is never sentimental, and clearly renders the intractable, often unpleasant, sometimes terrible realities. The plight of the Dedalus family, the loneliness of Bloom and Stephen, the pathos of Dignam's boy, the "dreadful catastrophe in New York" (10:90), and much else, show us a world bursting with sin and sorrow, and not one easily evaded by a mocking tale or a jibe. In identifying the art of this episode as "Mechanics," Joyce reminds us of his affinities with his great Irish predecessor Swift, whose satire flailed "the mechanical operation of spirit" and whose spirit is so potent in Joyce's last two books. Throughout "Wandering Rocks," machines like telephones, typewriters, and handbells keen and clack and barang, while human relations often seem equally mechanical, perfunctory, and heartless.

[4]Hugh Kenner, *Dublin's Joyce* (Boston: Beacon Press, 1962), 253; French, *The Book as World,* 124; Clive Hart, "Wandering Rocks" (Hart and Hayman 193). Hart also distinguishes "Wandering Rocks" from the "paralysis of *Dubliners,*" 193.

Simon Dedalus curses his daughters who struggle to put food on the table, Blazes Boylan automatically flirts and leers, Lenehan regales M'Coy with old stories of "bumping up against" (10:559) Molly's breasts, Bloom reads softcore pornography, and Buck scoffs at Stephen's artistic aspirations. A casual exchange summarizes this brutal aspect of the city: "How are things going?" inquires Mr. Crimmins. "Just keeping alive," replies Mr. Kernan (10:722). The connections between people seem merely arbitrary or coincidental; one thing happens to occur at the same time as another, as the narrative interpolations suggest. Other hopes of connection are frustrated, like Mr. Kernan's desire to catch the procession: "Too bad! Just missed that by a hair" (10:797). Movement appears awkward, like the "lazy jerks" of the onelegged sailor "swinging himself onward" (10:7) or enforced, like that of the H.E.L.Y'S men "plodding towards their goal" (10:311), or random, like Farrell's "glassyeyed" (10:919) lurch from pole to pole.

To some extent, then, Bloomsday Dublin is still the locus of paralysis, what Alvin Kernan might term a "scene of satire,"[5] a land of spiritual as well as literal drought. Humanity is often exposed at its basest: appetitive, reductive, and acquisitive. Dublin is crowded, yet individuals are isolated. Many are conventionally pious, but godless; talk and thoughts are saturated with Catholic idiom and symbols, but uninformed by spiritual discipline and uninspired by aspiration. We observe sentimentality but little feeling, business but no progress, a mélange, not a community. Yet none of this is remarked with the outrage, or the controlled fulmination or frenzy of pure satire, with its sense of ideals flouted or violated; instead, "Wandering Rocks," with its detached view of many small sagas taking place concurrently, has the comic effect of displacing absolute standards and implying relative values. The focus on individual drama yields to comic spectacle and panorama, so that Bloom and Stephen are no longer the center of concern but part of the stream of life. This Dublin is neither a stinking bedlam nor the center of moral paralysis, but a busy community, an atmosphere, as Joyce once characterized the real Dublin, "drab, yet glistening."[6] The city bustles and vibrates with activity: the morning's electric failure

[5]See Alvin B. Kernan, *The Cankered Muse: Satire of the English Renaissance* (New Haven: Yale University Press, 1959), especially the introduction.

[6]Arthur Power, *Conversations with Joyce,* 98.

(7:1047) serves to underscore how much *motion* is temporarily stilled.

"Wandering Rocks" dramatizes its citizens' fellow-feeling, as in this passage, near the middle of the episode.

> —He's a hero, he said simply.
> —I know, M'Coy said. The drain, you mean.
> —Drain? Lenehan said. It was down a manhole. . . .
> Going down the path of Sycamore street beside the Empire
> musichall Lenehan showed M'Coy how the whole thing was. One
> of those manholes like a bloody gaspipe and there was the poor
> devil stuck down in it, half choked with sewer gas. Down went
> Tom Rochford anyhow, booky's vest and all, with the rope round
> him. And be damned but he got the rope round the poor devil and
> the two were hauled up.
> —The act of a hero, he said. (10:492–503)

This anecdote is related with none of the usual Dublin "idle mockery" (1:661). Except in this scene, Lenehan is virtually incapable of anything but banal jesting. Here, though, he expresses unqualified admiration for a humble but definite act of selfless courage. Apparently we *can* find humanity in its best suit on the streets of Dublin—under it, even, where it is most disgusting. The simple specificity of place, citing the street and the music hall, locates the extraordinary within the ordinary—erecting, as it were, a commemorative plaque in the local neighborhood. The details of Lenehan's account are finely designed (and radically changed from what actually happened on May 6, 1905, to the historical Tom Rochford)[7] to suggest that this action is a secular reenactment of redemption: "be damned but . . . the poor devil" is saved. Almost too conveniently for my argument, and part of a pattern I will elaborate as comic revival, the key sentences begin with "down" and conclude with "up."

"Wandering Rocks" depicts not vices but follies, and shows more than paralysis or merely mechanical movement. A good deal of

---

[7]"In the real-life rescue Rochford was the third of twelve men down the sewer; all twelve were overcome by gas and dragged out unconscious—two died" (Gifford 184). Robert Martin Adams recounts the story in detail in *Surface and Symbol,* 92–95, stressing that the fictive Rochford's role is far more heroic than the actual Rochford's.

compassion in this episode belies its reputation as cold and heartless. The chapter opens with Father Conmee on a merciful mission to alleviate the distress of Dignam's widow and children. Father Conmee has been judged very severely as servile, fatuous, and complacent, as though his charity was as automatic and unfeeling as the movement of a gramophone. With his "indeeds" and "to be sures," his deference to an M.P., his regard for appearance and "cheerful decorum" (10:121), and his insularity and isolation, he deserves a degree of Chaucerian irony. But the satire is Chaucerian and indulgent, not Swiftian and ferocious, for Conmee's sins are venial; like most of his fellow Dubliners, Conmee is foolish, not iniquitous, prone to some self-satisfaction and self-justification. Father Conmee believes that "one should be charitable" (10:71) and, by his lights, does his best.[8]

The first character we meet in "Wandering Rocks" acts charitably, and the last episode, the viceroy's parade, is "to inaugurate the Mirus bazaar in aid of funds for Mercer's hospital" (10:1268–69). In between are other acts of charity and generosity. The one-legged sailor begs for alms from the sisters of charity, and receives an offering flung by a "generous white arm from a window in Eccles street" (10:222, etc.) belonging to Molly, in her first endearing gesture. And we are privy to this conversation:

> —Look here Martin, John Wyse Nolan said . . . I see Bloom put his name down for five shillings.
> —Quite right, Martin Cunningham said, taking the list. And put down the five shillings too.
> —Without a second word either, Mr Power said.
> —Strange but true, Martin Cunningham added.
>   John Wyse Nolan opened wide eyes.
> —I'll say there is much kindness in the jew, he quoted, elegantly.
> (10:973–80)

Considering his lack of intimacy with Dignam, Bloom's act is truly magnanimous. The fact that Joyce decided not to dramatize it adds to the decency of Bloom's unself-conscious charity, in contrast to

---

[8]In *A Portrait,* Father Conmee is hailed as "the decentest rector that was ever at Clongowes" (*P* 59), where he stood up for young Stephen Dedalus, as the real Father Conmee did for young James Joyce.

Father Conmee's conscious charity. Like the exchange between Lenehan and M'Coy concerning Rochford's heroism, this is a notably sincere appreciation of a figure who is more often mocked than admired by his peers. Nolan, Cunningham, and Power certainly consider it wonderful, though their surprise is fueled by distrust of the stereotypical avaricious Jew.

Nor is this the first time in "Wandering Rocks" that we hear praise for the much put-upon Bloom. The earlier instance of a kinder evaluation is especially telling, since it emerges out of exactly the kind of reductively satiric scene so often regarded as characteristic of "Wandering Rocks." Lenehan is recounting to M'Coy a "gorgeous winter's night on the Featherbed Mountain" when he shared a carriage with the Blooms. "Every jolt the bloody car gave I had her bumping up against me. Hell's delights! She has a fine pair, God bless her" (10:558–70). After elaborating on the ample curves of this "gamey mare," he says, "Bloom was pointing out all the stars and the comets in the heavens . . . But, by God, I was lost, so to speak, in the milky way" (10:567–70). Reducing Molly to a mare and Bloom to a cuckold, like characters in a Restoration farce, Lenehan is a type of jeering gargoyle. Yet even his attitude is the folly of a dunce, not the viciousness of the wicked. What is most remarkable is not that Lenehan is callow enough to be amused by such an old and trite story, but rather that M'Coy is plainly not amused. In response to his interlocutor's disapproval, Lenehan grudgingly adds, "He's a cultured allroundman, Bloom is, he said seriously. He's not one of your common or garden . . . you know . . . There's a touch of the artist about old Bloom" (10:581– 83). Lest we romanticize our hero beyond recognition, "Wandering Rocks" remains comic satire, true to the "law of falling bodies" (5:44–45): what goes up must come down. No sooner has Bloom risen in our estimation than we see him arousing himself with pornography—including one story by Sacher-Masoch, which reminds us that Bloom has, besides a touch of the artist, a touch of the masochist.

The characters' feelings in "Wandering Rocks" are neither perpetually paralyzed nor generally repulsive; they are in motion, often in contrary directions. "Wandering Rocks" acknowledges oscillation or, as Lenehan says, that "one good turn deserves another" (10:484– 85). The force between members of the family, for example, is necessarily one of simultaneous attraction and repulsion. Take, for instance, the awful scene between Simon Dedalus and his daughter, Dilly—most of which illustrates the space between people: he curses her and seeks refuge in bitter self-pity: "I'm going to get rid of you. Wouldn't care if I was stretched out stiff. He's dead. The man upstairs is dead" (10:684–85)—a nicely ironic echo of Boody's blasphemy. Yet for all his posturing and brutality, Simon too is suffering, and can be touched. "Here, Mr Dedalus said, handing her two pennies. Get a glass of milk for yourself and a bun or something. I'll be home shortly" (10:706–7). It seems typical of the relationships in *Ulysses* that feelings are shared only temporarily, tenuously; it is not the case, however, that in "Wandering Rocks" nobody wishes to connect and that every character lives in irremediable squalor. A portrait of Joyce's city would be more appropriately painted by Pieter Brueghel than by William Hogarth.

Numerous figures in *Ulysses,* besides Father Conmee, are treated with "plenitude of sufferance" (14:863), laughing at human folly rather than lashing at unforgivable vice—Simon Dedalus, D. B. Murphy, Blazes Boylan, and a host of other extravagant characters. For my purpose, to distinguish between the harsh rigors of pure satire and Joyce's mirthful love of the ludicrous, Gerty MacDowell commands attention, for she continues to be regarded too stringently. Joyce's description of his style in "Nausicaa" as "namby-pamby jammy marmalady" (*L* 1:135) is often cited as authorial justification to patronize or assail Gerty. Stanley Sultan, for instance, characterizes Gerty as a "libidinous girl whose persistent sentimentalizing keeps her from the proscribed normal sexual activity and yet causes her to act scarcely less immorally."[9] S. L. Goldberg remarks that "so hostile and so extended is Joyce's satirical attack . . . that we may wonder if she is quite worth twenty pages of his powder and shot."[10] Even a critic as astute as Karen Lawrence, more interested in language than in morality, describes "Nausicaa" as an "indictment of Gerty" and "condescending."[11] Such assessments make an important "mistake in the valuation" (13:1125), and implicitly regard Joyce as violating the fish-in-

[9]Stanley Sultan, *The Argument of "Ulysses"* (Columbus: Ohio State University Press, 1964), 272.

[10]S. L. Goldberg, *The Classical Temper,* 141.

[11]Karen Lawrence, *The Odyssey of Style in "Ulysses"* (Princeton: Princeton University Press, 1981), 122.

a-barrel rule of satire, which forbids attacking easy prey—especially those less empowered than the writer. Joyce is not one, in Pope's phrase from *Epistle to Dr. Arbuthnot,* "Who breaks a Butterfly upon a Wheel" (l. 308).

Gerty's powers are considerable enough to warrant generous attention in *Ulysses;* Molly Bloom, she to whom all things tend, is awarded scarcely more than twice as much, and in some ways, the first half of "Nausicaa" is a dress rehearsal for "Penelope." In a work uniquely receptive to folly, Gerty is both privileged and parodied, enabled and mocked. The hyperbolic inflations in "Nausicaa" depict Gerty as a classic mock-heroic figure, akin to Belinda in *The Rape of the Lock,* satirically diminished yet wondrously magnified. The reason the mock-heroic is such a congenial genre for Jocoserious Joyce is precisely that it humorously yokes apparently antithetical attitudes, suspending polar opposites—the sublime and the ridiculous. The sustained comparison between Gerty and Mary is an epitomal mock-heroic juxtaposition, cutting two contrary ways. The most obvious effect is satiric, stressing the disparity between the Mother of God and this naughty girl. As in *The Rape of the Lock,* however, the mock-heroic denigration has a reverse effect: like Bloom at the end of "Cyclops," Gerty is simultaneously celebrated and mocked, for the Joycean mock-heroic eschews any simplified emphasis upon either side of the hyphen, or even some comfortable resting point upon the fulcrum, but requires bifocal attention to both sides.

Unfortunately for Gerty's reputation, her deficiencies have regularly been emphasized at the expense of her attributes. Gerty's most obvious failings—preoccupation with trivia and narcissistic self-absorption—are follies with which Joyce naturally sympathized. His whole book is testimony to the potential significance of life's "flotsam, jetsam" (17:1686), junk, and throwaways. And he considered narcissism a virtual condition of his own art. One might speculate that Gerty MacDowell, like Austen's Emma Woodhouse or Flaubert's Emma Bovary, inspired some degree of authorial projection, for the stuff of Gerty's consciousness is Joyce's fundamental *matière,* lovingly rendered and relentlessly disavowed. Writing, Joyce is constantly running into himself, inscribing his name, or painting his face. "His own image to a man with that queer thing genius," Stephen says in the library, "is the standard of all experience, material and moral" (9:432–33)—words comically appropriate to Gerty, that keen student of her own image. She is constantly posing, preening, practicing her feminine wiles in front of an imagined mirror: "She did it up all by herself and what joy was hers when she tried it on then, smiling at the lovely reflection which the mirror gave back to her!" (13:161–62). Actually, again like Stephen, with his borrowed words, she is rarely on her own or doing it up by herself but usually imitating styles prescribed by such mavens of fashion as "Madame Vera Verity, directress of the Woman Beautiful page of the Princess novelette" (13:109–10). For both Stephen and Gerty, style is a way "to be tall increase your height" (13:113–14).

Since Gerty so thoroughly sees herself as a character in the Princess novelette,[12] and Joyce surreptitiously identifies with her folly, it is doubly apt that she intuits, in a sense, the propinquity of her author, teasingly hinted at by the pun upon Joyce's name: "The pretty lips pouted a while but then she glanced up [literally at Edy, figuratively at the writer] and broke out into a joyous little laugh . . . what joy was hers . . . " (13:125–27, 161). When she refers to "the gentleman opposite" (13:267) and "the gentleman opposite looking" (13:365), she of course means her looking-glass Bloom—but Joyce also suggests the proximity of her maker, gazing upon his creation and feeling it is good.[13] In regarding his two major female characters, Joyce is much less judgmental than many readers are toward women who make spectacles of themselves.[14]

An implicit bond between author, Gerty, and Bloom is that all have a touch of the artist. The "scene there in the gathering twilight" is so "picturesque" (13:624, 628) that Gerty wishes she could paint it. Unschooled, "she loved to read poetry" (13:634–35), devours *The Lamplighter,* and harbors literary aspirations; she's sure she has a story to tell "if she could only express herself" (13:643). Everything is seen as a picture, and Gerty invariably senses that "you could see there was a story behind it" (13:337). Consequently,

[12]Cf. Bloom: "Ask yourself who is he now. *The Mystery Man on the Beach,* prize titbit story by Mr Leopold Bloom" (13:1059–60).

[13]Another connection between Gerty and Molly is that when the latter begins to menstruate, she too seems to sense her fictivity: "O Jamesy let me up out of this" (18:1128–9).

[14]"Making a spectacle of oneself," writes Mary Russo, "seemed a specifically feminine danger. The danger was of an exposure." See "Female Grotesques: Carnival and Theory," in *Feminist Studies/Critical Studies,* ed. Teresa de Lauretis (Bloomington: Indiana University Press, 1986), 213.

when she gets a closer look at Bloom's face, she is creating as much as describing him: "the face that met her gaze there in the twilight, wan and strangely drawn, seemed to her the saddest she had ever seen" (13:368–70) because, in part, she's already written the story and typecast Bloom. From his dark eyes and pale intellectual face she could see that he was "a foreigner, the image of the photo she had of Martin Harvey, the matinée idol" (13:416–17).[15] In reading Bloom's face, Gerty writes her own story, dreaming of a braver, freer self: "Come what might she would be wild, untrammelled, free" (13:673). Though in this study of folly I don't wish to claim higher moral ground than critics who deride or undervalue Gerty, I'll say parenthetically that, like so many of Joyce's *Dubliners*, Gerty must make do with shoddy dreams. Pathetic, silly, she is not deplorable, as when she muses over poetry, "so sad in its transient loveliness" and skirts away from specifying "that one shortcoming . . . she always tried to conceal" (13:648–51). Making herself the heroine of trite romances and sentimental melodramas is her means of muddling through a reality that is likely to become more painful still.

Certainly fatuous, self-deluded, and pathetic, Gerty is foolish but not contemptible—contempt, noted Meredith, being "a sentiment that cannot be entertained by the comic intelligence."[16] She does provide relief to "the stormtossed heart" (13:8) of poor Bloom and might justly be regarded as "most merciful, compassionate" like the Virgin. Bloom sees in her eyes "an infinite store of mercy" (13:748), and repeats the word, "Thankful for small mercies" (13:789–90). She is "just like a second mother in the house" (13:325–26), a comforter. A particularly Popean aspect of the Joycean mock-heroic is that in "Nausicaa" the "heroic" plane of reference is never treated with unqualified admiration; neither Pope nor Joyce imagines a peerless past yielding to a degraded present. In *The Rape of the Lock,* Belinda at her toilette is a reincarnation of Achilles arming for battle—a sorry come-down, to be sure, but not the opposite of "greatness," for Pope also implies amused reservations toward the Homeric ideal; similarly, Joyce directs considerable irony toward the cult of the Virgin.

[15]Identifying Harvey, or helpfully specifying the allusion, distinguishes this naive narrator from others in the novel. It's the kind of gesture that Joyce mocked in George Moore, one of whose characters looks up the local train's schedule, to tell the reader information the character would surely have known.

[16]George Meredith, "Essay on Comedy," in *Comedy ,* 33.

The initial description of Gerty beautifully balances the tongue-in-cheek "heroic" and clear-eyed "satiric" elements, as though Joyce, often more fiercely antic, were trying out Pope's neoclassical mock-heroic mode: "What mighty contests rise from trivial things!" (1:2) exulted Pope's narrator of Belinda. Gerty's mind, like Belinda's, is a potpourri in which one might discover anything from throwaways to theology, from Bibles to billet-doux. (One might say the same of *Ulysses,* and note that the word *satire* derives from the Latin for "hash or mishmash.") At one point, describing Gerty's "toilettable," Joyce's Popean perspective alludes coyly to Belinda: "It was there she kept her girlish treasure trove, the tortoiseshell combs" (13:638–9).[17] Along with all the paraphernalia of a modern girl and "matters feminine" we find several traces of Gerty's Homeric and royal lineage: she imagines herself "graceful"—"The waxen pallor of her face was almost spiritual in its ivorylike purity though her rosebud mouth was a genuine Cupid's bow, Greekly perfect"— while her hair is her "crowning glory." She treats her skin with "queen of ointments" and has tiffs with her friends "like the rest of mortals." She has a "languid queenly *hauteur,*" imagines herself "exquisitely gowned with jewels," and reads "the Princess novellette" (13:83–116).

"Nausicaa" tolerates, even affectionately appreciates, the heroine's follies: "If to her share some female errors fall, / Look on her face, and you'll forget 'em all!" (*RL* 2:17–18). Yet as in *The Rape of the Lock,* only a slight tip of the prism reveals the heroine's ludicrous aspects. How Gerty imagines Bloom, for instance, is accurate, touching, and funny. Gerty's Bloom exists in the shadowy twilight of romantic idealization. "He was in deep mourning, she could see that, and the story of a haunting sorrow was written on his face" (13:421–22) is indirectly true; elsewhere she projects wildly and comically. Jilted by the young cyclist Reggy Wylie, she imagines Bloom betrayed by a lady cyclist! In one of the funniest sequences of the chapter, she is carried by her fantasy to the point of sexual contact, only to veer away: "No, no: not that. They would be just good friends like a big brother and sister" (13:664–65). She ingen-

---

[17]See also Pope: "And now unveiled, the toilet stands displayed. . . . The tortoise here and elephant unite, / Transformed to combs, the speckled and the white" (*The Rape of the Lock,* canto 1, 121 and 134–35).

uously describes our hero, masturbating at the moment, as "a man of inflexible honour to his fingertips" (13:694). Then she fastidiously distinguishes this special scene from a story she heard about a gentleman lodger doing something not very nice: "But this was altogether different from a thing like that because there was all the difference because she could almost feel him" (13:706–7). The desperate "becauses" are the substitutes for logic like those one finds in a dull freshman's composition. Yet Gerty, for all her easily elaborated fatuity, has "a charm few could" or should "resist" (13:106–7). Especially after the harsh masculine combativeness of "Cyclops," "Nausicaa" *is* a comforting feminine embrace, "nice snug and cosy" (13:239), wrapping us safely back in familiar, all-too-familiar, discourse: "The summer evening had begun to fold the world in its mysterious embrace" (13:1–2). Hers is a comic world not antipathetic but completely pathetic, where the day "lingered lovingly . . . dear old Howth guarding as ever the waters of the bay" (13:3–4). Like Bloom, the narrator of "Nausicaa" is slightly smitten by her, if not in everlasting love, happy to flirt temporarily, to play love's fool. This is not altogether fool.

Revival

Joyce's comic vision is fond of folly and rooted in the trivial, vulgar, and low. We see it in his extensive use and defense of that lowest form of wit, the pun: "The Holy Roman Catholic Apostolic Church was built on a pun. It ought to be good enough for me" (Ellmann 546). Charged with being "trivial," he nodded and added that he was also "quadrivial."[18] "What's up" (7:233) in *Ulysses* is immediately, incessantly deflated, in perennial comic fashion. The quick transition from high to low, sacred to profane, serious to silly, is a staple of humor from rude burlesque to elegant mock-heroic, from Aristophanes to Stoppard. A similar tendency toward degradation pulses through the notorious 1909 letters to Nora, in which Joyce consecrates "my dark-blue rain-drenched flower" and desecrates "my little fucking whore" (*SL* 181). Even in his most inti-

[18]Cited by Frank Budgen, "James Joyce," in *James Joyce: Two Decades of Criticism,* 24.

mate correspondence, author and reader share apotheosis and degradation: "Are you too, then, like me, one moment high as the stars,
the next lower than the lowest wretches?" (*SL* 167).

"From the sublime to the ridiculous is but a step" (15:2401–2),
notes Virag, that notable abaser, and for all his disgusting and disorienting palaver, truer words are never uttered in *Ulysses*. Many of
the novel's most vivid scenes or memories fuse the sublime and the
ridiculous, like the conception of Rudy, provoked by the sight of
dogs humping, or the climactic moment on Howth Hill, punctuated
by the sound of goat's droppings. Like Yeats's Crazy Jane, Joyce
never forgot that "love has pitched his mansion in / The place of
excrement."[19] A skeptical conception of the heroic, romantic, and
transcendent, with a solicitous, respectful regard for the ordinary,
ridiculous, and base, is the heart of folly and of Joyce's jocoserious
vision. Comedy is, as Aristotle stressed, "an imitation of characters
of a lower type"[20] who, unlike their epic and tragic counterparts,
will regularly be found farting, burping, shitting, peeing, screwing,
generally enduring, and often enjoying, life in their bodies.

What is characteristically Joycean about this traditional comic
predilection is the continual movement between high and low, up
and down, apotheosis and degradation. The juxtaposition of sublime and ridiculous, and the possibility of synthesizing jocose and
serious, are constantly underscored at the conclusion of episodes,
where farts compete with political oratory, ben Bloom Elijah ascends like a shot off a shovel, and J. Alexander Dowie peddles
salvation like a carnival huckster. Sharply conceived polarities, such
as the mock-epic inflations and satirical deflations of "Cyclops," or
Gerty's romantic longings—"*Art thou real, my ideal?*" (13:645–
46)—and Bloom's realistic grounding—"Up like a rocket, down
like a stick" (13:895)—tend to merge, like so many Joycean opposites, as in the climax of "Cyclops" or the "all melted away dewily" (13:741) paragraph of "Nausicaa." Cosmic and comic are distinguished, notes Joyce's great jocoserious successor Nabokov, by a
single sibilant.

Consider the postcard that Bloom reads in "Lestrygonians" as a
typically ambiguous pointer. Bumping into his old flame Josie
Breen, now married to a disturbed man, Bloom hears that "someone

---

[19]William Butler Yeats, "Crazy Jane Talks with The Bishop" (ll. 15–16).
[20]Aristotle, *The Poetics,* chap. 5.

taking a rise of" Dennis Breen has sent him an anonymous card, reading, "U. p" (8:258).[21] To the callous Dubliners who enjoy Breen's distress, the message is some sort of vulgar insult, like "you pee" or "up yours." In correspondence, Joyce used the phrase "U. p: up" in an ominous sense, as in "the jig is up," or "it's all over" (*L* 3:182). Both Bloom and Mrs. Breen read the card, "U. p: up" and Bloom mulls over it the rest of the day. "U. p." is thus a sign of cruelty and pain—or could it be another mundane sign of aspiration or ascent, in the last place we'd expect to discover it? Just when Bloom is downcast by the marks of woe on his friend and the signs of insanity on her husband, he gets the message: do but look Up.[22]

If "from the sublime to the ridiculous is but a step," the reverse is also true, for a step, of course, can go up or down, so that the cliché nicely accommodates Joyce's perpetual cycle, rising and falling. Degradation and apotheosis, "life's upsomedowns" (*FW* 49:24), are "seriocomic" analogues for fall and resurrection, and they are structural principles of both *Ulysses* and *Finnegans Wake*. Anything high will tumble, anything low may rise. Instead of one irreparable Fall— "the great fall" (*FW* 3:18)—and one inimitable Resurrection, *Ulysses* presents a comic series of falls and recoveries. For instance, to enter home without his key Bloom climbs the railing. "Did he fall?" (17:90); of course. "Did he rise uninjured?" (17:100); naturally, inevitably, always. As the punning title of Joyce's last novel suggests, this perpetual oscillation is an image of the life cycle from birth to death. "Ithaca" views that process as a whole even in depicting heavenly bodies: "of moribund and of nascent new stars" (17:1050–51) or in comparing the attributes of the moon and woman, "rising, and setting . . . waxing and waning" (17:1161–62).

Earlier I noted that comic heroes such as Falstaff, Don Quixote, Odysseus, and Bloom have powers of recuperation that protect them from any irreparable fall and suggest perpetual, miniature resurrections; in *Candide*, characters are literally brought back from death. Now I want to elaborate on this point, to argue that Bloom's capacity for revival is not peculiar to him but shared by others in his world,

[21]It is also characteristic of the reading in and of this novel, a subject I will pursue in my last chapter, that we are not entirely certain whether this simple message reads "U. p." or "U. p: up."

[22]Is it too ingenious to see in the letters U and P the initials of Ulysses and Penelope?

and in a sense by the book itself. If Northrop Frye's emphasis on comic plot structure is not particularly relevant to *Ulysses,* Joyce's June 16, 1904 is in other ways a "mythos of spring."

Stephen, during a rare playful moment in "Proteus," offers a working definition of the jocoserious cycle of fall and regeneration: "Down, up, forward, back" (3:123). Indeed, Stephen's experience in that episode is a surprising illustration of the comic tendency toward revival, unexpected because he is such a self-consciously tragic figure. The title of this episode (rather, the putative title dropped just before publication) is usually taken to mean the fluid, elusive nature of reality with which Stephen struggles. But "Proteus" also suggests Stephen's capacity for change, indicated by a fairly marked development. Reading the first half of the chapter, we may be as impatient as Buck Mulligan, or even fear for Stephen's survival; the second half, while it guarantees nothing, substantially raises our hopes. Heretofore, I've argued, Stephen appears adamantly rigid, and thus humorous in the Bergsonian sense of embodying a mechanical inelasticity of the spirit. His surprising recovery in "Proteus" is small, not generally noticed, but discernible and significant, for it suggests a new capacity to respond to flux, the sort of resilience, flexibility, and adaptability more often associated with comic than tragic figures.

At almost the exact center of "Proteus," when Stephen is tempted by the flood, the tide turns literally and metaphorically.[23] Stephen senses his feet "beginning to sink slowly in the quaking soil. Turn back" (3:268–69). To punctuate the reversion, the next paragraph begins, "Turning . . . " and the word recurs near the end of the paragraph. His gesture is expressive: he climbs upon a rock to watch "the flood . . . flow past" (3:282). Joyce depicts the stream of life, or, perhaps more precisely, the tide of life. Now Stephen thinks, "Down, up, forward, back" (3:123). Until now, he has viewed the depths as his perpetual reality, and failed to imagine the possibility of a larger cycle.

A measure of Stephen's progress in "Proteus" is his shifting attitude toward the dogsbody. He first spots "a bloated carcass of a dog" (3:286) as part of the blighted, deteriorating landscape. Stephen fears that realities are static and stagnant; Joyce knows they are

---

[23]Richard Ellmann observes that "Proteus" has a "caesura," but he does not connect the break to the shift in Stephen's mood. See *Ulysses on the Liffey,* 23.

mutable, "soultransfigured and of soultransfiguring" (7:771). Sure enough, a live dog appears, only to make a series of Protean metamorphoses from hare to buck to pig to serpent. Like "the buck himself" (1:42) in "Telemachus," this creature has no substantial identity. The live dog sniffs the dead dog, much as Stephen has been contemplating his mortality, or his fate as "dogsbody." The dog pisses, as Stephen will urinate; he digs for "something he buried there, his grandmother" (3:360–61), which recalls Stephen's riddle; and he is described as "vulturing the dead" (3:363–64), a phrase that fits both Stephen and the dog. It is also significant that Stephen is at first afraid of the dog, then musters enough courage to watch it. In "Proteus," he seems to take heart generally.

There are other omens, vague and ambiguous like Delphic oracles, but far from hopeless. Stephen recalls his dream of the previous night: "Remember. Haroun al Raschid. I am almosting it. That man led me, spoke. I was not afraid. The melon he had he held against my face. Smiled: creamfruit smell. That was the rule, said. In. Come. Red carpet spread. You will see who" (3:366–69). Stephen's dream seems to predict Bloom's invitation to spend the night, with the hint of a sexual liaison with Molly. Bloom is regularly associated with the exotic East, and "the melon" is a figure for Molly, and the kind of trope we find in the green world; at the end of "Ithaca," Bloom "kissed the plump mellow yellow smellow melons of her rump" (17:2241), which reiterates both "melon" and "smell," and makes the comic connection between the grotesque body, in Bakhtin's phrase, and vital fecundity. There are other harbingers to indicate that Stephen is not necessarily doomed, but "almosting it." Frightened by a vision of drowning, a vision that blends into a reproach for not "saving" his mother, Stephen suddenly wonders, "Who's behind me?" (3:325). He has a similar intuition at the end of the episode: "Behind. Perhaps there is someone" (3:502), which presages Bloom, for if we turn the page "behind," lo, "there is someone": "Mr Leopold Bloom" (4:1).

Stephen also seems to envision or predict Molly Bloom. Watching the gypsies, he thinks: "A tide westering, moondrawn, in her wake. Tides, myriadislanded, within her, blood not mine, *oinopa ponton,* a winedark sea. Behold the handmaid of the moon. In sleep the wet sign calls her hour, bids her rise" (3:393–96). Though Stephen is generally inclined to imagine The Eternal Feminine, these lines point more particularly toward Molly, often characterized in terms of the sea and the moon, and the daughter of Lunita Laredo (18:848). The sentence "In sleep the wet sign calls her hour, bids her rise" seems especially pertinent, since Molly both urinates and menstruates in "Penelope."

It is also striking that Stephen is now emboldened to essay a poem. That it is, to judge from the fragment we hear, conventional, maybe partly plagiarized, is less important than that Stephen ventures something. Perhaps inspired by the handmaid of the moon, his poem seems less precious and more earthy than his earlier cogitations. Stephen now feels impatient with his worship of the eternal feminine: "She, she, she. What she?" (3:426). And he makes his most poignant, overt statement of loneliness, with less protective irony: "Touch me. Soft eyes. Soft soft soft hand. I am lonely here. O, touch me soon, now. What is that word known to all men? I am quiet here alone. Sad too. Touch, touch me" (3:434–36). The word, as Ellmann speculated and Gabler's text confirms (9:429–30), seems to be love. Stephen remembers the Yeats song he sang to his dying mother, "*And no more turn aside and brood*" (3:445), and recalls his mother, this time not as a reproach but as consolation.

He sees the waters flowing gently, calmly, and has another portent of Bloom: "It flows purling, widely flowing, floating foampool, flower unfurling" (3:459), which foreshadows Bloom's vision of his bath at the end of "Lotos Eaters." To balance the drowning vision in the first half, he now has a vision of "raising" the dead: "A corpse rising saltwhite from the undertow, bobbing . . . landward. There he is. Hook it quick. Pull. Sunk though he be beneath the watery floor. We have him. Easy now" (3:472–75), which gives way to a vision of the cycle of nature, contemplated without dread: "God becomes man becomes fish becomes barnacle goose becomes featherbed mountain . . . " (3:477–79). Things definitely seem brighter, even if we don't notice the word, or name, *barnacle*: Stephen sounds less obsessive, more relaxed, playful, even self-ironic. He articulates his perceptions, at least to himself, with remarkable clarity and precision. He anticipates next Tuesday, "the longest day" (3:491), and leaves a sign of his mortal body, a bit of dry snot.

Though Stephen retains some characteristic bravado and rigidity—"As I am. All or not at all" (3:452)—he clearly perks up; pain modulates and yields to salutary energies. At this juncture, some optimism for the progress of Stephen Dedalus seems perfectly warranted, even divinely ordained. It is difficult, for instance, to ignore repeated references to the crucifixion and resurrection throughout the early episodes. Some of these allusions may be adventitious, as when Bloom helps the blind stripling across the street—and the word *cross* is thrice repeated (8:1076, 1077, 1081), or when Bloom makes the sign of the cross to illustrate his advertising illustration (7:132). But so insistent is the motif that the hints seem portentous, as in the recitation of "Lycidas" or the oft-noted "crosstrees" at the end of "Proteus."

The pattern of revival that begins to enforce itself in "Proteus" gathers momentum and power in "Hades." In Chapter 1 elaborated on Bloom's capacity for recuperation, a comic trait that is most rigorously tested and forcefully affirmed in "Hades." Like many fundamentally comic writers, Joyce finds our ultimate resolution, death, ever-present and infinitely funny: "funferall," as it is frequently termed in *Finnegans Wake* (13:15, 111:15, etc.) and he is "the faunayman at the funeral" (*FW* 25:32). In "Hades," Joyce fully develops the essentially comic rhythm of Bloom's first three episodes: the Law of Falling Bodies balanced by that other natural law, Couldn't Sink If You Tried. We sense the counterpoint, "down, up, forward, back" (3:123), or "life's upsomdowns" (*FW* 49:24) everywhere, as in the anecdote about Reuben J. Dodd and his son, who had fallen into the Liffey: "A boatman got a pole and fished him out by the slack of the breeches and he was landed up to the father on the quay more dead than alive" (6:282–84). Here a young man falls and rises—"more dead than alive," returned "to the father"—in a mini-comic resurrection.

This movement "down, up" is not only Bloom's temperament, but a structural principle or rhythm of "Hades" and other episodes. As Bloom moves from the "womb" at the end of "Lotus-Eaters" to the "tomb" of "Hades," his mood oscillates markedly. In this episode the hero confronts a challenge to his instinctive acceptance of flux, the body, the stream of life. Intractable realities associated with tragedy and satire figure prominently and balance comic optimism: decay vs. sensuality, termination vs. continuity, despair vs. hope, death vs. life, distance vs. connection, loss vs. return. Joyce typically views things as provisional contraries, but ultimately suggests that clear-cut dichotomies are much more closely connected than previously assumed: "by the coincidance of their contraries reamalgamerge in that indentity of undiscernibles" (*FW* 49:35–50:1). It is a severe test from which Bloom emerges a bit steeled or (in keeping with the organ of the episode) heartened.

Especially in the first two-thirds of "Hades," life is seen in its negative aspect, more as Stephen typically depicts it. A body that may give pleasure in a "womb of warmth" (5:567–68) is now characterized as a "trunk" or a "stiff." Things fall apart. Spotting Blazes Boylan, Bloom begins to feel older and more vulnerable: "Body getting a bit softy. I would notice that: from remembering" (6:204–5).[24] He, and everybody else, has the blues; the scenes they see are bleak, chilly, drab, "a treacherous place" (6:657), as Mr. Kernan remarks. In the first section of "Hades" almost everything Bloom encounters or remembers is painful, debilitating, demoralizing. The deceased are "so much dead weight" (6:521–22); the memory of his father is virtually a siren call to self-destruction. After enduring the horror of hearing his carriage-mates (save Cunningham) denounce suicides, feeling more estranged than ever—"They have no mercy on that here . . . Refuse christian burial. They used to drive a stake of wood through his heart in the grave. As if it wasn't broken already" (6:345–48)—Bloom is lured by the temptation of self-slaughter, as Stephen had been in "Proteus": "No more pain. Wake no more. Nobody owns" (6:365). In his descent, the cycle of nature provides no comfort to Bloom, but appears meaningless: "Every mortal day a fresh batch" (6:623–24) are buried. The mourners' humor appears either as grotesque and disgusting, or as hopeless attempts to whistle through the dark. Bloom imagines Paddy's "return" from a coffin bumped out upon the road, but envisions no spiritual release from the body; the corpse is redfaced from alcoholism, the insides decomposing quickly, the sphincter loose. Like so many other reminders in "Hades" of our last end, Paddy's corpse is a *memento mori*.

Even for Bloom's ostensibly Christian cohorts there is no comfort to be found in spiritual forms. The caretaker's joke typifies the general attitude toward the hope of redemption:

—They tell the story, he said, that two drunks came out here one foggy evening to look for the grave of a friend of theirs. They asked for Mulcahy from the Coombe and were told where he was buried. After traipsing about in the fog they found the grave sure enough. One of the drunks spelt out the name: Terence Mulcahy. The

[24]It is possible that Bloom is thinking here of Molly's body, or of both their bodies. He sometimes omits pronouns that would distinguish between them, as in the phrase "Could never like it again after Rudy" (8:610).

other drunk was blinking up at a statue of Our Saviour the widow had got put up . . . . And, after blinking up at the sacred figure, *Not a bloody bit like the man,* says he. *That's not Mulcahy,* says he, *whoever done it.* (6:722–31)

Yet, along with a laugh at the expense of sacred figures comes a kind of stubborn faith in banal, mundane life as we ordinarily live it, without promises of regeneration. Such horseplay reveals the bias of comedy: trivial, silly, reductive, yet buoyant, energetic, therapeutic. Even Joyce's drunks play their positive role in the casual comedy, as Martin Cunningham's aside seems to suggest.

—That's all done with a purpose, Martin Cunningham explained to Hynes.
—I know, Hynes said, I know that.
—To cheer a fellow up, Martin Cunningham said. It's pure good-heartedness: damn the thing else. (6:735–38)

Cunningham's defense of humor conveys the authoritative (possibly authorial) resonance; like many utterances in *Ulysses,* it helps guide our reading of the novel.

Humor in such a moment measures the distance between "Our Saviour" and the Dubliners, but also connects all mortals (as Kernan says to Bloom) "in the same boat" (6:663). "Hades" simultaneously illustrates the distance and affinity between people, a paradox raised to a principle I will elaborate upon (or belabor) in the next section. Bloom thinks often of the unbreachable gap between himself and his dead son, yet the persistence of his memories connects them too; eventually Bloom "raises" Rudy and "transforms" him into Stephen. Again, throughout, the rhythms are seesaw, an "oscillation between events" (17:428), a "counterbalance" (17:691); just when Bloom regrets losing Rudy—"My son. Me in his eyes" (6:76)—he takes pleasure in the reincarnation of his wife: "Molly. Milly. Same thing watered down" (6:87). The water image recalls the sea as mighty mother in "Telemachus" and flows into Bloom's reiterated vision of the "stream of life," which establishes another link between Stephen and Bloom.

Many varieties of "connection" are made in "Hades," often emerging from a bit of play. Bloom, fighting the despairing notion that the dead are soon forgotten (a notion belied by his own ruminations), thinks of a scheme to "reconnect" the dead and the living: "Have a gramophone in every grave or keep it in the house. After dinner on a Sunday. Put on poor old greatgrandfather. Kraahraark! Hellohellohello amawfullyglad kraark awfullygladaseeagain" (6:963–65). Bloom's whimsy itself is an extension of, and link with, Stephen's fantasy—for him, a rare humorous interlude—in "Proteus": "The cords of all link back, strandentwining cable of all flesh. . . . Hello! Kinch here. Put me on to Edenville. Aleph, alpha: nought, nought, one" (3:37–39).[25]

The pattern of descent and reascent, that jocoserious sine curve, not only recalls the lost but revives the living. In "Hades," Bloom descends into the gloom and returns, enabled by the experience. Toward the end of the episode, the language of "Hades" begins to include more insistent echoes of Bloom's heroic predecessors, as in his Dantesque "how many! All these here once walked round Dublin" (6:960) or in the narrator's Virgilian portrait, "quietly, sure of his ground, he traversed the dismal fields" (6:876–77). In "Hades," Bloom makes the Joycean passage "from one extreme to the other" (6:382), from despair to conditional affirmation.

Bloom is saved, or at least brought back, by his unself-conscious, simple faith in life. This faith is neither romantic nor spiritual, and it includes a keen sense of the banal and the ludicrous, because, as we have seen, "from the sublime to the ridiculous is but a step" (15:2401–2). So the life force is closely associated with its many opposites, as when Bloom remembers the engendering of Rudy: "Just a chance. Must have been that morning in Raymond terrace she was at the window watching the two dogs at it . . . And the sergeant grinning up. She had that cream gown on with the rip she never stitched. Give us a touch, Poldy" (6:77–81). The memory concludes with an almost oxymoronic fusion between sacred and profane, eros and thanatos: "God, I'm dying for it. How life begins" (6:81).

In "Proteus," the third chapter of Stephen's triad, Stephen makes a notable recovery; so too in this, the third of Bloom's episodes, does Bloom recuperate markedly. Another manifestation of a "retrospec-

[25]Robert M. Adams gives several other connections between the thoughts of Bloom and Stephen. Adams also notes that Stephen's jest may suggest that he can bring something (one) from "nought" (Hart and Hayman 109). Another critic elaborating on parallels between Bloom in "Hades" and Stephen in "Proteus" is Richard Ellmann, in *Ulysses on the Liffey,* 47–48.

tive arrangement," perhaps implying some providential design, is the triadic structure, or pattern of trinities. In the last third of "Hades," life, which had seemed so fragile, so ephemeral, begins to appear more resilient and permanent. Earlier, there were numerous jokes about redemption, resurrection, and return; pubs, for instance, offer "elixir of life" (6:430–31). The final movement of "Hades" breathes new life into tired figures of speech and old jokes; its movement is back to the world, up rather than down. For example, Martin Cunningham had said, "In the midst of life," which underscores the *memento mori* theme: in the midst of life we are dying. Now, with considerably more optimism, Bloom reformulates that Christian reminder: "In the midst of death we are in life. Both ends meet" (6:759–60). Felix blunder! The graveyard seems less menacing: "Chilly place this. . . . Must be an infernal lot of bad gas round the place" (6:604–8) gives way to "gentle sweet air blew round the bared heads in a whisper" (6:839). Instead of bitter exile, Bloom senses almost mystical attachment: "If we were all suddenly somebody else" (6:836). Similarly, the mourners seem to have progressed beyond forced jocularity and formulaic pieties: "The mourners took heart of grace, one by one, covering themselves without show" (6:874–75). Humor seems funnier, certainly less defensive or offensive. Where Bloom "smiled joylessly" at Simon's satiric assaults and thought "His jokes are getting a bit damp" (6:57), now he appreciates the caretaker's way of "cracking his jokes . . . warms the cockles of his heart" (6:786–87). In this meditation, he virtually defines the Joycean human comedy: "You must laugh sometimes so better do it that way. Gravediggers in *Hamlet*. Shows the profound knowledge of the human heart. . . . Seems a sort of a joke. Read your own obituary notice they say you live longer. Gives you a second wind. New lease of life" (6:791–96).

In his prosaic fashion, Bloom has touched upon some "profound knowledge" and has experienced a renewal or "new lease of life." His trip to the cemetery is a modern visit to the underworld in which the hero confronts the significance of mortality and the possibilities of limited but precious life. As I have argued, Bloom the outsider, a *schlemiel* or Pierrot figure to his contemporaries,[26] begins to appear somewhat grander to us, on the way to the status of holy fool—although the border between the ridiculous and the sub-

---

[26]Hynes, who has borrowed money from him, doesn't even know Bloom's first name.

lime is always open: Hynes collects names of mourners for the newspaper and Bloom kindly remembers to add the name of the absent
M'Coy, only to find, later that night, that his own name has been
botched by the typesetter.

Not even Odysseus or Falstaff enunciated the comic credo so
forcefully as Joyce's hero: "I do not like that other world she wrote.
No more do I. Plenty to see and hear and feel yet. Feel live warm
beings near you. Let them sleep in their maggoty beds. They are
not going to get me this innings. Warm beds: warm fullblooded life"
(6:1002–5). Bloom surely takes heart from his descent; he has gone
down to the depths and returned with a touch of comic grace. It
gives him spirit to survive John Henry Menton's gratuitous snub, in
a manner that specifically recalls the resilience and self-control of
Homer's hero, snubbed by Ajax and often exhorting himself, "Down
my heart!" Like Hamlet in the graveyard, he feels less anguish and
more equanimity, and sees life as a larger cycle, with death an inte-
gral aspect of it. "The Botanic Gardens are just over there," he
observes. "It's the blood sinking in the earth gives new life" (6:770–
71). *New lease of life, new life, warm fullblooded life*—the refrain
indicates the direction of the episode, of Bloom's mind, and the
novel's early sections. The hero has made a passage and returned,
descended and reascended: "The gates glimmered in front: still
open. Back to the world again. Enough of this place" (6:995–96).
He does not recover any sentimental bromide, nor does he pretend
to ignore any painful realities: "Poor papa too," he thinks, passing
through those glimmering gates. "The love that kills" (6:997). The
love that binds may also be the love that kills, and even an extraordinary heart is vulnerable. Yet to look clearly into that abyss, and still
to look up, is far closer to the sublime than to the ridiculous.

If in large measure it is the comic spirit—buoyancy, vitality, sympathy, capacity for recuperation—that sustains Bloom, it is also his
humor that thoroughly roots him. When Mr. Kernan, the other
non-Catholic at the service, makes a gesture toward Bloom by quoting the language of "the Irish church"—"*I am the resurrection and
the life. That touches a man's inmost heart*" (6:670)—Bloom po-
litely assents but inwardly demurs.[27]

[27]Robert M. Adams notes that "strangely enough, the connotative meaning
of the word 'heart' has been turned around by Mr Kernan's quotation of Jesus'
words on the occasion of the raising of Lazarus (John 11:25); and henceforth in
Hades it almost always has a favorable implication" (Hart and Hayman 105).

Your heart perhaps but what price the fellow in the six feet by two with his toes to the daisies? No touching that. Seat of the affections. Broken heart. A pump after all, pumping thousands of gallons of blood every day. One fine day it gets bunged up and there you are. Lots of them lying around here: lungs, hearts, livers. Old rusty pumps: damn the thing else. The resurrection and the life. Once you are dead you are dead. That last day idea. Knocking them all up out of their graves. Come forth, Lazarus! And he came fifth and lost the job. Get up! Last day! (6:672–79)

Bloom's characteristic fatalism and scientific bent are evident here, and much of the novel might be said to justify his skepticism. Interestingly, he uses the same expression employed by Cunningham moments later, when he defines the purpose of the caretaker's joke: "To cheer a fellow up . . . It's pure goodheartedness: damn the thing else" (6:737). Speaking of the heart, favoring humor, they echo each other's idiom and appear to be privileged viewpoints. Though the text seems to endorse Bloom's rejection of "the resurrection and the life," Bloom's joke about Lazarus, which sounds like standard schoolhouse humor, is not the book's final word on regeneration, redefined in the gospel of joyicity. "As to his religion, if any?" (*FW* 89:13). Whatever Joyce's own religious convictions or doubts, in *Ulysses* there is a kind of grace beyond the reach of Bloom—at least the hope of metaphoric resurrection. In "Hades" Paddy rises; in "Circe" numerous spirits return, including souls most dear to Bloom and Stephen. The dead may indeed come forth. And there are other ways to "get up!" as "Hades" dramatizes, possibilities outside of the strictly theological, afforded to Bloom precisely because his heart is so much more than "a pump." That the book does not regard "the resurrection and the life" with Kernan's solemnity does not necessarily mean that we must abandon hopes for "knocking them all up." On the basis of these early episodes, we might be regarded as foolishly skeptical not to entertain the possibility of some "new lease of life" (6:796). Or, as Joyce proclaimed in his last comic gospel, "Phall if you but will, rise you must" (*FW* 4:15–16).

The movement down and back up is implicitly and variously manifest throughout Molly's soliloquy. Her method of assessing Bloom and others follows that rhythmic pattern. Her first impulse is always a nasty barb or cynical remark to cut people down to size or bring them down to earth; she is, like her own view of Simon

Dedalus, "such a criticiser" (18:1088), eager to size others down. But her evaluations, like her mood generally, modulate or rise.[28] In working through her own moods, Molly demonstrates another kind of descent and revival. Remarkably unsentimental, she sees life without illusions or saving euphemisms, and determines to muddle through. Like the whole novel, Molly is haunted by death and loss, yet she counterbalances them, sometimes quite consciously. Rudy's death, she says, "disheartened me altogether I suppose I oughtnt to have buried him in that little wooly jacket I knitted crying as I was but give it to some poor child but I knew well Id never have another our 1st death too it was we were never the same since" (18:1447–50)—a moment of pathos compelling enough, one would think, to give pause to her most vociferous critics. Most striking is the force with which she wills herself out of the "glooms": "O Im not going to think myself into the glooms about [Rudy] any more" (18:1450–51). Implicitly, too, she takes "heart" in Milly, not only as a compensation for the loss of her son but as a "reincarnation" of herself. In thinking of her daughter, she as much as says, "This is my body," as when she recalls her budding breasts "like Millys little ones now" (18:850) or excuses Milly's impudence because "I was just like that myself" (18:1077–78). So intense is her experience of simple life, so persistent is her will to endure, so powerful her sense of continuity, that we experience Molly as some kind of life-force. "I suppose he thinks Im finished out and laid on the shelf well Im not no nor anything like it well see well see" (18:1021–23). Molly's last turn seems emphatic. Thinking again of her end, "stretched out dead in my grave" (18:1103), she makes a comic ascent, which turns her imagined death into *funferal.* Her No to despair is nearly as emphatic as her famous Yes to life.

Life is "alternately stimulating and obtunding" (17:25), inspiring and depleting, transcendent and imminent, as Molly's mundane instincts remind us here amid the ecstatic: "and I knew I could always get round him . . . and I thought well as well him as another" (18:1579–1605). *Ulysses* grounds us as strongly as any novel in the intractably comic conditions of existence, yet looks up. The pattern is played out unto the last, as Molly remembers Bloom's

[28]James H. Maddox, in *Joyce's "Ulysses" and the Assault upon Character,* 210, points out that "once she has gained that dominance, she is willing to grant sympathy and sometimes admiration."

proposal, when she "drew him down to me" (18:1607). Molly's "melons" are associated with the "melonfields" of the promised land and with the homeland kissed by the returning Odysseus. Thus Bloom is brought home one final time, abased and exalted. This hero, for all his foolishness, is potent enough to compel the assent of nature, wise enough to adore "everything connected with [her] glorious Body" (18:1176–77), while the heroine, for all her silliness, is wise enough to love her husband with his follies, in part because of them. "Penelope," that episode of contradictions, denies the distinctions between ups and downs in the sublimely inconsistent, perfectly apt culmination of Joyce's jocoserious vision.

Magnetic Influence

Far from being irrevocably doomed to tragic isolation or satiric paralysis, Joyce's Dubliners exist, at least potentially and intermittently, in a world of comic centripetal force, drawing individuals together. Confluence is a basic, ubiquitous force in many comedies, seen in its most familiar and purest form in Shakespeare's comic romances, in which some beneficent spirit draws everybody to one place, such as the woods outside Theseus's Athens, the forest of Arden, or Ephesus, and reshapes the configuration of characters. Here, unlikely coincidence and good hap abound: paths cross, the lost are found, the bad repent, and innocent youths meet and mate. Fielding, making sport of the strain upon credulity and disingenuously professing strict realism, finds ways to get nearly all of his characters, right at the middle of *Tom Jones,* to the famous Inn at Upton. There, he stages a farcical acceleration of the comic tendency to merge, with rapid and unexpected entrances and exits. The law of comic confluence is still provoking thoughtful laughter in David Lodge's *Small World,* where the international airport or the MLA conference provides the space in which to intersect. As Jimmy Durante used to proclaim, "Everybody wants to get into the act!" The classic comic finale wants to draw as many figures as possible into its revivified community.

For Jocoserious Joyce, the conventional comic entelechy is far too optimistic, so he both renders and undercuts the law of confluence. A splendid instance of all-too-human yet nearly uncanny bonding in *Ulysses* is the "magnetic influence" between Bloom and Gerty on which Bloom muses, and which gives a Joycean twist to the old comic turn. As Bloom contemplates the extraordinary coincidence that his watch stopped at "about the time" Blazes and Molly met, he ponders "magnetic influence . . . Back of everything magnetism. Earth for instance pulling this and being pulled. That causes movement" (13:984–88). Explaining the "phenomenon" of attraction in roughly scientific terms, Bloom also defines a comic law operating implicitly throughout *Ulysses* and emphatically in "Nausicaa," for "magnetic influence" is even more potent than Bloom realizes. (Also funnier: "pulling this and being pulled" being an apt description of Gerty's effect upon him). "Suppose there's some connection. . . . Mysterious thing too. . . . the evening influence" (13:1014–15, 1088).

"Magnetic influence" acts upon the spirits as well as on the bodies of Gerty, the gushy romantic, and Bloom, the rational skeptic. Apparent opposites, they not only attract each other but blend together in oxymoronic "amalgamation" (17:1121). This quintessentially Joycean union of opposites reaches its culmination, appropriately, at their simultaneous orgasm,[29] on the page that turns from Gerty's to Bloom's point of view, where "all melted away dewily" (13:741). As we approach Bloom's consciousness, he "coloured like a girl," as though she had entered him. For that transition paragraph of third-person objective narration, Bloom is still rendered in the stilted style of Gerty's *Lamplighter* vision: "it is he . . . A fair unsullied soul had called to him . . . An utter cad he had been" (13:744–47). Then we return to Gerty's mind for her curtain: "Their souls met in a last lingering glance and the eyes that reached her heart, full of a strange shining, hung enraptured on her sweet flowerlike face" (13:762–64). Patently the sort of parting she needs to imagine, with a cherished self-image of "her sweet flowerlike face," she reflects Bloom ("flowerlike") just as he had "coloured" (13:743), Gertylike. Whatever it is, magnetic influence or romantic magic, some potent force marks the moment with fireworks and stopped watches.

That Gerty and Bloom are on the same wavelength is suggested by numerous connections between their sections. Bloom is certainly right that there is "a kind of language between [them]" (13:944).

[29]Whether Gerty actually has an orgasm is debatable. Bloom, who is right about other aspects of their encounter, seems to think she climaxed: "Took its time in coming like herself, slow but sure" (13:1016).

"Ah!" thinks each, (13:741, 821). Bloom guesses that her period is imminent, she suspects that he is aroused; he intuits what she intuited: "Did she know what I? Course" (13:908). He terms his penis "that little limping devil" (13:851–52), which is also the way he thinks of himself—"Devil you are," (13:929)—and of limping Gerty—"Devils they are when that's coming on them" (13:822) and "Hot little devil" (13:776). Both Bloom and Gerty refer to menstruation by the euphemism "that." She views his face as "wan" (13:369), then bids him farewell, smiling "wanly" (13:764). Opposites, they are doubles, each seeing the self reflected in the idealizing eyes of the other. Each seems to say, as Bloom thinks of the pool of seawater, "see my face there, dark mirror" (13:1260). Bloom realizes their mutual empathy, and he suspects its origin, in a variation on the law of magnetic influence: "Daresay she felt I. When you feel like that you often meet what you feel" (13:828–29). A second homey iteration of his notion is, "So it returns. Think you're escaping and run into yourself. Longest way round is the shortest way home" (13:1109–11), which is, incidentally, also a neat summary of Stephen's Shakespeare lecture.[30]

Bloom's "magnetic influence" (13:984–85) is thus a comic law of the novel, for Joycean characters emanate energy that draws them together in decidedly unscientific ways. "Coincidence" is not a sufficient explanation for some manifestations of this force in *Ulysses*. Bloom and Stephen cross paths three times, visit the same bookstall, roam the same beach, and have common thoughts, themes, concerns. Not only do they seem providentially arranged to receive one another but, sharing nearly verbatim bits of consciousness, they sometimes seem to be mystically bonded. For instance, Stephen stumbles upon a very mysterious discovery while perusing the same stall of books explored by Bloom:

> what is this? Eight and ninth book of Moses. Secret of all secrets. Seal of King David. Thumbed pages: read and read. Who has passed here before me? How to soften chapped hands. Recipe for

[30]Brook Thomas comments, "Even if the *Shakespeare Quarterly* would reject Stephen's theory as too idiosyncratic, the *James Joyce Quarterly* might consider it as the best piece of criticism on *Ulysses* yet written. It is an important part of the tale of the telling." See Brook Thomas, *James Joyce's "Ulysses": A Book of Many Happy Returns* (Baton Rouge: Louisiana State University Press, 1982), 60.

white wine vinegar. How to win a woman's love. For me this. Say
the following talisman three times with hands folded:
—*Se el yilo nebrakada femininum! Amor me solo! Sanktus! Amen.*
(10:844–49)

Bloom, our latter-day Moses, has "passed here before" Stephen, and
at the end of "Circe" will muse over the prostrate form of Stephen
that a girl is the "best thing could happen him" (15:4951). In
"Circe," this bit of Stephen's private consciousness will be echoed by
the apparition of Molly to Bloom: "Nebrakada! Femininum"
(15:319). Other bits of one character's consciousness preternaturally
appear in that of another; for example, in "Lestrygonians," musing,
"Never know whose thoughts you're chewing" (8:717–18), Bloom
forsakes "rawhead and bloody bones" (8:726)—the very phrase ex-
claimed by Stephen in the brothel. Throughout *Ulysses,* "magnetic
influence" brings people back or closer together, often humorously,
sometimes outlandishly; Joyce winks even while he uses this hoary
comic convention. When Bloom puzzles over the identity of the man
in the macintosh, he thinks, "Always someone turns up you never
dreamt of" (6:807), and the novel won't let us forget this mysterious
figure. Flowers upon a grave offer wishes "for many happy returns"
(6:227) in a book where the dead need no encouragement to return;
bodies pop up like so many jacks-in-the-box.

In "Penelope," the power of "magnetic influence" (13:984–85)
seems to obtain, but only barely and not without considerable resistance. The Ithacan voice defined this process as "the alternately
stimulating and obtunding influence of heterosexual magnetism"
(17:25–26). Molly's spouse provokes considerable animosity. She
scoffs his "plabbery kind of manner" (18:195), pedantry—"hed say
its from the Greek" (18:241), perversity—"hes not natural like the
rest of the world" (18:268), arrogance—"he thinks nothing can
happen without him knowing" (18:281–82), duplicities—"20
pockets arent enough for their lies" (18:1236–37), blather—
"talking his usual trash and nonsense" (18:384), stubbornness—
"Poldy pigheaded as usual" (18:528), lack of focus—"for all the
plans he invents" (18:989), and obliviousness—"living with him so
cold never embracing me" (18:1400). Sometimes it seems that
Bloom can do no right; she criticizes him for being too meek and for
being too assertive. She feels ambivalent about his "feminine" aspects; he is gentler, more sensitive, more empathetic than studs like

Blazes, but he lacks her father's attractive forcefulness. So insistent, even strident, are her complaints that one suspects they emerge from a powerful need for self-justification: "I could have been a prima donna only I married him" (18:896), and "serve him right its his own fault if I am an adultress" (18:1516).

Yet after eleven years of sexual alienation and this day's crisis, Bloom and Molly still attract and hold each other. Even in her private meditations, at a moment when she is most likely to feel self-righteous and defensive, she finds in Bloom much to admire. Having faced and defined everything she dislikes about her marriage and her life—Molly's version of descending into the abyss—she, like Bloom in "Hades," begins a return. No sooner does she deliver her ecstatic paean to Blazes' Rabelaisian organ than she acknowledges, "but I dont know Poldy has more spunk in him yes" (18:167–68).[31] She may mock Bloom's learning but she also admires it (especially when his knowledge relates directly or indirectly to herself): "still he knows a lot of mixedup things especially about the body and the inside" (18:179–80). Sexually estranged, she remembers his appeal: "he was very handsome at that time . . . though he was too beautiful for a man" (18:208–10). Other signs of comic confluence or "magnetic influence" bloom: Molly seems to come home to Bloom. Although she resents his carousing late, she appreciates that "he had the manners not to wake me" (18:927–28). Amazed that he had the audacity to order breakfast—this must be the most critically scrutinized meal since the Last Supper—she immediately thinks of shopping and seemingly assents to his request. Since we met her, she has moved from an ambiguous "Mn" (4:57), interpreted by Bloom as a negative, to at least a conditional affirmation.

Another humorous version of the "magnetic influence" linking characters and author together is that in "Ithaca" Bloom's urination forms a Y, Stephen's an S, while Molly's rendition of the train's whistle, "eeeee" (18:908), makes sure we find the missing E to form the word that begins and ends her episode: YES. Thus Penelope stays home. Or, figuratively, returns home, for Molly, without ever

---

[31]Rabelais is another comic author with whom she is very roughly familiar: "those books he brings me the works of Master Francois somebody supposed to be a priest" (18:488–89). For a perceptive analysis of the Rabelaisian connection, see Zack Bowen, *"Ulysses" as a Comic Novel.*

leaving, has made an odyssey as dramatic as "the voyages those men have to make to the ends of the world and back" (18:853–54). If marriage is obtunding, it is also stimulating; magnetic influence never quite ceases to operate, and eventually it brings Molly back— lured and comforted by the presence of his body, ludicrously upside down but *there*. Without sentimentalizing *Ulysses* into a domestic sitcom, we can perceive its deep domestic roots and tendencies; like *The Odyssey* it begins and ends with "the home life, to which Mr B attached the utmost importance" (16:1177). For all his aimless meandering and halfhearted philandering, Bloom spends most of his day reflecting upon his family, his children, his father, and especially his wife. Even when Bloom is giving free rein and plentiful energy to fantasy, it is neither erotic adventure nor heroic glory that he enjoys, but a cozy suburban dream house. He is, in this way, a perfect match with Molly, whose freewheeling fantasies and vivid memories begin, end, and center on her husband and family.

Joyce's variation on this principle of comic confluence is to suggest movement toward all those happy R's—reunion, recognition, reconciliation, regeneration, rebirth, revival—movement that is later parodied, to some extent frustrated, but never quite precluded. With its comic disdain for rules, this book never quite rules out anything. One way *Ulysses* teases the reader is to fool us into expecting characters to come together more harmoniously and happily than they necessarily will. It is no accident that so many readers exaggerate the significance or implication of the meeting between Stephen and Bloom, for the text encourages precisely such hopes that something substantial, if not miraculous, might occur. Similarly, it is not simply one's optimistic predisposition that leads to sentimental interpretation of the Blooms' future together. Magnetic influence, drawing both husband and wife, evidently moves them or keeps them in conjunction. Though it guarantees nothing about tomorrow, and indeed is part of a larger cyclical pattern of ascent and descent, perpetually reiterated, magnetic influence is a palpable, potent comic force—like Prospero's powers, marvelous yet local, transient, and limited.

Incomplete

Though unfixed and isolated, Joyce's characters do connect, or appear destined to come together. Often depressed, grieved, or burdened, they have notable powers of recuperation; frequently pathetic or ludicrous, they seem occasionally to exist under some aegis or comic analogue of providence. Always grounded in the intractable conditions of existence, such as the loss of parents and offspring, the first ten episodes, more so than the next seven, provide numerous and compelling grounds for hope. Few readers, noting the emphatic pattern of recovery in episodes such as "Hades," or Molly's reaffirmation of her connection with her husband, will utterly despair for the characters. But the cycle of falls and recoveries is not likely to give way to a climactic regeneration, so that the power of revival and magnetic influence will be limited, intermittent, and ultimately "Incomplete" (17:598); enabling motion, *Ulysses* avoids consummation. A world always subject to "equal and opposite power" (17:253) does not tend to closure, but toward the "vital continuity" or "essentially contingent" nature of comedy.[32]

Tom Jones and *Tristram Shandy* are English fiction's competing paradigms of comic closure. Fielding's ending provides what most people expect and all of us want—the happy ending, where the good characters are recognized and rewarded, and the bad are exposed and punished. Like so many comedies, its festive nature is celebrated by a marriage and the promise of proliferent continuance—ending, that is, with the guarantee that life will continue. Yet in another sense, Fielding's resolution is the emphatically closed mode of comic romance, the tradition of *As You Like It* and *Pride and Prejudice,* where all's well that ends well, because the protagonists' lives have attained their shapes or fulfilled their essential destinies. Of this mode Henry James disapproved, because of its "distribution at the last of prizes, pensions, husbands, wives, babies, millions, appended paragraphs, and cheerful remarks."[33] Though Fielding continually asserts the verisimilitude of his "history," *Tom Jones* is obviously propelled by romantic energies, its hero banished from Paradise Hall on a quest for wisdom, attained in the person of his Sophia. One of Joyce's least ambiguous opinions was disdain for romantic solutions: "I am nauseated by their lying drivel about pure men and pure women and spiritual love and love for ever: blatant lying in the face of truth" (*SL* 129).

Joyce found more truth in Laurence Sterne, who took the ex-

[32]The phrases are those of Susanne K. Langer, in *Feeling and Form,* 335.
[33]Henry James, "The Art of Fiction," in *The Portable Henry James,* ed. Morton Dauwen Zabel (New York: Viking Press, 1951), 396.

treme step of dying to avoid resolving *Tristram Shandy,* for such a narrative could only be finished by violating its premises. (One might say the same of Byron's *Don Juan*). Tristram's "transverse zig-zaggery," associative connections, and wacky incongruities will not abide closure. Indeed, frustration, failure of connection, is one of Sterne's primary themes as well as a principal technique. It is thus fitting, if accidental, that this great shaggy-dog story ends with the tale of an infertile bull: "A COCK and a BULL," says Yorick, "—And one of the best of its kind, I ever heard!"[34] In this less romantic mode of Sterne and Joyce, comedy promises "vital continuity," life will be continually interrupted and resumed: "in the end the world without end" (15:2236).

Since the happy, closed ending is such a widespread expectation in comedy, exploring and spoofing resolution becomes central to Joyce's comic project. More so than *Tristram Shandy, Ulysses* depends on our familiarity with the various conventions of closure, for it tries, or pretends to try, several possibilities. As an encyclopedia of comedy, *Ulysses* naturally surveys the field and mocks the artificial, happy endings that Henry James deplored, thus highlighting the problematic nature of comic closure more deliberately and fully than Sterne. It has been my argument that humor is intrinsically unstable and that Joyce exaggerates this tendency. Nowhere is the inherently mercurial quality of comedy more apparent than where it is supposed to come to rest, for it resists solution. In varying degrees, all comic denouement is untidy, random, and arbitrary.

It is only by a particularly willing suspension of disbelief that we accept the pretense of happy ending, for pure comic closure is nearly always gerrymandered or illusory—which is why readers are often troubled by the endings in Aristophanes, Molière, Shakespeare, Twain, and so many comic writers. Comedy is notoriously partial to the young and innocent, so that the perspectives of Malvolio ("I'll be reveng'd on the whole pack of you!") in *Twelfth Night* (V.i.387), Jaques ("I am for other than for dancing measures") in *As You Like It* (V.iv.199), Lady Catherine de Bourgh in *Pride and Prejudice,* and Blifil in *Tom Jones* are largely elided in the triumphant celebration. Yet it is not only the fools and villains who are excluded from the merriment; as Frye notes, *Pride and Prejudice* would quickly cease to amuse if the married life of Charlotte and Mr. Collins were given

[34]Sterne, *Tristram Shandy,* 9:xxxiii.

more attention. While comedy provides a release from strictures, a holiday from social norms and private scruples, it also stresses temporality: we know exactly what comes the morning after revelry. Indeed, the fifth act of *Twelfth Night* already seems like a hangover for Malvolio, Toby, and Sir Andrew. The spectre of change, loss, and mortality may be blinked away during the party, but is not thereby banished. Prospero, uncomfortably contriving the comic denouement, knows this. "O brave new world," Miranda wonders, "that has such people in't." To which her father replies, sagely and sadly, "Tis new to thee" (*Tmp*.: V.i.184–85). Comic closure rarely sustains careful scrutiny, least of all inquiries about the future, for happily ever after can only be in never-never land. A modicum of common sense or mature reflection reveals not only the transience but the fundamental artificiality, or "blatant lying," of comic closure. Touchstone makes the eminently comic assertion, "but as all is mortal in nature, so is all nature in love mortal in folly" (*AYL*: II.iv.56–57). How is a man capable of such insight going to converse with Audrey—a question that might very well have occurred to the man whose wife offered to sell his gift of the first copy of *Ulysses*.

The random, forced aspects of comic denouement are most evident in the inevitable marriages. In *Twelfth Night,* the wonderful Viola weds the dreadful Orsino, Sebastian and Olivia can hardly be said to have met, and poor Maria is saddled with Toby. Similarly capricious and vexing matches are formed at the end of *As You Like It.* Oscar Wilde's ironic description is apt: "Tragedy ends in death; comedy, in marriage." Congreve's Millamant is one of many vibrant figures whose fate is to "dwindle" into a spouse. In *Emma,* one can only hope that the heroine will qualify her professed intention to be always schooled by Knightly, and that their marriage can withstand the irritating presence of Mr. Woodhouse. Comic resolution regularly asks us to take a great deal on faith, such as the hope that Tom Jones has truly learned the value of prudence and will not soon be caught with a chambermaid. Fielding's ending is typical of comic resolution in ignoring compunctions and qualms: Sophy, at the behest of her father, abandons her condition that Tom demonstrate his supposed maturity for a year before she will consent. Thus the voice of common sense, indeed of the prudence Tom supposedly affirms, is simply forgotten in the festive rush.

Jocoserious Joyce plays with the possibility of comic closure by blending Fieldingesque providential design and Shandyean fortuitousness. Thus *Ulysses* seems both heavily determined, conveying "a retrospective kind of arrangement," and indeterminate, suggesting the dimension of contingency. The former, that sense of "retrospective patterning"[35] is especially evident at the conclusion of "Scylla and Charybdis," where, it will be recalled, Bloom passes between Stephen and Buck, and we are left with the benediction from *Cymbeline,* "*Laud we the gods . . .* " (9:1223–25). Of course, "Scylla and Charybdis" is the ninth episode, "the end of the first half of *Ulysses*" as the author specified on his working draft.[36] At such junctures Joyce is most literally an Arranger, one who learned from his Jesuitical training, as he put it, "to arrange things so that they are easy to survey and to judge" (Ellmann 27), obedient to the Augustinian precept that "we should not underestimate the significance of numbers, since in many passages of sacred scripture numbers have meaning for the conscientious interpreter." The conscientious interpreter, alerted to the significance of numbers, particularly sacred ones, might connect the closing prayer of the ninth episode of *Ulysses* with the "threemaster, her sails brailed up on the crosstrees, homing" (3:504–5), at the end of episode 3, and Molly's hymn to nature, concluding episode 18. It might be only a bit too ingenious to recall that one of Bloom's most tonic affirmations comes at the end of "Hades," chapter 6.[37] I have argued that only a resolutely skeptical reader would ignore or distrust the many hopeful signs placed so strategically. Though it might be hasty or naive, it would not be utterly foolish, after completing ten chapters, to anticipate something akin to conventional comic closure.

In the second half of the novel, though, the endings of episodes are far more obviously parodic, like the mock-heroic ascension of ben Bloom Elijah (12:1916), or Alexander J. Christ Dowie's apocalyptic "coughmixture with a punch in it for you" (14:1590). In-

[35]The phrase is that of Barbara Herrnstein Smith, *Poetic Closure: A Study of How Poems End* (Chicago: University of Chicago Press, 1968), 119.

[36]See A. Walton Litz, *The Art of James Joyce: Method and Design in "Ulysses" and "Finnegans Wake"* (London: Oxford University Press, 1964), and Michael Groden, *"Ulysses" in Progress.*

[37]Numerology has always struck me as "a happy hunting ground" for minds like that of the teller of Swift's *A Tale of a Tub*: "The profound number THREE is that which hath most employed my sublimest speculations, nor ever without wonderful delight." See Jonathan Swift, *"Gulliver's Travels" and Other Writings,* ed. Louis Landa (Boston: Houghton Mifflin, 1960), 272.

stead of cryptic intimations of immortality, we get bathetic plunges, the sublime giving way to the ridiculous, as at the end of "Sirens," when Emmet's patriotic proclamation merges with Bloom's gargantuan fart. That the Arranger has become a Deranger, the master of the anticlimactic climax, is evident in his playful self-reflection, suggesting his implied presence and mockery of closure.

> *Written. I have.*
> Pprrpffrrppffff.
> *Done.* (11:1291–94)

Each of the last four episodes entertains a conventional comic closure, as though the novel were trying out every known way, short of authorial demise, to end. "Circe" stages dramatic catharses for Bloom and Stephen, then a black mass, an apocalypse, Stephen's metaphoric rebirth, and a resurrection. "Eumaeus" presents a recognition scene between the protagonists and a metaphoric consummation or marriage. "Ithaca" provides a return home, reunion between husband and wife, the hero's revelations or epiphanies, abundant heavenly signs, and elaborate consecration of hero and heroine. "Penelope" ends with Molly's spectacular benediction.

What this brief catalog of endings omits is, of course, the bristling parody. Amid the farcical mélange of "Circe," for instance, the final moments stand out of the whirligig as a vivid spoof of comic closure. The "strong curtain" in "Circe" is a recognition scene between Bloom and Stephen/Rudy, yet its purport is highly bewildering. What strikes one most forcefully is not the union but the distance between the characters. Bloom, eager to provide "exactly what Stephen needs" (15:4916), solicitously, tenderly awakens Stephen by calling his name and Stephen groans "Who? Black panther. Vampire" (15:4930). Whatever he might mean by this, it can't be heartening. Then he passes out again, murmuring bits of Yeats's "Who goes with Fergus," which gives rise to Bloom's misperception that he is singing about "some girl" named Ferguson. As so often in this sad comedy, characters proceed on misperceptions, for better and for worse: communication is as comically fractured as in the conversations between Sterne's My Uncle Toby and My Father.

The resurrection of Rudy sometimes excites unduly optimistic theological interpretations. Sultan, for instance, says that Stephen, "having accepted God's dominion . . . has put himself in a position to accept His grace."[38] Much is made of his foetal posture. Blamires, always excited by any signs of impending grace, concludes that "the home-rule Son will yet arise in the north-west."[39] Gracehopers (to make a category out of the figure in *Finnegans Wake*) argue that Bloom, with a touch of the artist, has resurrected Rudy through the power of love. But too many details in this scene qualify, complicate, and gaily mock that possibility. Rudy is depicted *very* sentimentally, dressed in an Eton suit because that is Bloom's notion of respectability, "with glass shoes and a little bronze helmet" (15:4958), like a fairy-tale figure. Certainly Rudy has otherworldly detachment, for he doesn't even pause to speak to his father, but pointedly "gazes, unseeing, into Bloom's eyes and goes on reading" (15:4964). Like Bloom's "atonement" with Stephen in "Eumaeus," this reunion is only partial, fragmentary, temporary, and amusing. Both compelling and ludicrous, this recognition scene reenacts, yet parodies, conventional completion. Don Gifford's suggestion that Rudy is associated with Hermes seems particularly appropriate, for the little messenger of the gods is both the spirit of interpretation and a notorious trickster. To end "Circe" with his appearance, a kind of *deus ex machina,* is a wonderfully melodramatic climax that raises, yet defies, the possibility of completion.

Amid that book of howlers, "Eumaeus," is a telling stylistic tic— the ellipsis. Of course speakers in the cabmen's shelter are regularly interrupted or simply trail off, as in ordinary conversation, but the ellipsis appears so frequently in this episode that a further implication suggests itself: narrators, unable to close sentences or conclude thoughts, give up, despair of completion. In one passage (16:1440– 80) that moves in and out of Bloom's mind (though the distinction is far from clear throughout this episode), we find several ellipses,[40] that are only partly accounted for by the subject matter: Bloom is thinking about sexual desires, "a kind of need there" (16:1462–63),

[38]Sultan, *The Argument of "Ulysses,"* 345.

[39]Harry T. Blamires, *The Bloomsday Book: A Guide through Joyce's "Ulysses"* (London: Methuen, 1983), 207.

[40]The ellipses are less marked in Gabler's Corrected Text than in the 1961 Random House edition, where several omissions needed to complete the construction or sense are flagged by dots (. . .). Other ellipses are avoided in the new edition. For instance, "Stephen, who confessed to still feeling poorly and fagged out, paused at the, for a moment . . . the door to . . . " (Random House 1961 edition, 660); the preposition "to" at the end of the sentence is now omitted (16:1707).

and pressing troubles he wishes to evade. Yet the vexing nature of the subject does not explain why the narrator abandons so many perfectly simple sentences, such as, "he took out his pocketbook and, turning over the various contents it contained rapidly finally he" (16:1422). Ellipses imply that one might continue indefinitely and never get anywhere. Perhaps this should not surprise us, for in "Eumaeus," that black hole for identity, there are not even any dependable doors, only "the, for a moment, the door" (16:1707). Consequently any narrative assertion, like motion generally in this episode, is halting, awkward, stymied. Sentences that do not trail off vaguely tend to stop arbitrarily: "That worthy, however, was busily engaged in collecting round the. Someway in his. Squeezing or" (16:681–82). When the language of "Eumaeus" does move fluently, it meanders mindlessly, such as the epic sentence beginning "for instance" and ending, finally, hilariously, "in a word" (16:1585–1602). Like any great clown, from Falstaff to Robin Williams, the narrator of "Eumaeus" plays the fool to the hilt. His ellipses and the never-ending sentences, like the mock-epic catalogs of "Cyclops" and "Circe," are indications of the novel's comic fecundity and capacity, or need, for infinite supplement.

If "Eumaeus" generally repudiates the possibility of getting anywhere, it also spoofs completion of the movement between Bloom and Stephen, for the central action of "Eumaeus," the coming together of the protagonists, is rendered as a mock communion, or perhaps a recognition through a glass darkly. Together at last for a sustained period, Stephen and Bloom are constantly misunderstanding each other, as humorously mismatched as Don Quixote and Sancho Panza. When they do connect, it is usually about something wonderfully incidental, as when Stephen wonders why cafés put chairs upside down on tables at night, to which "the neverfailing Bloom replied without a moment's hesitation, saying straight off" (16:1711–12). More often they are "poles apart" (16:774). Stephen says, in a characteristic declaration, "I suspect . . . that Ireland must be important because it belongs to me" (16:1164–65), and Bloom does not even pretend to get it. "What belongs queried Mr Bloom bending, fancying he was perhaps under some misapprehension. Excuse me. Unfortunately I didn't catch the latter portion . . . " (16:1166–68).[41] Stephen speculates that "sounds are impos-

---

[41]Conversely, one might say that Bloom's clownish bewilderment is the perfect response to Stephen's preposterous egocentricity.

tures, . . . Like names" (16:362–63); Bloom "concurred" without knowing why and moves irrelevantly from the abstract question to the personal: "Our name was changed too" (16:365–66).

Trying to raise the level of conversation, Bloom makes another amusingly inapt assumption, referring to Stephen ("Non serviam!") as "a good catholic" (16:748). Though "the mystical finesse involved was a bit out of his sublunary depth" (16:761–62), Herr Professor questions Stephen's catechistic definition of the soul as a "simple substance": "Simple? I shouldn't think that is the proper word" (16:764), although he concedes "you do knock across a simple soul once in a blue moon" (16:765) (over a cup of coffee at a shelter, one might say) and he tries to salvage the conversation with his favorite two-dollar word, "phenomenon" (16:769).

At one point, Bloom preaches "mutual equality" to Stephen, who responds with some facts and names that do not pertain in any clear way to what Bloom has been saying.

> —Memorable bloody bridge battle and seven minutes' war, Stephen assented, between Skinner's alley and Ormond market.
>   Yes, Mr Bloom thoroughly agreed, entirely endorsing the remark, that was overwhelmingly right. And the whole world was overwhelmingly full of that sort of thing.
> —You just took the words out of my mouth, he said. A hocuspocus of conflicting evidence that candidly you couldn't remotely. . . . (16:1104–10)

Bloom eagerly seizes Stephen's "remote" reference as confirmation for his generalizations, despite the obscurity of Stephen's remark and the "hocuspocus of conflicting evidence" the world provides. Pointing out the "B.A." after his name to Stephen, Bloom is confused by Stephen's response, which is a private reference to Deasy's letter about hoof-and-mouth.

> —Is that first epistle to the Hebrews, he asked, as soon as his bottom jaw would let him, in? Text: open thy mouth and put thy foot in it.
> —It is, really, Mr Bloom said (though first he fancied he alluded to the archbishop till he added about foot and mouth with which there could be no possible connection). (16:1268–72)

Stephen yawns a lot, even for someone overtired, and must be bored, possibly embarrassed by Bloom. Practically every effort he makes to lift his style to Stephen's level results in a Bloomism or a blooper; trying to stand tall, Bloom walks tiptoe and falls flat. He botches Marx—"Everyone according to his needs or everyone according to his deeds" (16:247); after overhearing a haggle in Italian about money, he suggests that Stephen write poetry in beautiful Italian—*Bella Poetria* (16:346) indeed; and he gets the titles wrong for what he specifies are "to his mind, the acme of firstclass music as such, literally knocking everything else into a cocked hat" (16:1739–40). Based on what Bloom says, why should Stephen see him as anything more than a genial buffoon? Just about the only time these two come together is in a brief glance after somebody remarks ignorantly about the park murders: then "Mr B. and Stephen, each in his own particular way, both instinctively exchanged meaning glances, in a religious silence of the strictly *entre nous* variety" (16:594–96).

Otherwise their communion is comically stymied, as when Bloom recounts his exchange with the Citizen: "So I without deviating from plain facts in the least told him his God, I mean Christ, was a jew too and all his family like me though in reality I'm not. That was one for him. A soft answer turns away wrath. He hadn't a word to say for himself as everyone saw. Am I not right?" (16:1083–87). An unanswerable inquiry. Again, the Eumaean assertion of Plain Facts, collapsing in the utterance: "God, I mean Christ" being more or less the same thing, both "jews"—albeit not exactly "orthodox," not to put too fine a point on it. Then the kind of self-definition one finds in recognition scenes, only muddled: "a jew . . . like me though in reality I'm not" (16:1084–85). We know what he means, more or less, but how could Stephen? Then another adorning Scriptural allusion ("A soft answer") giving way to adversarial triumph and self-assertion.

Stephen's response continues to be taken as the anagogic heart of *Ulysses*: "*Ex quibus,* Stephen mumbled in a noncommittal accent, their two or four eyes conversing, *Christus* or Bloom his name is or after all any other, *secundum carnem*" (16:1091–93). Of this a recent commentator writes: "Perceiving Bloom as something other than an ordinary man, as a divine principle . . . is an indication that Stephen is in the process of becoming the Joyce who will write *Ulysses*."[42] Rather than revelation, I find revelry. Pointedly asked to

---

[42]Daniel R. Schwarz, *Reading Joyce's "Ulysses"* (New York: St. Martin's Press, 1987), 239.

reply in the affirmative, Stephen takes refuge in a mumbled quotation out of Bloom's sublunary depth. Typically, it is not a response at all but borrowed words he does not believe: the fragment alludes to the Vulgate, *Romans* 9:5, which translates "and from that race [the Israelites] is Christ, according to the flesh" (Gifford 549). Stephen is going on automatic, citing what he has been taught or memorized, regardless of the context; he is explicitly "noncommital."

How substantial is their communion? Bloom lectures Stephen with botched Latin and platitudes, while

> Over his untasteable apology for a cup of coffee, listening to this synopsis of things in general, Stephen stared at nothing in particular. He could hear, of course, all kinds of words changing colour like those crabs about Ringsend in the morning burrowing quickly into all colours of different sorts of the same sand where they had a home somewhere beneath or seemed to. Then he looked up and saw the eyes that said or didn't say the words the voice he heard said, if you work.
> —Count me out, he managed to remark, meaning work. (16:1141–48)

"Things in general" means nothing in particular, I think. Stephen is daydreaming and barely present here. "Count me out" is as emphatic a rejection as this tired, surly youth will permit himself, and the murky moment is a lucid view of muddle. If you are looking for atonement, completion, or just a "plausible connection" (16:386), "to cut a long story short" (16:1691), Eumaeus well look elsewhere.[43]

The possibility of a "plausible connection" or of things coming together is a major consideration in "Ithaca," told by a kind of *alazon,* a pedantic, self-deceived object of ridicule who is also a source of humor, albeit somewhat rarified. The episode is not exactly *"Everybody's Book of Jokes* (1,000 pages and a laugh in every one)" (17:442), though giddy verbal play such as we heard in "Sirens" creeps into the textbook discourse, along with mordant, impish, and donnish jokes. Full of what used to be called "learned

---

[43]Though it breaks this clown's heart to spell out the joke, "you may as" well know that nobody who has read this sentence hears the pun. Still I persist in folly, awaiting that ideal reader who most resembles me.

wit,"[44] "Ithaca" is comic in the madcap encyclopedic tradition of *Tristram Shandy*, which is also full of lists, catalogs, and documents, paradoxically conveying inadequacy, frustration, and incompletion. As Tristram famously lamented, reality moves too fast and includes too much for the writer to capture.[45] The Ithacan pedant, like Tristram, tries to include everything, and his efforts, like the motions of Freud's clown, are "extravagant and inexpedient. We are laughing at an expenditure that is too large."[46] If in tragedy life is constricted and truncated, in comedy life goes on, in full stream, like the water celebrated in "Ithaca." So when water is defined by its attributes and connotations, its qualities require over a page to document, until it becomes a trope for the whole fecund world of *Ulysses* itself. The very length of this entry implies that defining and characterizing water adequately and comprehensively would, like Bloom's scheme for squaring the circle, require "33 closely printed volumes of 1000 pages each of innumerable quires and reams of India paper . . . in order to contain the complete tale . . . " (17:1075–77). Thus "Ithaca" parodies its own obsessive inclusiveness, mocks meaning as a quest to square the circle. Yet, like Beckett's tramps who can't go on but will go on, the encyclopedist continues.

The answers in "Ithaca" tend to be authoritative assertions—usually scientific, technical, and clinical, overwhelming us with facts but frustrating our imaginative comprehension. Probably the most important single fact divulged in "Ithaca" is the date of the last "complete carnal intercourse" (17:2278) between Bloom and Molly. Yet even that paragraph, with its repetition of the words "con-

---

[44]For example, "an aorist preterite proposition (parsed as masculine subject, monosyllabic onomatopoetic transitive verb with direct feminine object) from the active voice" (17:2218–20), etc., etc. to signify what Blazes did to Molly.

[45]"I am this month one whole year older than I was this time twelvemonth, and having got, as you perceive, almost into the middle of my fourth volume— and no farther than to my first day's life—'tis demonstrative that I have three hundred and sixty-four days more life to write just now, than when I first set out; so that instead of advancing, as a common writer, in my work, with what I have been doing at it—on the contrary, I am just thrown so many volumes back . . . at this rate I should just live 364 times faster than I should write—It must follow, 'an please your worships, that the more I write, the more I shall have to write—and consequently, the more your worships read, the more your worships will have to read." Sterne, *Tristram Shandy*, 4:xiii.

[46]Freud, *Jokes and Their Relation to the Unconscious*, 190.

summated," "complete," "incomplete," and "circumscribed," mocks our desire to wrap things up or simplify in the discredited manner of "Eumaeus." Doubtless the most debated fact in "Ithaca" is the "series" of Molly's—well, what are they: lovers, suitors, admirers, Bloom's fantasies or jealousies? Before we can figure out what to make of it, we must decide what it purports to be.[47] Two generations of critical scrutiny demonstrate that such facts are inconclusive, that even a simple list entails a complicated hermeneutical process. (Oh rocks! More jawbreakers!)

The text holds open the possibility that Bloom might have smiled in jocoserious recognition that "he is neither first nor last nor only nor alone in a series originating in and repeated to infinity" (17:2130–31). In a comic reversal of the divine revelation, "I am the first and the last," our hero approaches his mock-apotheosis in his degradation. It is the sort of archetypal completion *Ulysses* so often parodies, especially in this episode, which gives us the word "jocoserious" at the moment that Bloom and Stephen are imbibing their cocoa (17:369). Antic Joyce, I have reiterated, insists on contrary possibilities, tottering between the two sides of the oxymoron, resisting, repudiating the fine balance of earlier comic masters such as Pope or Fielding, who prefer to depict apparent incongruities as ultimate syntheses. Instead of an artful, elegant resolution, reconciling the mighty and the trivial, mockery and affection, as in *The Rape of the Lock,* Joyce (often, but not always; "Nausicaa" is exceptional) stresses the continuing disparity and tension between discordant elements.

Although "Ithaca" is frequently characterized as catechistic, its purpose is the opposite of dogmatic revelation. Its perpetual, unresolved play between antitheses, or "peripatetic intellectual dialogues" (17:965) makes a comic critique of dialectic, with the question and answer format underscoring the rhythm of give-and-take, back-and-forth. Blake-like, Joyce dissolves rigid dichotomies between sublime and ridiculous, sacred and profane, cosmic and trivial, lyric and banal.

---

[47]Rather like a generic approach to literature, as defined by C. S. Lewis: "The first qualification for judging any piece of workmanship from a corkscrew to a cathedral is to know *what* it is—what it was intended to do and how it is meant to be used. . . . The first thing the reader needs to know about *Paradise Lost* is what Milton meant it to be." See *A Preface to "Paradise Lost"* (New York: Oxford University Press, 1961), 1.

A principle of Joycean humor is the traditionally comic insistence that the underprivileged terms in the binary oppositions be given equal importance: sublime, sacred, cosmic, and lyric are not valorized. The characteristic Joycean twist is that parity does not bring equilibrium. In this readiness for reversal or perpetual antithesis, *Ulysses* obeys a favorite decree of folly, which in scientific "Ithaca" is a law of nature, indicated by numerous references to oscillation or antagonism.

> Both admitted the alternately stimulating and obtunding influence
>   of heterosexual magnetism (17:25–26)
> an equal and opposite power of abandonment and recuperation
>   (17:253–54)
> counteracting influence (17:291–92)
> oscillation between events (17:428)
> counterbalance (17:691)
> foreward and rereward respectively (17:2308)
> obverse meditations (17:1057)
> neverchanging everchanging (17:233–34)
> antagonistic sentiments (17:2154)
> a nature full and volatile in its free state, was alternately the agent
>   agent and reagent of attraction. Because action between agent
>   and reagent at all instants varied, with inverse proportion of
>   increase and decrease (17:2163–66).

The "fluctuating incertitude" (17:557) felt by Bloom when wondering whether he had already said "he had frequented the university of life" is typical of "Ithaca,"[48] both in its movement and mood, for it is in this learned and authoritative discourse that we are most explicitly confronted with the limits of what we can know. One question asks, "What rendered problematic" Bloom's plans, and the answers include "the irreparability of the past . . . The imprevidibility of the future" (17:973–80). Stephen proceeds "from the known to the unknown . . . between a micro- and a macrocosm ineluctably constructed upon the incertitude of the void" (17:1013–15). The *parallax* motif recurs: "parallactic drift of socalled fixed stars, in reality evermoving . . . " (17:1052–53). Instead of being

---

[48]In fact, Bloom *had* used the phrase, but not to Stephen. It occurs in "Circe," when he defended himself against Beaufoy, which is a rare reference to the events of that chapter.

The Rock, "Ithaca" turns out to be more wandering rocks. Repudiating our need for closure, the novel maddeningly refuses to conclude. We cannot reach any firm conclusion about Stephen's fate or the Blooms' future, "there being no known method from the known to the unknown" (17:1140–41). What meaning or hope we derive depends as much upon the premises we bring as upon anything we find in the text, but all prior conceptions or instincts are "as possible of proof as of confutation" (17:1153). Reading "Ithaca" in quest of either positive or negative signs, as either a "Gracehoper" (*FW* 414:21) or a "tragic jester" (*FW* 171:21), is like moving a magnet through a vast heap of iron filings; fragments will cluster in an apparently ordered pattern but heaps will inevitably remain overlooked. One of Joyce's Ithacan coinages is "monoideal" (17:582), meaning something like "prolonged fixation on one idea" (Gifford 575); as readers of *Ulysses,* we all become monoideal. We find and interpret the sign, with attention to one idea (comedy, say), but ignore or slight the contrary possibilities.

"Ithaca" often sounds less like the voice of scientific authority than like a poststructuralist critic, entertaining infinite possibilities and asking us to create our own novel. The Ithacan word for "textuality" is "ipsorelative" (17:1350), meaning reflexive, a self-contained organization of cross-references. As in this word, the novel (like the Freudian self) always seems to be talking about itself, regarding its ipsorelativity. Stephen and Bloom discuss "the general text" (17:768), including translation, letters, vocabulary, kinds of literature, modes of writing. Almost everything in "Ithaca" reverts to textuality, like the ideas both Stephen and Bloom have for snappy ads. Bloom's two smartly dressed girls might be "engaged in writing" while, in Stephen's scenario, a young man reads what a young woman has written on hotel paper (17:612–17)—hence, two miniature texts about texts within a larger text about texts.

What seems to matter most to "Ithaca" is not the product of analysis but its unending process, so that supplement or criticism has the same status as the text itself. "The supernatural character of Judaic scripture" (17:1900) does not mean that The Word is self-evident or sufficient unto itself; on the contrary, Talmudic commentary is as sacred as scripture because there is no such thing as "the letter of the law" (17:1627). Whether the text is the Bible, Shakespeare, or Joyce, due to "the difficulties of interpretation" (17:343), we may derive only "imperfect conviction from the text" (17:390).

"Stephen's commentary" on the ballad of Little Harry Hughes, for example, is so contorted and confused that the commentary needs commentary, as the narrator indicates by asking several "follow-up" questions.

Eventually "Ithaca" appears to be talking about little except textuality; the characters have been metamorphosed into "characters" and "narrators." Advertisements and legal documents are cited "in textual terms" (17:1824, 1868), indicating first, that nothing happens without being rendered in one or another textual term, and second, that the terms themselves are multiple and arbitrary: examples are the scriptural archetypes (burnt offering, rite of Onan, atonement) or some other thesis you or I wish to enforce. Even when something is not narrated our attention is drawn to its "potential narration" (17:638), the sense that it is "unnarrated but existent by implication" (17:642–43). Life itself is seen as narrative, subject to "generic conditions" (17:995).[49]

As "Ithaca" moves to a close, or rather stops going, its "narrativity" seems more pronounced than ever. Once Molly awakens, neither she nor Bloom is referred to by name for the rest of the chapter, and very rarely in the last chapter. They become "narrator" and "listener." Having "recapitulated" his day to himself in "terms" of Biblical archetypes, Bloom narrates another highly selective version of his day to Molly, prompting the question, "Was the narration otherwise unaltered by modifications?" (17:2267). The answer "Absolutely" is a joke, since we have been so thoroughly taught that everything is narrative, which requires editing and demands commentary, even when the text is as ostensibly simple as a list. The textuality of *Ulysses* defies completion, although resolutions have been "anticipatorily consummated" (17:2277) for hundreds of pages. Closed textuality is as rare as complete sexuality, "inasmuch as complete mental intercourse between himself and the listener had not taken place" (17:2285–86). This passage refers not just to Bloom's relationship with Molly but to our relationship with "Ithaca," however much the interested parties imagine "consummation" (17:762, 2120, 2287).

The plethora of parodies on "Sinbad the Sailor" suggests not so much the hero's infinite capacity for metamorphoses as the text's

---

[49]John Barthes once commented that of course God is an artist; unfortunately he is a realist.

capacity to interpret him variously. In this last list of "Ithaca" is recapitulated the novel's abasement and exaltation of Bloom and the free play that delights and nourishes. After all is said and done, to the extent that all is ever said and done, "Darkinbad" is the "Bright-dayler," a mock-heroic name and epithet that perfectly suits the hero of Joyce's oxymoronic vision. The punch line of "Ithaca" is that dot, suggesting closure or symbolizing Q.E.D. "Ineluctably constructed upon the incertitude of the void" (17:1014–15), no reading or writing can ever be definitive, even if each of us fondly imagines himself "to be first, last, only and alone" (17:2129) in our vision of the text. One of many things that distinguish Joyce from other modernists and "anticipatorily" (17:2277) connect him with postmodernism is his relatively relaxed, even amused perception of inevitable incompletion. Far from dismayed, he usually seems delighted by the unending task of doing and undoing, narrating and commenting. *Ulysses* is like that home without Plumtree's potted meat: Incomplete. In this sense, there is no Ithaca—or, if there is, it need not be an end but a voyage, like that envisioned by Joyce's contemporary Constantine Cavafy.

> Always keep Ithaca in mind.
> Arrival there is your destined end.
> But do not hasten the journey in the least.
> Better it continue many years . . .
>
> Ithaca granted you the lovely voyage.
> Without her you would never have departed on your way.
> She has nothing else to grant you any more.
>
> And though you find her squalid, Ithaca did not cheat you.
> So wise have you become, so experienced,
> you already will have realized what they mean: these Ithacas.[50]

In Joyce's view, incompletion frustrates the tendency of magnetic influence and parodies the atonement "so devoutly . . . to be wished for" (16:1031). Thus *Ulysses* makes comedy, in some traditional ways, of both connections and lack of connections. To some extent, *Ulysses* brings characters like Bloom and Molly back together à la *Tom Jones;* conversely the novel is a chronicle of frustration, like *Tristram Shandy.* In Sterne's world, the spectre of impotence hangs

[50]Constantine Cavafy, "Ithaca," trans. Peter A. Bien.

about every male in the Shandy household, including the bull: Tristram is "circumsised or worse" by a falling window sash, My Uncle Toby sustained a debilitating wound at Namur and in parts crucial and unmentionable, and My Father's attention to his nuptial duties is interrupted, so that the hero's sensibility is dispersed everywhere and goes nowhere. Nobody in Shandy Hall can communicate anything.

Like Sterne and other humorists who lament and love frustration, Joyce finds incompletion abounding and amusing. A full catalog of Bloom's lack of connections would be extensive and redundant: he fails to ogle the lady's legs, meet Martha, enter Molly, get the ad renewed, and so on and so forth. What is striking is that Bloom doesn't dwell on this litany of frustrations, certainly not as grounds for despair; as in *Tristram Shandy*, the failure to connect is not disastrous but amusing, the source of mirth and pathos. Indeed, Bloom considers his daily budget balanced, a nicely comic balance of give and take, profit and loss. Moreover he notices, in true comic fashion, that many connections that *are* made on this day are based on accident or coincidence. Studying what Bloom experiences and thinks, we observe further instances of gratuitous connection, such as the reappearance of that throwaway touting Dowie's arrival, and of possibly portentous connection, for Bloom's nocturnal mumbo-jumbo about a "roc's auk's egg" (17:2328–29) seems to have been felicitously misunderstood by Molly as a request for "breakfast in bed with a couple of eggs" (18:1–2).[51] And whether this will bring the Blooms closer to a marital revival or merely become another lost opportunity and disappointment, "who can say?" (14:1063), for in *Ulysses,* as in Joyce's characterization of a Chekhov play, "there is no beginning, no middle, and no end, nor does he work up to a climax; his plays are a continuous action in which life flows onto the stage and flows off again, and in which nothing is resolved."[52]

The *Fools Step in Where Angels* Principle

Probably the grandest pratfall in *Ulysses* is "Eumaeus," in which Antic Joyce plays the fool with such fidelity, precision, and gusto that he—like any fool worth his sceptre—provokes ridicule and

[51]As Fritz Senn speculates, *Joyce's Dislocations,* 105.
[52]Power, *Conversations with Joyce,* 58.

animosity. This may be the book's most frequently maligned chapter, toward which even dedicated Joyceans profess disappointment, impatience, ennui, and irritation.[53] We seem to have been handed over to an egregious fool, one who, finally given his moment in the spotlight, will remain on stage until he is yanked off. A chapter of throwaways, "this gratuitous contribution of a humorous character" (16:1358), longer than the entire "Telemachiad," challenges and provokes readers by sustaining folly beyond "reasonable" limits, all the while subjecting the idea of authorship to severe, sustained mockery. Yet nothing is more typical of *Ulysses* than to challenge itself by vigorous comic questioning—spoofing authorial authority and implying that writing is folly, through exaggeration, parody, mimicry, burlesque, degradation. A bizarre blend of sustained self-indulgence and relentless self-irony, flaunting its own excess and inadequacy, "Eumaeus" is joyously foolish, a canny sham.

Because the narrator of "Eumaeus" tries so hard to be an author, I will dub him the Penman, someone who fancies himself (like Bloom) "a bit of an artist in his spare time" (16:1448–49), capable of pursuing "a literary occupation" (15:801).[54] He is certainly a lard-witted author, waging an endearing, losing battle with language: "From inside information extending over a series of years Mr Bloom was rather inclined to poohpooh the suggestion as egregious balderdash for, pending that consummation devoutly to be or not to be wished for, he was fully cognisant of the fact that their neighbours across the channel, unless they were much bigger fools than

[53]Stanislaus Joyce disliked "Eumaeus" for "its weak effort to be witty" (*L*, 3:58). Edmund Wilson refers to "Eumaeus" as "the interminable letdown . . . colorless and tiresome . . . too heavy a dead weight," in *Axel's Castle: A Study in the Imaginative Literature of 1870–1930* (New York: Charles Scribner's Sons, 1931), 216. Arnold Goldman says "the 'tired' cliches of 'Eumaeus' strike most readers as a letdown. . . . The effect of the 'imitative form' (tired characters: tired prose) appears disastrous . . . " in *The Joyce Paradox: Form and Freedom in His Fiction* (London: Routledge & Kegan Paul, 1966), 100. Hugh Kenner says "the episode has incurred the displeasure of those who don't read closely, and imagine that Joyce is conveying the sense of exhaustion by exhausting the reader for fifty pages," in *Dublin's Joyce,* 260.

[54]In "Eumaeus," Bloom muses about penning "something out of the common groove . . . *My Experiences,* let us say, *in a Cabman's Shelter*" (16:1229–31). Don Gifford nicely describes the narrator of "Eumaeus" as someone like Bloom, only more so.

he took them for, rather concealed their strength than the opposite" (16:1029–34). This sentence is characteristic of our Penman in several ways. He claims authority ("From inside information . . . fully cognisant of the fact . . . ") to make sweeping generalizations, expressed in a dissonant blend of pomposity ("rather inclined . . . egregious") and breeziness ("poohpooh . . . balderdash"). The grand allusion to Shakespeare collapses when two separate passages from *Hamlet* are clumsily yoked ("consummation devoutly to be or not to be wished for"), with a gratuitous final preposition to grate the ear. Everything is elaborated ("neighbours across the channel" for "English"), nothing is edited ("rather concealed their strength than the opposite" instead of "rather concealed than revealed their strength"). If *Ulysses* is the book we read with pen in hand, "Eumaeus" is the chapter we attack with a busy blue pencil.

In writing badly with such brilliance, Joyce offers readers the fun of picking apart the Penman's bloopers and has rather concealed his strength than the opposite. "Eumaeus" is prime Irish Bull.[55] Inspired fatuity abounds, such as "never beyond a certain point where he invariably drew the line" (16:92–93), or, of a knife, "that the point was the least conspicuous point about it" (16:819–20). As an encyclopedia of clichés or primer on "The Art of Sinking," the chapter is amusing, not least in the Penman's earnest delusion that he is writing grandly; meanwhile Joyce has inscribed self-reflexive comments about getting to the point, never getting beyond a certain point, consummation always pending.

"Eumaeus," the great book of blarney, provides many synonyms

---

[55]Defined by the *OED* as "a ludicrous inconsistency unperceived by the speaker. The epithet *Irish* is a late addition." For example, Sir Jonah Barrington delights in documenting "the bulls of Sir Boyle Roche . . . the most celebrated and entertaining anti-grammarian in the Irish Parliament." See *The Ireland of Sir Jonah Barrington: Selections from His Personal Sketches,* ed. Hugh B. Staples (Seattle: University of Washington Press, 1967), 246–47. Roche once asked Parliament, "Why should we put ourselves out of our way to do anything for *posterity*—for what has *posterity* done for *us?*" (249). Incidentally, the editor, Hugh Staples, compares Sir Jonah Barrington to John Stanislaus Joyce "who seems in some respects to have modeled his life on Sir Jonah's" (xviii). The modern master of Irish Bull is of course Yogi Berra: "Line up in a circle," "It's not over till it's over," "That restaurant is so crowded no one goes there any more," and "You should go to other people's funerals or else they won't come to yours."

for foolishness, including "blandiloquence" (16:231), "the usual blarney" (16:1635), "obviously bogus" (16:1045), "pure buncombe" (16:1286), and "a lot of shillyshally" (16:1340). Speakers do not just "say," but perform, and these "doughty narrator[s]" (16:570), including our Penman, invariably insist that they are telling gospel truth, a reliability devoutly to be wished (for) but rarely attained. Because everybody now claims unimpeachable narrative authority, the words "fact" and "facts" are repeated thirty-four times in "Eumaeus," more often than they appear in all the other episodes combined. Often the word occurs as an intensifier, in a phrase such as "in point of fact" (16:195) or "as a matter of fact" (16:178). Facts per se are considered telling, "the eloquent fact" (16:638), even in some dubious contexts. Ireland is described as "the richest country bar none on the face of God's earth . . . and all agreed that that was a fact" (16:988–95). We even hear of "actual facts" (16:324), which in "Eumaeus" is less redundant than it appears, since so often we are given nonactual facts or actual nonfacts, such as Kitty O'Shea's Spanish background. There are also various and numerous assertions that something is "true" or "genuine," or that something is "reason," "evidence," "proof," and so forth; my favorite instance is Bloom's Utopian plan for "education (the genuine article)" (16:1653). Repetition of words such as "matter," "thing," "substance," "object," and "shape" convey the hope or pretense that one has gotten a handle on this narrative business, nailing things down, getting to the brass tacks, sticking to "strict history" (16:1514) or "the historic story" (16:1361).

Faith in any strict distinction between "history" and "story," though, is humorously undermined by the *Telegraph* account of Dignam's funeral. Typically, the point is underscored by a strained pun on the name of the newspaper, "tell a graphic lie" (16:1232). This poor pun, a miniature bit of folly, turns out to be surprisingly pertinent because the newspaper version contains several "nonsensical howlers of misprints" (16:1267). Bloom, who was of course present, is pathetically, comically reduced to "L. Boom," while the absent C. P. M'Coy and Stephen are listed—along with M'Intosh. So basic facts are incorrect, and this historical record partly fictive.[56]

---

[56]O Tempora! O Mores! Department: fact-checkers at respected magazines rely on newspapers like the *New York Times,* which usually trust the reporter's accuracy. If the fact appears in a book, fact-checkers ordinarily assume it is correct.

In "Eumaeus," everybody has trouble seeing and understanding clearly, so that this episode imitates Homer's in rendering a perpetual series of disguises; here comes everybody "sailing under false colours" (16:496). Rumors like those of stones in Parnell's coffin pass for facts, "innuendo" (16:1209) thrives, trivialization, circumlocution, and deception abound. Roughly speaking, everyone in "Eumaeus" resembles Odysseus. That inedible bun is "like one of our skipper's bricks *disguised*" (16:786, my emphasis); everybody deserves Skin-the-Goat's derisive description of Captain O'Shea as a "cottonball" (16:1357), that is "having the appearance but not the actuality of something" (*OED*). Nothing substantial is evident "on the face of it" (16:539), especially not expressions. Faces are masks: [Murphy] "turned his body half round, shut up his right eye completely. Then he screwed his features up someway sideways and glared out into the night with an unprepossessing cast of countenance" (16:395–97). Limiting one's own vision is a way to hide oneself, and "ever conceal, never reveal" (15:4952).

Bloom "could by straining just perceive" (16:932) the old boozer, and the same sentence reiterates that Bloom is "rather out of his depth." Stephen is "altogether too fagged out" (16:189) to remember or perceive anything very clearly, not even whether he is handing Corley pennies or half crowns. What stands out most clearly in "Eumaeus" is obscurity. Typical of the dimness through which everything is perceived in "Eumaeus" is the head of the horse "suddenly in evidence in the dark quite near" (16:1782). Lots of things are seen dimly in the dark. Stephen "could just make out the darker figure" (16:105). Bloom's glance at Stephen's features "did not throw a flood of light, none at all in fact, on the problem" (16:302). We hear comments from "somebody who was evidently quite in the dark" (16:589–90) both literally and figuratively.[57] Very vaguely Stephen rambles on "to himself or some unknown listener somewhere" (16:885–86); "furtively" scrutinizing Stephen, Bloom fails "to throw much light on the subject" (16:1180–83). Mulling over Bantam Lyons's eagerness to place a bet (another example of misunderstanding), Bloom considers the difficulty of gambling: "Guesswork it reduced itself to eventually" (16:1293–94). The old sailor reads with the dubious help of a pair of "greenish goggles" (16:1672), which prompts the question, "Are you bad in the eyes?"

---

[57] A distinction rarely observed by the speakers who constantly say the former when they mean the latter.

He replies, "One time I could read a book in the dark, manner of speaking" (16:1679–80). Oblivious to their imperceptions, everybody is reading in the dark, manner of speaking.

Because "Eumaeus" is in this sense itself "a book in the dark," it has recently been rescued from its longstanding disrepute and become rather a favorite text for poststructuralists, who view its verbal glop as our linguistic condition. But it seems to me inapt to say that this episode "reveals a more general anxiety about writing as an echo of other writing and language that has been tainted by its prior use."[58] Such anxiety characterizes a modernist like T. S. Eliot[59] but not Joyce, who gaily quotes, distorts, imitates, and spoofs his predecessors. Where the narrator of *The Four Quartets* is lamenting or self-lacerating, agonizingly conscious of his belatedness, Joyce's Penman is sublimely oblivious. Certainly "Eumaeus" demonstrates the ubiquity of folly, an "actual fact" that we should not lament but celebrate.

To say this is not only to note that "Eumaeus" is subject to the "generic conditions" of comedy I have been elaborating, but also to argue that its folly is both exposed and enabled. The buffoonery of "Eumaeus" emerges from precisely the comic tendencies we have been tracking. The Penman is a forger, almost completely dependant upon borrowed words, worn-out figures of speech, clumps of thought. Like Buck and The Nameless One in "Cyclops," this narrator is a notable disabler or discrediter; through his perception we see everything reduced to lowest-common-denominator terms, or Murphy-like, with one eye shut. It is here that Stephen is perhaps most obnoxious, and Bloom most embarrassing. Here, too, Bloom makes a gesture that may be construed as offering his wife to Stephen. Having attained his apex at the end of "Circe," Bloom in "Eumaeus" succumbs to the law of comic gravity.

Let me recall once more the climactic Circean scene just prior to "Eumaeus," in light of which the association of Rudy with Hermes

[58]Karen Lawrence, *The Odyssey of Style in "Ulysses,"* 173.

[59]For example, "That was a way of putting it—not very satisfactory: / A periphrastic study in a worn-out poetical fashion . . . " (*East Coker,* 2). Or the message of the ghost in *Little Gidding,* II: "For last year's words belong to last year's language / And next year's words await another voice." Or, "Words strain, / Crack and sometimes break, under the burden, / Under the tension, slip, slide, perish, / Decay with imprecision, will not stay in place, / Will not stay still" (*Burnt Norton,* 5).

is especially apt. As Socrates reminds us, "Hermes has to do with speech . . . he is the interpreter, or messenger, or thief, or liar . . . all that sort of thing has a great deal to do with language."[60] Hermes flows from Greece via Rome into Irish "Mercurial Malachi," whose spirit is indirectly evoked at the opening of "Eumaeus": "Mr Bloom *brushed* off the greater bulk of the *shavings* and handed Stephen the hat and ashplant and *bucked* him up" (16:1–3, my emphasis).[61] Buck and "Eumaeus" are off-putting for some of the same reasons, primarily their clowning gratuitousness or excess. Much too much is said in "Eumaeus" for so little matter, for "a fool also is full of words" (Eccl.10:14), the verbal equivalent of that expenditure of energy which Freud recognized as comical. It is almost as if that emphatically mute Rudy had spawned his opposite and double, the voluble teller of the next episode. Language is not only hypertrophied but apparently random; there is no standard—what goes here, as the bishop said to the actress, could just as well go here. Virtually anything might be picked up, so that the "throwaway" ascends from motif to symbol. Whatever is at hand, or foot, may provide stuff for improvisation—as with that chaffering clown Buck Mulligan. The essence of the throwaway sensibility is the pun, but we might generalize beyond punning to note in "Eumaeus" (and of course in *Finnegans Wake*) a kind of Pollylogia, after "pollylogue" (*FW* 470:9), which I'll define as an antic predilection for ambiguity; delight in the tadpole slipperiness of language; a comical tendency, at the risk of obfuscation and nonsense, to imply an incongruous possibility in any word, anytime, anyhow. It goes without saying that this affinity for banality involves us with a lot of junk, the low stuff of culture that has always been the material of comedy.

In a simple way, then, the newspaper featured prominently in this episode indicates the chapter's receptivity to the stuff of life, erroneous, barely differentiated, hardly evaluated, almost arbitrarily collected and rendered in what Stanislaus recognized as "flabby Dublin journalese" (*L* 3:58). But the *Telegraph* is true to the spirit of folly in another way, for it is a Lost and Found Department—rather like *Ulysses* itself, one of the book's principles being that in any pile

---

[60]Plato, *Cratylus,* trans. Benjamin Jowett, in *Plato* (Chicago: Encyclopaedia Britannica, 1952), 97.

[61]Fritz Senn makes this point, in *Joyce's Dislocutions,* 135, as does Hugh Kenner, in *Joyce's Voices,* 35.

of junk something we recognize is liable to turn up. Like Shakespeare's great clown Autolycus, "as said before" (11:519), this book is a snapper-up of unconsidered trifles. Amid the bitched type, "*eatondph 1/8 ador dorador douradora*" (16:1257–58), we spy Simon Dedalus's "one and eightpence too much," the punch line to the yarn spun at the cemetery; since it is "too much," it logically appears as excess gibberish, perhaps the purest form of folly, in the newspaper. Not even a stray letter is lost in *Ulysses*: the "l" that disappears from the hero's name, metamorphosing him into "L. Boom," turns up in Martha's typo, "I do not like that other world."[62] Such whimsical returns imply that we are reading at once an antic book where anything goes and a book where certain rules or laws obtain.

These patterns or tendencies include the four I have delineated as generic conditions of the novel: comic acceptance, revival, confluence, and contingency. Banality, vulgarity, and stupidity are viewed for what they are and treated without sentimentality or evasion: the stream of life, with all its "flotsam, jetsam" (17:1686) is regarded with "that plenitude of sufferance" (14:863) or comic equanimity. In "Eumaeus," petrified, abased, exhausted language gets a "new lease of life" (6:796); dead words rise. The most minute, least consequential fragments connect in comic confluence, through "magnetic influence" or the Arranger's magic. And the episode's comic contingency reveals both the anticlimactic, interrupted, or frustrated nature of human experience, and its inexhaustible fecundity, the prodigious wealth of basic phenomena; those unavoidable ellipses imply that the speaker and life itself may well keep on going. Just as Bloom is subjected to rigorous mockery and survives with a measure of dignity and grace, so is language, and by extension all of "Dear Dirty Dublin," ridiculed and redeemed by this great fool.

[62]In becoming, as it were, El Boom, Bloom is comically inflated into God, Stephen's "shout in the street." Bernard Benstock interprets "L. Boom" very differently: "The missing 'L' in his printed name in the newspaper is the loss of the Hebraic God, El, from his life. Bloom is a wanderer, the Wandering Jew, exiled from Beth El." See Bernard Benstock, "L. Boom as Dreamer of *Finnegans Wake*," *PMLA* 82 (1967): 97.

$$3$$

Carried Away by a Wave of Folly

Re: Doublin'

As a primary subject, value, and method in *Ulysses,* folly provides a scale on which to comprehend and evaluate the characters. I began with and devoted considerable attention to Buck both because he is relatively neglected and because his roistering impiety, extravagant whimsicality, and manifold mirth draw attention to a striking development, the giving over of the stage increasingly to apostles of folly. In this chapter I survey the emergence and reign of folly in the various narratives. To trace what Tristram Shandy terms "transverse zig-zaggery," that wild pirouetting every which way, without oneself falling into folly, is probably impossible, but I have limited the perils by focusing upon ways in which Joyce's narrative impersonations entitle and empower folly: wordplay, *bagatelle,* abusive gibing, gusto, bawdy, nonsense, self-parody, apparently purposeless fooling—all that glorious, ridiculous clowning which Buck Mulligan introduces as master of the revels and embodies as abbot of unreason.

Whatever bright or dark powers Buck exerts in his strong opening turn seem contained or displaced for several episodes after "Telemachus." Indeed, the narrative is generally controlled, precise, and fluent enough to resemble, as James H. Maddox argues, the kind of discourse Stephen Dedalus wishes to create.[1] This style blends Flaubertian or Eliotic verisimilitude with interior monologue, re-

[1]Maddox, "Mockery in *Ulysses,*" in Newman and Thornton, 141–56.

sulting in a sharply focused vision of individual psychology and Jamesian "felt life." Though Joyceans tend to agree that this "initial style" is abandoned in favor of what more and more readers are now considering a very different discourse, tantamount to a whole new book, there are disagreements about where this development is first perceptible and what defines it.

With folly as our guide, we might notice a movement toward both broader spectacle and narrative shenanigans implicit from the outset and associated with the strange potency of Buck Mulligan. The first occasion this puzzling capacity enforces itself on our attention is the "Chrysostomos" (1:26) interpolation, usually understood to be the connection Stephen makes between Buck and the "golden-mouthed" Greek rhetorician. If so, it is odd that the word is not at least set off in a separate paragraph, signaling a change in point of view. The word comes right after Buck has given a "long slow whistle" (1:24), which is mysteriously answered by "two strong shrill whistles" (1:26). I'd argue that this is an intimation of the disruption that will become more apparent in "Aeolus" and flagrant in "Scylla and Charybdis" and "Wandering Rocks." Another Chrysostomos, St. John Chrysostomos, was a Church father, best remembered for his insistence that laughter came from the devil. Perhaps this interpolation and the doubling echo from Buck's single whistle to two answering whistles reveal a fault line in the discourse, or an omen of the fissions to come. If so, we might construe Buck's "Thanks, old chap . . . That will do nicely. Switch off the current, will you?" (1:28–29) as his private and privileged exchange with the maker of the novel, for whom he has stood, delivering the mock-invocation to the epic, conjuring up Stephen, and playing preacher-shaman; Buck is the first of the novel's many sham authors, endowed with the power to disrupt and control the discourse.

Another place where the "initial style" exposes a gap or disjunction is this puzzling sentence in "Aeolus," amid J. J. O'Molloy's stirring rendition of Seymour Bushe's "polished periods" (7:747), but attributed neither to O'Molloy nor to any of his auditors: "I have often thought since on looking back over that strange time that it was that small act, trivial in itself, that striking of that match, that determined the whole aftercourse of both our lives" (7:763–65). It is as though Pip or David Copperfield, with their mannered elegance and sentimental styles, had suddenly materialized in the Dublin newsroom. Though in "Hades" Bloom is off-camera for several brief intervals, the narrative heretofore has generally clung to the perspective of our two protagonists; "Aeolus" separates itself from Stephen and Bloom for sustained periods, and steps back to view them in the broader panorama of city life. As if to punctuate the break between narrator and protagonists and to proclaim the emergence of a separate narrative consciousness, "Aeolus" prominently displays its headlines or captions in boldface and presents a bit of consciousness that doesn't "belong" anywhere we recognize: someone else is now perceiving and presenting in a spirit distinct from the initial style and perspective of the novel. If the initial style represents Stephen's ideal discourse, such rifts as "Chrysostomos" and this Dickensian sentence announce a second self or jesting double of the first narrator: some clowning performer, or Buck Mulligan about to be raised to unimagined heights, as though the court fool had been designated King or Pope for the holiday revelry.

Like the unexplained echo and splitting of Buck's whistle, the sentence both causes and is itself a double take, juxtaposing past and present, marking what is "trivial in itself," yet fatal, punning on "match," and emphasizing "both our lives."[2] Since in "Aeolus" Stephen and Bloom cross paths for the second time, the interpolation may kindle hopes that the striking of the match between the protagonists will ameliorate "the whole aftercourse" of their lives. Simultaneously, such hopes, intermittently encouraged by the opening six episodes (especially the tonic resolution of "Hades"), begin to be treated as sentimental, articulated in suitably old-fashioned diction and rhythm: a convention of comedy or melodrama is now presented as an object of scrutiny. Disorienting in itself because it comes out of nowhere, the cryptic sentence is a Joycean Cheshire cat, pointing in contrary directions; it is precisely the "whole aftercourse" of life that Joyce refuses to summarize in an epilogue à la *Middlemarch* or *Great Expectations*. As with so many narrative gestures in *Ulysses,* it at once encourages and mocks optimism, so that the reader "*mostly sees double*" (7:580).

"The doubling aspect of comedy," says Zack Bowen, "so pervades

[2]The last phrase makes the sentence sound like part of an intimate letter, and I would not be surprised to learn that the sentence was something Joyce wrote to Nora in recalling June 16, 1904. If so, it would be another kind of doubling that I will explore in the last chapter, the double-duty of autobiographical material pointing outside the text or back toward the real maker of the fiction.

Ulysses that there is scarcely a theme or situation which does not have its low counterpart."[3] For instance, the initials of the esteemed "Member of the Royal Irish Academy" are modified to "K. M. R. I. A." (for "kiss my royal Irish arse"). Such instincts, originally Buck's, are gradually and strikingly apparent in the narrator, until he begins to appear less like the scrupulous, faithful clerk and more like a court jester, with an irrepressible instinct to bring low anything high, or to degrade authority. This Arranger is also a deranger.

Though we can spy intimations of folly as early as the first page, it is "Aeolus" that especially requires us to don folly's lenses and perceive doubles everywhere: "Antithesis, the professor said nodding twice" (7:952). In this view of Dear Dirty Doublin', and eventually in the novel generally, we see and hear everything twice: "Grossbooted draymen rolled barrels dullthudding out of Prince's stores and bumped them up on the brewery float. On the brewery float bumped dullthudding barrels rolled by grossbooted draymen out of Prince's stores" (7:21–24). Repetition creates an echo-chamber or hall-of-mirrors effect, reinforced by words and names featuring double letters: grossbooted, rolled, barrels, dullthudding, Bloom, J. J. O'Molloy, and O'Madden Burke. Since "Aeolus" is the episode of doubling, its organ is the dual lung; its icon is the advertisement for Alexander Keyes: "Like that, see," says Bloom, "Two crossed keys here. A circle" (7:142). The ad, of course, is a pun, appropriately the favorite humor of the chapter. *"The Rose of Castille.* See the wheeze? Rows of cast steel. Gee!" (7:591). Clam Dever Lenehan's puns serve Joyce's larger purpose of playing with the double meanings of words: "wheeze," slang for "gag," suggests the winds blowing constantly through the halls and air in the lungs, while "rows of cast steel" depicts the parallel lines of track and suggests the Aeolian principle of doubling. To Lenehan's joke O'Madden Burke responds, "Help! . . . I feel a strong weakness" (7:594).[4] Jeems Jokes loves the wordplay of his wheezing Dubliners because puns and oxymora insist upon simultaneous antitheses. Fusion and fission of meanings "by the coincidance of their contraries reamalgamerge in that indentity of undiscernibles" (*FW* 49:35–50:1). Seeing double

---

[3]Bowen, *"Ulysses" as a Comic Novel,* 26.

[4]Samuel Beckett appropriates and extends this gag into "a strong weakness for oxymorons." See "Ding-Dong," in *More Pricks Than Kicks* (New York: Grove Press, 1970), 38.

requires the fool's ability to contradict oneself, to sustain contrary possibilities, until "the supposed opposites appear to change places and switch valences and in so doing call up a virtual third term constituted by their interaction."[5]

ULYSSES AN OXYMORONIC VISION!

There is one other early episode in which the Buckean spirit of folly appears to enforce itself notably, and that is "Scylla and Charybdis": here, in earnest, "the play begins" (9:164). I argued earlier that Buck's entrance about halfway through the chapter first daunts, then seems to inspire Stephen, whose theory and spirits become more playful. It is worth returning briefly to that sequence to note the "doubling" implicit in its presentation. The narration is consistent with what precedes it, in its movement between the protagonist's consciousness and external reality. What is peculiar here, though, is the increased pressure upon the narrative made by another, more antic disposition. Continually, for example, Stephen or some impish presence mocks the names and utterances of the participants: "Piper! Mr Best piped" (9:275), "A shrew, John Eglinton said shrewdly" (9:232), "Quoth littlejohn Eglinton" (9:368), and so on. Arguably this is Stephen's somewhat weak wit. But no sooner does Buck appear than the language goes berserk, as though the force of folly were irresistible. Because Stephen is busy lecturing and debating, it cannot plausibly be he who is thinking in musical notations, arranging the typography for the passage beginning "He faced their silence" and ending "Woa!" (9:683–707), and presenting dialogue in playbook form (9:893–934), and envisioning Buck's "play for the mummers" (9:1167) as the title page and *dramatis personae* of a published text (9:1171–89). With such emphatic ploys, the discourse, initially divided between Stephen's interior and the external reality, seems split once more, between Stephen's consciousness and some Buck-like presence, a "Maister Gatherer" (9:895) for whom, in an apposite phrase for which I wish I had more synonyms, "All events brought grist to his mill" (9:748).

[5]The latter formulation is that of John Paul Riquelme, *Teller and Tale in Joyce's Fiction: Oscillating Perspectives* (Baltimore: Johns Hopkins Press, 1983), 145.

If I had to mark the spot in *Ulysses* where folly, implicit from the outset, now plants her flag and proclaims her dominion, I think it would be at the word *"Entr'acte"* (9:484). Though one might well understand this as Stephen's thought in response to Buck's sudden entrance, the word seems trickier than that. Stephen has just completed a major section of his argument, with a resounding conclusion: "a voice heard only in the heart of him who is the substance of his shadow, the son consubstantial with the father" (9:480–81). To be interrupted just then, not in midsentence or after awkward silence, seems fortuitous; we are also suspiciously close to the middle of the chapter, which, as we have seen, is often an important juncture for the organizer of the episodes; the entrance of Buck and Stephen's emphatic silence for one hundred lines make it impossible to ignore the pattern of episodic division, another version of doubling. But, of course, Stephen has no way of knowing that this is a frequent arrangment of a book he is in. From the note sheets we know that James Joyce wrote, upon the completion of "Scylla and Charybdis," "the End of the First Part of *Ulysses*."[6] I am suggesting that he inscribed within the text a hint of his authorial presence in the motley that is evident for the rest of "Scylla and Charybdis" and throughout many subsequent episodes, a declaration that he will perform comic turns in the Jamesian "sacred office."

One of the major implications of the transition to this jesting mode of narration, what Virginia Woolf deplored as the book's "tricking, doing stunts," is the tendency (hinted at by the headlines and the interpolation in "Aeolus") to view Dublin from a more detached, comic vantage point. Henceforth, through its culmination in "Ithaca" and with exceptions like "Nausicaa," there is a marked movement away from attentively recorded personal feelings; in "Wandering Rocks," Stephen and Bloom are, surprisingly, no more important than other Dubliners. The narrative view is suddenly wider and more distant, rendering much of life as spectacle, and enabling comic satire.

It would be foolish to pretend that the novel's gradual abandonment of the sense of felt life in favor of life as spectacle is accomplished without cost. As we are reminded by Bergson's emphasis on the "momentary anaesthesia of the heart" and by Walpole's formulation that "life is a tragedy to those who feel, a comedy to those who

[6]See Michael Groden, *"Ulysses" in Progress,* 7.

think," humor limits empathy and exaggerates detachment. Although the narrator of "Wandering Rocks" continues to look over the shoulders of his subjects, adapting their styles and values, the process now seems less generous, more stinting. The vantage point, far above the city, is more remote, objective, less colored by feeling than in previous episodes. Here, more than ever, Joyce seems absent, like the God of poor Boody Dedalus: "Our father who art not in heaven" (10:291). More than usual thus far in *Ulysses,* the narrator appears to leave the Dubliners to their own devices. His style is meticulously precise and clinical, as if the narrator were not touched by his perceptions; "Wandering Rocks" almost seems to have been written by a computer. We encounter "a onelegged sailor" on the first page, but when he reappears he is still "a onelegged sailor," not "the onelegged sailor," as though we had never met him.[7] The verbatim reiteration of many other interpolations in some ways denies meaningful progression or even gradual discovery and clarification, and emphasizes the sense of automatic repetition, which is itself a humorous trait.

A second marked development in this episode is that its narrator emerges as a persistent trickster, so that "Wandering Rocks" is a more perilous passage than its placid surface suggests. There are, to mix the metaphor or trip over tropes, a number of red herrings and false leads. We hear of a Mr. Bloom the dentist who is unrelated to our hero, and an "Old Russell" (10:812) who is not the A. E. of the previous chapter. The text begins to tease us by hinting that its hints are unreliable. Boylan's secretary Miss Dunne wonders, "Too much mystery business in it. Is he in love with that one, Marion?" (10:371). This refers not to the liaison between her boss and Marion Bloom (nor is Miss Dunne Bloom's "Martha") but to the Wilkie Collins novel she is reading. From "Wandering Rocks" we get abundant information—such as the date, typed by Miss Dunne on her keyboard—but much else is what the FBI calls "raw unevaluated data." Clive Hart distinguishes various kinds of error that any attentive Dubliner would instantly perceive, such as the cavalcade crossing the wrong canal.[8] Many internal inconsistencies or bald errors cast doubt on the narrator's omniscience and reliability, or suggest

[7]Karen Lawrence makes this nice point in *The Odyssey of Style in "Ulysses,"* 84–85.

[8]Clive Hart, "Wandering Rocks" (Hart and Hayman 181–216).

that he is fooling us. In "Wandering Rocks" the reader may begin, like Stephen, to fear mockery, to worry that he is being gulled by some "masterbilker" (*FW* 111:21). This fear turns out to be not unwarranted, since conning, gulling, and fooling become principal games in later episodes.

For these reasons, I consider the last section of "Wandering Rocks," the cavalcade, a celebration of the ascendance of folly. In the tradition of stage comedy, nearly everybody gets into the act; always fond of mock-epic catalogs, Joyce mounts this one with special gusto. It includes Gerty MacDowell, whom we haven't yet met, the charming soubrette on the poster, the H. from H.E.L.Y'S, jaunty Blazes Boylan, Artifoni, the blind stripling, the man in the brown macintosh, and Mr. Eugene Stratton. Everybody, including the personified river, seems animated by the parade: "Poddle river hung out in fealty a tongue of liquid sewage" (10:1196–97). Staging this procession signals that the latter half of the book will be more performative, not only in shifting focus from the characters toward a broader, wider panorama, but also in featuring self-regarding antics. In this way, too, the novel becomes increasingly Buck-like, holding up that jester's prop, the mirror, not only to life but to itself or selves. Earlier chapters ("Aeolus," the most heavily revised, being a partial exception) elaborate on character and situation; most of the latter nine chapters play with modes of narration. The novel becomes more and more its own subject, quoting itself, spoofing itself. The self-reflexivity in the "striking of that match" sentence is not an isolated in-joke, but a characteristic manifestation of the jester's hand. While such "jestures" shatter the verisimilitude of the initial style, they contribute to an alternative, comic effect: the reality of a composing presence, grounded in an actual world, writing the book that we hold in our hands.

It is, of course, a tried and true comic strategy to have intrusive, manipulative narrators grab the limelight in *Don Quixote, Gargantua and Pantagruel, Tristram Shandy, Tom Jones,* and *Don Juan.* Everybody will recall Cervantes' *trompe l'oeil* with the origin of the manuscript, Tristram's digressions on the writer's woes, and Fielding's magisterial gamesmanship, repudiating yet reincarnating the *deus ex machina.* What gives *Ulysses* its peculiar comic thrust is that its implied author, unlike the projected versions of, say, Fielding or Byron, is at once mysteriously absent and flagrantly present. While Tristram Shandy subordinates himself for long periods, as in the Widow Wadman sequence, we can never forget that we are in *his* book, in which a dominant figure presides. Joyce initially maintains the pretense of self-effacing objectivity, only to turn it topsy-turvy. The proliferation of narrators as diverse as those who deliver "Eumaeus" and "Ithaca," not to mention the glitches within each episode, can be nearly as jarring as beginning another book on a similar subject. "The Arranger" is less a defining consciousness, in the tradition of Fielding or Byron, than a ringmaster introducing numerous, sometimes simultaneous, acts that compete for attention: he has, one might say, the "sweetly varying voices" (9:1170) of Buck Mulligan. Or, to vary the comparison, Antic Joyce resembles Donald Barthelme's dolt, comically asserting and denying his selfhood, in a modern motley made of two hundred transistor radios tuned to different stations.[9]

Echo

If folly is crucial in *Ulysses,* it is by no means an unqualified or unexamined value. Much of Joyce's humor is music hall mayhem, of the "what will they think of next" or the "you hadda be there" variety, humor so patently silly or so pervasively disorienting that it is hard to determine how seriously or playfully one should consider it. For example, I have presented "from the sublime to the ridiculous is but a step" as a jocoserious credo; among the virtues of *moly* Joyce specified to Budgen (along with chance, agility, presence of mind, and power of recuperation) is "a sense of the ridiculous" (*SL* 272). Yet this cardinal tenet of *Ulysses* is delivered by that abrasive and bewildering figure, Virag: "(*With a dry snigger.*) You [Bloom] intended to devote an entire year to the study of the religious problem and the summer months of 1886 to square the circle and win that million. Pomegranate! From the sublime to the ridiculous is but a step. Pyjamas, let us say? Or stockingette gussetted knickers, closed? Or, put we the case, those complicated combinations, camiknickers? (*crows derisively.*) Keekeereekee!" (15:2399–2404). In this context, obscure though it is, the figure of speech is part of the derisive sniggering or comic ranting stressed by the stage direc-

---

[9]See Donald Barthelme, "The Dolt," in *Unspeakable Practices, Unnatural Acts* (New York: Farrar, Straus & Giroux, 1968).

tions. Virag's repulsive cynicism, aimed at just about everything, makes him an unlikely point of reference, much less a source of revelation: if we wish to see the novel as a healthy acceptance or affirmation of life, Virag rubs quite the wrong way. As we have noticed, from his opening paragraph Joyce likes to put insights on the tongues of scalawags and rogues.

The occasionally unstable, sometimes off-putting, nature of Joycean comedy is illustrated by a comparison to humor in *Tom Jones,* where Fielding's narrator approvingly resolves hostilities: "The good People now ranged themselves round the Kitchin Fire, where good Humour seemed to maintain an absolute Dominion."[10] Instead of that neoclassical, benevolent and perceptive "good humour," we get Virag's dry snigger and derisive crowing— characteristic of laughter in "Circe," like the scornful jeer of Mrs. Mervyn Talboys (15:1098), Bello's *"guffaws"* (15:2999), even the mocking "Haw, haw" (15:3733) of THE BOOTS. In "Circe," as elsewhere, Bloom is usually excluded from the fun, and regarded as the object of humor: "They think it funny. Anything but that" (15:593). Bloom's rueful remark could describe a very good deal of the joshing, jesting, clowning, and mocking that takes place this day in Dublin, such as the raucous and callous banter of the young men in "Oxen of the Sun." We might make a similar point regarding Stephen's relationship to humor. Though he badly needs a more flexible, tolerant "sense of the ridiculous" in life and in himself, the novel's first prophet of play, that incorrigible jester Mulligan, is as much anathema as panacea.

The first episode in which folly's fundamental riskiness seems pushed to the limits is "Sirens." The narrator of "Sirens" wears motley, wreaks havoc, and nearly obscures the pathos of Bloom's plight. Joyce's new role as the manic maestro, a virtuoso performance in which the clowning narrator manages "to keep it up, To keep it up" (15:3446–47) with remarkable agility, variety, and persistence, is the very opposite of his self-effacing, meticulous, "initial style." The spirit of folly embodied in Buck Mulligan and intermittently evident in the first ten episodes, especially in "Aeolus" and "Wandering Rocks," now prevails; folly predominates for the rest of the book, though never closer to self-demolition than in "Sirens."

I have stressed that in this epic of Dear Dirty Doublin', repetition

[10]Henry Fielding, *Tom Jones* (9:4).

is an important means of organization and comic confusion. Doubling has intrinsically satiric possibilities, as a jester like Buck Mulligan knows when he mocks Stephen's refusal to wear grey pants because he is still in mourning: "He can't wear them, Buck Mulligan told his face in the mirror. Etiquette is etiquette. He kills his mother but he can't wear grey trousers" (1:121–22). With his usual inventiveness, Buck employs several varieties of doubles: he echoes Stephen's "I can't wear them" (1:120), speaks to his own image in the mirror as though it were a separate entity, and reiterates the word etiquette. Simple repetition of virtually anything, as in a child's echo, is potentially humorous and usually annoying.

The "Echo" (11:634), introduced by Buck and frequently heard in "Aeolus," is a prominent feature of "Sirens"; nothing is a single thing, everything is doubled, echoed, paralleled, recapitulated. Consider this description: "Miss Kennedy sauntered sadly from bright light, twining a loose hair behind an ear. Sauntering sadly, gold no more, she twisted twined a hair. Sadly she twined in sauntering gold hair behind a curving ear" (11:81–83). Whatever musical effect Joyce is imitating, what we hear is repetition—or near-echo, for the reiteration is not exact: "sauntered sadly . . . sauntering sadly . . . twining a loose hair . . . twined a hair . . . a loose hair . . . a hair . . . gold hair." As we discover, the introductory fragments are rarely reiterated verbatim: "Tink cried to bronze in pity" (11:11) is a version of "Tink to her pity cried a diner's bell" (11:286). Perceptions, memories, data are usually slightly askew in "Sirens": Bloom reads Figatner and always thinks Figather. So, too, the narrator makes associations or recapitulates material in ways that don't quite match our experience. For example, he contributes to our confusion between "that old fogey" and Bloom by connecting their eyes, gratuitously but emphatically. To Kennedy's "Will you ever forget his goggle eyes?" Douce chimes in, "And your other eye!" (11:148). The impulse to chime in, to join together, to pair or match or twine, seems irresistible. Probably a snatch of song, "your other eye" becomes one of the countless notes that resonate throughout "Sirens." This narrator refuses to ignore any throwaway, as though he were a stand-up comedian in an improvisational theatre. A few lines later, "in a giggling peal young goldbronze voices blended, Douce with Kennedy your other eye" (11:158–59). Their laughter seems infectious, not to us but to the clowning narrator, who begins to mimic their mindless humor. Kennedy cracks Douce up by terming the old fogey "greasy eyes," which is pronounced "gracey" and furthers our suspicion that the old fogey is a double for Bloom. This passage typifies the narrator's antics.

> Douce gave full vent to a splendid yell, a full yell of full woman, delight, joy, indignation.
> —Married to the greasy nose! she yelled.
> Shrill, with deep laughter, after, gold after bronze, they urged each to peal after peal, ringing in changes, bronzegold goldbronze, shrilldeep, to laughter after laughter. And then laughed more. Greasy I knows . . .
> Married to Bloom, to greaseabloom.
> —O saints above! miss Douce said, sighed above her jumping rose. . . . I feel all wet. (11:171–82)

Although we don't share their cruel glee, they surely share something, as the echoes suggest ("peal after peal . . . bronzegold goldbronze"). By the time we get to "Greasy I" we're unsure whether the narrator (the "I" in 11:176?) is speaking or whether the ladies are still pealing. Then the implicit association with Bloom is made explicit by "married to Bloom . . . " Evidently in "Sirens" almost anything goes. Sure enough, Bloom suddenly acquires a mock-heroic epithet: "Greaseabloom" (11:180). This narrator is happy to echo anything. Even more insistently than in "Wandering Rocks," we are receiving whimsy. The echo effect, so emphatic in the "shrill, with deep laughter" paragraph, becomes giddy, almost manic, and certainly obfuscating. Names become jokes. In "Wandering Rocks," Tom Rochford made a pun, "Boylan with impatience" (10:486), that, along with so much else, is picked up by the maestro when Blazes makes his exit from the bar: "I'm off, said Boylan with impatience" (11:426). Sometimes it's not even wordplay but sheer goofing, as when Miss Douce "douced her arm away" (11:203).

The echoes are incessant, inexact, and cumulative. Miss Douce serves Mr. Dedalus a drink "with the greatest alacrity" (11:213), which spawns this paragraph: "With grace of alacrity . . . With grace . . . Alacrity she served. He blew through the flue two husky fifenotes" (11:214–18). Douce's phrase blends with the previous motif, "Greasy," leading to a pun on Bloom/blew and another fusion: two fifenotes. The overall effect of so many echoes is definitely derisive, as though everything is being jeered back at us. Heretofore

Bloom has been the object of mockery from other characters, but implicit sympathy from the narrator; the maestro of "Sirens" sounds less partial, less solicitous toward Bloom and more concerned with his own performance. A related development is that events once reported objectively are now so thoroughly embellished, seen not through a glass but in a funhouse mirror, that we can't take anything for granted. The "authentic fact" (11:927) is disappearing, as the seashell signifies: "The sea they think they hear. Singing. A roar. The blood it is. Souse in the ear sometimes. Well, it's a sea" (11:945–46).

Bloom's recognition bears on the often confusing, sometimes antipathetic nature of the antics in "Sirens": "Your head it simply swirls," for goofiness runs wild. What begins as childlike wordplay eventually becomes alienating: "Pat is a waiter who waits while you wait. Hee hee hee hee. He waits while you wait. Hee hee. A waiter is he. Hee hee hee hee. He waits while you wait. While you wait if you wait he will wait while you wait. Hee hee hee hee. Hoh. Wait while you wait" (11:916–19). Before long, this presiding imp is mocking the blind stripling—for being blind! "Tap tap. A stripling, blind, with a tapping cane came taptaptapping by Daly's window where a mermaid hair all streaming (but he couldn't see) blew whiffs of a mermaid (blind couldn't)" (11:1234–36). If we don't laugh, it's not simply pity but a deeper identification that we feel: like the blind stripling, we grope and make our way, all the more tentatively because the essential landmarks suddenly seem unfixed, displaced, or dissolved; the comedy of "Sirens" is anarchic, sometimes profane, implicitly related to the diabolical glee of Buck Mulligan.

The maestro's gay abandon is complicated by suggestions that he knows the narrative is not so precise as it once was. Surprisingly, the maestro himself appears to have reached a comic recognition, or an insight out of folly: no narrator, who has gotta use words when he talks,[11] can be infallibly reliable. A sentence like this appears to reflect a new self-consciousness about the protean elusiveness of words: "Upholding the lid he (who?) gazed into the coffin (coffin?) at the oblique triple (piano!) wires" (11:291–92). Another sign of the narrator's waning confidence and waxing awareness is the real-

---

[11]Cf. T. S. Eliot, "Fragment of an Agon": "I gotta use words when I talk to you."

ization that he is repeating himself. "As said before," he says, "he ate with relish the inner organs . . . " (11:519–20); "Bloom ate liv as said before" (11:569). Or of Blazes' progress toward Molly: "Blazes Boylan's smart tan shoes creaked on the barfloor, said before. . . . jaunted as said before just now" (11:761–63). Such tics appear almost obsessively, as though the narrator were a music hall entertainer worried that his act is going stale, or some great writer weighing every word. We have seen that Stephen is heavily dependent on received wisdom and formulation.

Now, the idea that all discourse is reiteration, "as said before," seems to pertain not only to Stephen's condition but to language generally. This tendency of "Sirens" to repeat randomly makes comprehension and evaluation increasingly difficult. For example, Lenehan greets Blazes with characteristic bonhomie, "See the conquering hero comes" (11:340), which is instantly picked up by the narrator: "Between the car and window, warily walking, went Bloom, unconquered hero" (11:341–42). Lo, another mirror image or double of uncertain significance: Blazes is playing Bloom's role of Molly's lover with at least a degree of acquiescence by Bloom. But does "unconquered hero" magnify or mock the hero? Picked up and given back to us, the epithet is a throwaway joke that becomes ridiculously, sublimely appropriate.

The maestro of "Sirens" is maddeningly random or undiscriminating, yet surprisingly cogent. Prone to factitious associations mainly via the similarity of sound, his weak wit may have powerful implications, like Buck Mulligan's unreliable, inspired clowning. It is in this light, the potential relevance of the random, that I understand another interpolation in "Sirens" that often provokes attention, this piece, apparently, of Bloom's consciousness: "In Gerard's rosery of Fetter lane he walks, greyedauburn. One life is all. One body. Do. But do" (11:907–8). True to the tendencies of the chapter, this fuzzily echoes Stephen (9:651–52). That two men on the same morning in Dublin might both notice a cloud passing the sun, or walk the same beach, is perfectly plausible; but how do we understand this quite outrageous coincidence? If the ear to which we hold up this shell is full of hope, we might construe it as a sign of mystical or providential connection between Stephen and Bloom. Their musings have, after all, included many roughly similar instincts or thoughts; now we have an indication that some mysterious force, what I've termed "magnetic influence," links them. If, on the contrary, we are more skeptical, we might find this not an omen but a joke. After all, lots of details have been recapitulated in the book, never more insistently or with less regard for simple verisimilitude than in "Sirens." This need not necessarily be considered any more significant than any of the other echoes. With such reiterated interpolations as the "Gerard the herbalist" passages, the maestro is both reinforcing and making fun of the optimistic expectations cultivated by his more serious predecessor in the opening episodes.

Given this pattern of obfuscation, manic proliferation, obsessive reiteration, and arbitrary recapitulation, it's far from clear how we can take anything in "Sirens" only one way. Like Buck Mulligan, whose self-parodying performance simultaneously asserts and precludes meaning, the maestro is sometimes inspired, other times insupportable, and often both. It may be too narrowly optimistic to argue, as Jackson Cope does, that this is "the chapter in which the possibility of renewed communion is recognized and, as the final word of the prelude promises, the movement towards that renewal is begun."[12] He makes much of the "Siopold!" consummation—too much, I would say, given the maestro's high-jinks. If we are hoping that Bloom can become Stephen's surrogate father, then the fusion between Bloom and Simon is a "consummation devoutly to be . . . wished for" (16:1031). "Siopold! Consumed" (11:752) might thus represent the union of Bloom and Simon. Yet "Sirens" is full of fusions,[13] and this one, which after all takes place nowhere except in the wacky narrator's imagination, does not necessarily portend anything special, for another result of fusion is blended sense and nonsense. Is this moment before the Siopold consummation a lyric flight or a parodic put-down? "It soared, a bird, it held its flight, a swift pure cry, soar silver orb it leaped serene, speeding, sustained, to come, don't spin it out too long long breath he breath long life, soaring high, high resplendent, aflame, crowned, high in the effulgence symbolistic, high, of the ethereal bosom, high, of the high vast irradiation everywhere all soaring all around about the all, the endlessnessnessness" (11:745–50).

What one might very reasonably take as the high point of the chapter—a hopeful omen or even a magical transformation—might

[12]Jackson Cope, "Sirens" (Hart and Hayman 242).
[13]John Gordon, *James Joyce's Metamorphoses* (Totowa, N.J.: Barnes & Noble, 1981), 69.

with equal validity be regarded as burlesque—of Stephen's epiphany on the beach in *Portrait,* of any high-falutin' aspiration, or of the maestro's antics ("don't spin it out too long," he reminds himself). The reader's persistent problem of separating wheat from chaff, in this chaffering chronicle, is becoming ever more difficult, because the maestro is incessantly making capriciously "witty" connections between things. Locke's distinction between wit and judgment is useful here. Judgment is the ability to discern fine differences, while wit is the capacity to perceive likeness. The comic vision prefers to discover gross likeness, so Joyce's jesters specialize in fusions— puns, portmanteau words, and "reamalgamerged indentities" such as "Siopold." Even "reamalgamerge" (*FW* 49:36) includes the word "game."

Near the end of "Sirens," Bloom passes a sign with Emmet's last words and thinks of Meyerbeer's "Seven last words" (11:1275). Looking for prophetic revelations, especially those boding well for Bloom, we might note that the seven last words of the whole novel are particularly favorable to Bloom: "yes I said yes I will Yes" (18:1608). But a counterforce or tug of gravity operates persistently in the latter half of the novel, requiring wariness toward interpretations that buttress uncritical hope. In this chapter, when the narrator's antics are rampant and conspicuous, our perceptions and evaluations are less definite than ever, because the comic "Bringer of Plurabilities" (*FW* 104:2) insists on multiple, even contrary, possibilities. More and more, Joyce is playing with paradoxes, or insisting on both having and eating the cake. The notion of doubling or echoing has resonated through the chapter and, like all the other themes and techniques of the novel, is a subject for contemplation: "Rich sound. Two notes in one there. . . . Taking my motives he twined and turned them. . . . Echo. How sweet the answer" (11:632–35). The rapid oscillation from high to low, ups to downs, makes it difficult to interpret the implication even locally, much less generally.

"Sirens" uses humor and play to disorient, to destabilize. Fundamental distinctions, such as the separation between narrator and character, are confounded. Folly is fork-tongued, cross-eyed, and two-faced, so that her assertions are doubly dubious, free to cavort, doubleshuffle, and disappear, producing a liberating, exasperating proliferation of possibilities. Identity dissolves and reemerges, as the nonsense with names emphasizes: "Up the quay went Lionel-

leopold, naughty Henry with letter for Mady . . . went Poldy on"
(11:1187–89), so that the hero can justly be denominated, "Henry
Lionel Leopold dear Henry Flower earnestly Mr Leopold Bloom"
(11:1261–62). In this episode of fusions and consummations, Joycean comedy, tragedy, pathos, and farce jostle and mix. Appropriately, the culmination is Bloom contributing to the music of the
chapter with a prolonged fart,[14] which mixes with the song and
Robert Emmet's heroic rhetoric. His last epithet in "Sirens" is
"greaseabloom" (11:1284), which takes us back to the barmaid's
scorn for "greasy eyes" (11:169) but also suggests that this Bloom is
no longer any one thing; he is, so far as "Sirens" is concerned, a
composite of perceptions, a slippery, elusive series of possibilities,
and a remarkably rendered, fully realized, multifaceted individual.
One last echo in this chapter recalls and spoofs the omens planted in
earlier episodes. On the beach Stephen had sensed, "Behind. Perhaps there is someone" (3:502), and at the library Bloom had
"passed out between" Stephen and Buck. Now Bloom thinks, "No-
one behind. She's passed" (11:1289) and breaks wind. Confronting
the sublime with the ridiculous is a characteristic gesture for both
Bloom and Joyce, for it punctuates the valorized, vainglorious nature of folly. Like its clowning narrator, the text makes itself an
object of parody, a new and dangerous tactic, with riotously rich
consequences for interpretation, but one that seemed necessary for
an author who once defined literature as "a parody of life" (S. Joyce
91).

Playful Crossfire

Folly in "Cyclops" obeys two contrary tendencies: fission and
fusion. Inspired by the doubling of "Aeolus" and the manic echoing
of "Sirens," the discourse splits into two distinct viewpoints. Then,
in accord with the attraction of opposites—"Extremes meet"
(15:2098)—they collaborate upon a common project, the mockery
of Bloom. Each voice is comically hyperbolic and apparently untrustworthy, for opposite reasons. The "I" who begins narrating the

[14]I admire but can't document Richard Ellman's circumlocution, "a carminative effect." À propos this particular carminative effect, Joyce may have known
about a turn-of-the-century Parisian *artiste* whose specialty was farting music.

episode is an unnamed character in the bar, a Thersites-like figure I will call the Satirist, who reduces everything to its lowest common denominator; a second, parodic interpolator preposterously expands, dilates, magnifies. In referring to the "alternating asymmetry" of "Cyclops,"[15] Joyce underscored the counterpoint between these monocular and unreliable points of view, but neglected to mention that his novel always suffers fools gladly.

The satiric voice of "Cyclops," like that of Buck Mulligan, is difficult to fix and evaluate because of its mercurial ironies, its blended insight and blather. Sometimes the Satirist is simply sensible and accurate. But it is not always easy to untangle truth from the variety of satiric turns, for he speaks ironically, hyperbolically, sarcastically, wittily, foolishly, casually, ominously—with radically varying degrees of obliquity. Directly the Satirist tells us that there is many a true word spoken in jest, he makes a joke with some truth in it. Referring to Bloom's supposedly feminine qualities, such as fussing over Molly during her pregnancy, he says, "One of those mixed middlings he is" (12:1658–59). The Satirist's mockery is consistent with the episode's masculine premium on toughness, aggression, violence, and war; it is also penetrating. Bloom, with his feminine middle name, is first seen cooking breakfast and waiting on Molly. In "Circe," Bloom's "mixed middling" nature is exaggerated and enacted—culminating in the announcement that he is "the new womanly man . . . about to have a baby" (15:1798–1810). The Satirist scores other palpable hits just before Bloom delivers his "gospel": "Old lardyface standing up to the business end of a gun. Gob, he'd adorn a sweepingbrush, so he would, if he only had a nurse's apron on him. And then he collapses all of a sudden, twisting around all the opposite, as limp as a wet rag" (12:1476–80).

This is not altogether fool, but someone with a disconcertingly sharp focus on Bloom—malicious but often on target, rather like Buck's treatment of Stephen. Like Buck, the Satirist believes in little besides the law of falling bodies: old lardyface Bloom "is standing up . . . and then he collapses all of a sudden . . . Limp as a wet rag." To see Bloom as limp, of course, puts the case in the phallic terms favored in "Cyclops," but it also correctly intuits that Bloom is "the limp father of thousands, a languid floating flower" (5:571–

---

[15] So Joyce described his "technic" in the Linati scheme. See Ellmann, *Ulysses on the Liffey,* Appendix.

72). Embedded in the Satirist's nasty scurrility is another law of folly, perpetual antithesis: our hero is constantly "twisting around all the opposite," in his nature and in his attitudes. He is the latter-day man of many turns: in "Cyclops," the meek apostle of pacifism becomes the provocative adversary of the Citizen. Even the way Bloom speaks, defining love as "the opposite of hatred," is twisting and turning; no sooner asserting his presence more forcefully than ever, he suddenly absents himself.

For all his faults, albeit legion and egregious, the Satirist has redeeming virtues. He is undeniably bright, exuberant, witty, and well-informed. This is no droning drunk, but a gifted storyteller with impressive "powers of organization" and some "disturbingly right" insights.[16] His wit, sometimes formulaic—"Not taking anything between drinks, says I" (12:53)—is often acute. We find ourselves laughing at humor that we would not publicly endorse because it is too vulgar or bigoted or silly. Yet our laughter expresses a secret complicity, or a recognition that the Satirist offers a necessary (if not a sufficient) view of the world, sarcastic cynicism to counterpoise idealism, decorum, and pomp. After the Parodist renders "the image of a queen" (12:292–93) in all her majesty, through a tedious recitation of her titles, the Satirist endorses and elaborates on Joe's much less respectful picture of "the flatulent old bitch that's dead" (12:1392). Like Buck Mulligan, the Satirist stresses the lower bodily element to bring down any elevation.

As usual in literature, praise or panegyric is interesting only to the recipient, while abuse, flyting, or "sufficient evidence of malice" (12:1072), has a broad appeal. (Alice Roosevelt Longworth once said, "If you can't say something nice about somebody, sit with me.") It is no small praise of the Satirist to say that he is rarely dull; often he is truly entertaining, the engaging, backbiting rogue with whom one might wish to sit for an hour. Like Buck Mulligan, this Satirist is engaging, provocative, and endowed with a touch of authorial omniscience. For a two-bit drifter he is astonishingly knowledgeable, even if most of what he knows about people is detrimental. He somehow remembers Bloom's sale of bazaar tickets for the "royal Hungarian privileged lottery" (12:777) and, evenhanded in his dispersal of humiliations, recalls Boylan's father's sale of "the

---

[16]David Hayman, "Cyclops" (Hart and Hayman 261, 244). My treatment of the Satirist generally follows Hayman's.

same horses twice over to the government to fight the Boers" (12:999). Relentlessly nasty, the Satirist is also shrewdly perceptive, as when he deduces that Boylan and Molly are sexually involved (12:996–98). The Satirist's attacks on Bloom are made by a Joycean fool, which is to say they are often enabled: "there's many a true word spoken in jest" (12:1658). The spirit of Mercurial Malachi, that enigmatic, potent blend of malice, wit, acumen, and horseplay, has reappeared in a new guise.

Like Buck, the Satirist of "Cyclops" is a deeply ambiguous but richly endowed figure, simultaneously an authorial surrogate and a scapegoat. Michael Seidel comments that "Satiric knowledge is somewhat akin to taboo or illegal knowledge,"[17] which captures both the privileged and disreputable nature of the Satirist—like Tristram recounting the debacle of his engendering, or Swift's Strephon scrutinizing the lady's beshitted underwear. Such tellers are constantly divulging, with voyeuristic glee, other people's private business or trouble. Although the essential assertion of every satirist is that he is only describing what he sees, he is invariably suspected of loving profanation. Like the parodist intimately connected with the writer he mocks, the satirist is both attracted to and repelled by—indeed, could not exist except for—his victim. No wonder this genre, more than any other, so often needs "the persona" as its basic rhetorical ploy. Joyce's satirical speakers, like numerous narrators in Franklin, Rabelais, Byron, and Swift, are hit men, hired to do the dirty work and keep the boss's name clean. We might therefore regard doubling not simply as a technique but a necessity: in an early letter to his brother, the future inventor of the Satirist and Buck Mulligan worries, "Mother says I was a 'mocker.' Am I?" (*SL* 132).

While "Cyclops" employs a conventional Satirist for the unconventional purpose of deriding the hero, it introduces at the same time a second voice, that of the Parodist, whose methods are also quite traditional and whose effects are sometimes disorienting. In the tried-and-true comic fashion, the Parodist puffs everything until it bursts—describing the Citizen in a Rabelaisian series of heroic adjectives, thirty-two in succession, culminating in "ruddyfaced sinewyarmed hero" (12:154–55), or delivering an epic catalog of

[17]Michael Seidel, *Satiric Inheritance: Rabelais to Swift* (Princeton: Princeton University Press, 1979), 23.

"Irish heroes and heroines of antiquity" that lists, along with historical Irish personages, Dante, the Rose of Castille, Caesar, and Beethoven (12:176–99). In such instances we make a 180-degree turn, concluding that the Citizen and the Irish heroes are anything but larger than life.

The Parodist's favorite technique at such moments is to inflate, or, like Buck, to adapt incongruously elevated language to describe something ordinary. His inability to sustain the high style reveals that he is tall only by walking on stilts. For example, the second interpolation, beginning "In Inisfail the fair there lies a land, the land of holy Michan" (12:68), characterizes everything as "fair . . . holy . . . mighty . . . high . . . lovely . . . " but the weight of grandeur is too much for this ersatz bard, and his heroic style collapses into travelog clichés. A catalog of fish sporting in the "fishful streams" (12:71) deteriorates into "the mixed coarse fish generally . . . too numerous to be enumerated" (12:73–74); trees "wave in different directions their firstclass foliage . . . with which that region is thoroughly well supplied." As in "Eumaeus," these inflated interpolations, imitating epic and romantic language, are full of such pratfalls and blunders as "firstclass foliage." The mock-heroic parodies of "Cyclops" also resemble the "heroi-comic" poetry of Pope, or Fielding's "comic epic in prose," with an important difference: Joyce's Parodist, like his Satirist, does not believe in the heroic. Hence the usual effect in "Cyclops" is spoof or burlesque, without the complex mixture of irony, affection, and wonder of, say, *The Rape of the Lock* or the portrait of Gerty. Joyce's Parodist mockingly undermines anything high, transcendent, heroic, spiritual, or sublime. He makes fun of a seance, for example, by burlesquing a "message for the living" (12:357): mind, says the theosophist's voice, that Cornelius Kelleher doesn't pile it on, and tell Patsy that the missing boot is in the return room.

Like all raconteurs and performers, the Parodist isn't always funny and sometimes strains too hard for a gag, as when he spoofs the society wedding with all the tree names.[18] But the parodies are usually an amusing, effective, and eminently jocoserious "art of sur-

---

[18]For such lists, Robert Adams Day has coined the word "scatologue, or shit list." In that list of tree-names, for example, are numerous double-entendres, such as Kitty Dewey-Mosse, and doubled-names, such as Daphne Bays or Gloriana Palme.

feit" (9:626), a spirit of ludic lunacy and love of excess that pervades *Ulysses,* especially after "Sirens." This Parodist, like *Ulysses* generally, loves to pick up a verbal detail, a titbit, a throwaway, and give it new life, until it proliferates wildly and comically. In that catalog of Irish heroes we find "the Rose of Castille," Lenehan's wheeze in "Aeolus"; in a summary of titles is "M. R. I. A." (12:1895), another Aeolian gag, "S. O. D." (12:1894), and "F. T. C. D." (12:1895) for "Fellow of Trinity College Dublin." In the baby-talk parody of Bloom's gospel is hidden Gerty MacDowell, "M.B. loves a fair gentleman," and our old friend "the man in the brown macintosh" (12:1495–98).

The Parodist is usually, but not always, intent on inflation and burlesque; sometimes he simply mimics, producing pastiche, without a clear comic or evaluative purpose, as in the very first interpolation, beginning "For nonperishable goods bought of Moses Herzog . . . " (12:33). A fairly close imitation of legal jargon, this passage has no clear significance, which makes it both a cryptic and an appropriate introduction to "Cyclops," where there is no high road to stable meaning. The purpose and principle of selection of, say, the list of Irish heroes may be clear, but why cite the list of clergy (12:927–37)? Given the random nature of the Parodist's perspective, it is hard to justify selecting any particular detail for serious consideration. A sustained example of bizarrely disorienting parody is the long account of the hanging (12:525–678). By turns maudlin and farcical, it jumps blithely from the drama of the condemned's last moments to the antics of Lenehan and Mulligan; anything goes, such as the catalog (that convention of both epics and newspapers) that includes the Hungarian Countess Marha Virága Kisászony Putrápesthi (12:560–61). Like the crowd, the jarring styles body forth a "medley of cries" (12:599–600), the opposite of Thomistic *claritas, consonantia, integritas* that Stephen once endorsed. Just before the hanging is a wedding, so that the funeral can be *funferal* (*FW* 120:10). It is not enough to say that this long interpolation parodies journalism or Irish taste; it is closer to the heart of *Ulysses* in indulging "playful crossfire" (12:1292) and undermining the possibility of aesthetic clarity, harmony, and integrity.

Marilyn French notes that "Cyclops," like "Aeolus," contains virtually a whole newspaper, with sports, society, news, features, including the long report of the hanging. Unlike a newspaper, though, much of the "journalism" seems to know it is part of a larger fiction, and uses that realization to make fun of itself—as when boosterism puffs two local lads we can't fail to recognize, "the favourite Dublin streetsingers L-n-h-n and M-ll-g-n who sang *The night before Larry was Stretched* in their usual mirthprovoking fashion" (12:542–43). At such points, "Cyclops" anticipates "Circe" in resembling a music hall program, arranged and performed by "the Archjoker" (12:559) in a dizzying variety of performances.

Dazzled by two such gifted fools as the Satirist and the Parodist, it is understandable that many readers are to some extent fooled by "Cyclops." Because some of the attacks on Bloom are so patently unfounded—Lenehan, for example, jestingly asks if Bloom is "defrauding widows and orphans" (12:1622)—we take comfort in believing "the opposite of hatred." "Cyclops" seems to suggest exactly what the Citizen furiously scorns: "That's the new Messiah for Ireland" (12:1642). In order to understand "Cyclops," that is, we make a routine readjustment to irony by reversing the assertions and arriving at an appealing conclusion: Bloom is a prophet or Christ figure and his adversaries are knaves, fools, and "unfortunate yahoos" (12:1352–53).

As I discussed in an earlier chapter, "Cyclops" does have an unmistakable spiritual or anagogic thrust. To interpret "Cyclops" as Bloom's crucifixion and apotheosis is heartening and, as I've contended, partially compelling. Subjected to unrelenting scorn by flagrantly chauvinistic, sexist, anti-Semitic, macho, aggressive, and malicious barflies, Bloom appears more impressively heroic: "the absent balancing principle," "guiltless of all offence," "his real stature remains quite firmly established."[19] Yet if we wish to conclude that Bloom's stature in "Cyclops" is so thoroughly magnified, even consecrated, then we have to perform not simply a routine reversal but some agile interpretive tricks, for there are serious obstacles. Though it is true that in some ways our hero resembles Christ, exalted through abasement, the opposite, as folly would have it, is also true: Bloom is humorously spoofed by the exalted comparison. Categories in "Cyclops" are "heterogeneous terms" (12:570), and anyone wishing to cling to them will soon be beset with misgivings.

"Cyclops" makes perception and evaluation problematic by cast-

[19]Marilyn French, *The Book as World,* 139; Hayman, "Cyclops" (Hart and Hayman 245); and S. L. Goldberg, *The Classical Temper,* 283.

ing its lot with folly; we cannot be entirely confident we know what is "really" happening in the pub, much less how to judge it, for strict verisimilitude seems to have been abandoned, not only in the zany parodic interpolations but in the ostensibly realistic dialogue. Lines such as "He's a bloody dark horse himself" (12:1558), "That's the new Messiah for Ireland!" (12:1642), "Ahasuerus I call him" (12:1667), or "Bloody wars . . . I'll be in for the last gospel" (12:1849) implausibly suggest an anagogic dimension, as though all these figures are playing parts in a fiction; when J. J. O'Molloy joins a discussion of Bloom's religion by asking, "Who is Junius?" (12:1633), thus identifying one of the narrators of "Oxen of the Sun," one senses an authorial wink.

In standing up to the bullying Citizen, Bloom plays a substantially new role, and is not the only character in "Cyclops" to undergo a surprising metamorphosis, for not even the static, flat Citizen stays in character. Much of what he says is vividly ludicrous, like lambasting English "syphilisation . . . No music and no art and no literature worthy of the name" (12:1197–1200), while at other moments the language of this ignoramus is compellingly lyrical. Praising Irish manufacturing—"And our wool that was sold in Rome . . . and our flax and our damask" (12:1242–43)—he flows on and on, as though endowed with the "gift of tongues" (15:106).

"Cyclops" seems to have inherited the cap and bells from "Sirens"; as in the previous chapter, the cumulative effect of so many incongruities and inconsistencies casts into doubt our perception not only of its two narrative voices, but also of what Marilyn French calls its "actual scene" and David Hayman regards as "an elaborately realistic matrix."[20] Such an abundance of "satirical effusions" (12:728) or "playful crossfire" (12:1292–93) demands that we question, qualify, and supplement any one view; we are in a funhouse hall of mirrors, comically multiple and highly disorienting. Though we remain in touch with the reality of characters talking in a pub, we are uncertain what is perception, what is parody, what is serious, what is playful. "Cyclops" asks us to listen critically, carefully, and sympathetically to all its foolish voices. If Bloom is in some ways a holy fool, he is still simply foolish, as in his response to the Citizen, when he ludicrously cites several apostates as Jews, and describes God as Christ's father or uncle. In this chapter of "cod-

[20]French, 150, and Hayman (Hart and Hayman 246).

ding," there is no simple truth. As easy as it may be to patronize or pity the barflies, it is hard to deny that "many a true word is spoken in jest." If we admire Bloom's heroic resistance and spiritual flowering, we must also concede that for good reasons he is subjected to ironic inflation and satiric attack not just by the Parodist and the Satirist, but by much of the book.

Of course, some of Bloom's troubles in "Cyclops" are not his fault. Incorrectly rumored to have made a killing on the Gold Cup race, he is seen as too cheap a Jew to stand treats. Much of what he says and does is blameless, even admirable, such as his solicitude for Dignam's widow and children. But if Bloom is "a new apostle to the gentiles" (12:1489), "the new Messiah for Ireland" (12:1642), he is also silly and stubborn, someone who deserves, at least to some extent, the ridicule heaped upon him by the Parodist and the Satirist. When the talk turns to capital punishment, for instance, "of course Bloom comes out with the why and the wherefore and all the codology of the business" (12:450–52). Although Bloom is surely more competent than his interlocutors to take up such questions, he is rarely consistent, precise, or articulate, and he lacks basic awareness of his audience. They would rather discuss the erection than the rights of the accused, and do so, incidentally, not without wit: "Ruling passion strong in death, says Joe" (12:463). Uncharacteristically and persistently humorless in "Cyclops," Bloom becomes quite obtuse, lecturing where he should be bantering, trying to explain "by science . . . It's only a natural phenomenon" (12:464–65). Bloom's pet word, "phenomenon," allows him to sound modern and scientific without knowing any details; the Parodist later refers to him as "the distinguished phenomenologist" (12:1822) and Molly also complains about his "jawbreakers" (18:566). Our hero, "with his *but don't you see?* and *but on the other hand*" (12:514–15), ineptly addressing the blind and monocular, invites satiric ridicule. To his auditors he is a spoilsport, pontificating, patronizing, and sentimental—"Mister Knowall" (12:838) with a "programme" of "humane methods" (12:842–43) for everything: "Gob, he'd have a soft hand under a hen," remarks the Satirist, prompting the interpolating Parodist to ridicule Bloom with baby talk and hen talk (12:845).

By the climax of "Cyclops," when Bloom ascends as Elijah, we should know enough about the complexity of folly not to make any easy choices between the sublime and the ridiculous. Jocoserious duality—"two notes in one there" (11:632)—is as firmly established in "Cyclops" as it is anywhere in *Ulysses*. Its cumulative effect is not to create some golden mean between magnification and diminution, but to maintain the potential validity of contrary possibilities. When any view is possible, and none is precluded, we cannot make sense by staking out an imaginary mean.[21]

> When, lo, there came about them all a great brightness and they beheld the chariot wherein He stood ascend to heaven. And they beheld Him in the chariot, clothed upon in the glory of the brightness, having raiment as of the sun, fair as the moon and terrible that for awe they durst not look upon Him. And there came a voice out of heaven, calling: *Elijah! Elijah!* And he answered with a main cry: *Abba! Adonai!* And they beheld Him even Him, ben Bloom Elijah, amid clouds of angels ascend to the glory of the brightness at an angle of fortyfive degrees over Donohoe's in Little Green street like a shot off a shovel. (12:1910–18)

In his small way, Bloom deserves recognition for bringing a bit of (unappreciated) light to the gentiles. Elijah is of course an Old Testament type of Christ who will return to announce Judgment Day, an event about which we hear a good deal on Bloomsday. But who is comparing Bloom to Elijah, and how seriously should we take the consecration? The Parodic inflations have been punctured throughout the chapter, just as here apotheosis yields to bathos. Another way to put this is that the chapter ends with a conflation of the Parodic and Satiric voices. No evaluation of Bloom, not even a "voice out of heaven," is permitted to stand without complicating ironies. The Satirist's irony is nowhere near as stable as that of, say, Pope in *The Dunciad,* nor is the Parodist's irony as reliable as that of Fielding in *Tom Jones* or of Pope in *The Rape of the Lock*.[22] Compared to Fielding or Pope, Joyce is more mercurial, antic, and anarchic, with a comic instinct to mock every dogma, multiply pos-

[21]Colin MacCabe makes a similar point about the lists in "Cyclops": "In Joyce's text there are no possibilities which are excluded and with this overload of sense we fall into nonsense." Colin MacCabe, *James Joyce and the Revolution of the Word* (New York: Barnes & Noble, 1979), 98. He also speaks of the "mutual subversion of discourses" (100).

[22]Although the monochromatic authority of these neoclassical voices has been greatly overemphasized.

sibilities, and turn all things sacred and profane topsy-turvy. The ascension of folly in *Ulysses* renders dichotomies like high and low or sacred and profane provisional or moot. Is the ascension Bloom's martyred self-image, authentic heroic magnification, parodic mock-heroics, or "satirical effusions" (12:728)? "Cyclops" is true only to folly's contrariety and an endless series of comic reversals.

Proliferent Continuance

Devastating parody of the author's authority, and its implications for Joyce's "own" discourse, often confounds readers of "Oxen of the Sun," especially those prone to Stephen's anxiety of influence or wary of Joyce's promiscuous gaiety in absorbing "texts so divergent" (15:2090–91) and devouring his canonical predecessors. As if to lure readers into the intentional fallacy, Joyce specified his meaning with misleading simplicity when he identified "the idea" of "Oxen of the Sun" as "the crime committed against fecundity by sterilizing the act of coition," presented "by way of" a series of parodies and imitations of English prose writers (*SL* 251). If he was in earnest, and not speaking metaphorically, Joyce in this letter is guilty of the crime against fecundity by sterilizing the act of reading. I prefer to think that Joyce was playing the fool to illustrate why we should never trust the Author's "Word and Holy Breath" (9:61). In any event, Joyce's summary has discouraged consideration of the fundamental challenge of "Oxen": determining the authority of the parodied voice. Although Joyce's letter implies distance from some of the authors he recreates ("then a passage solemn as of Milton, Taylor, Hooker"), generally he does not specify his attitude toward the voices; he calls them neither imitations nor parodies, but "episodes by way of" Bunyan, Dickens, Carlyle, and so on. In my view, the effects of Joyce's impersonations are considerably more various than his professed intention—as he seemed to acknowledge when he wrote to Harriet Weaver that "Oxen" was "the most difficult episode in an odyssey . . . both to interpret and to execute" (*SL* 249).

The authority of the voices in "Oxen" is too often understood to be uniform, as though each voice were Joyce speaking in various styles. For example, Harry Levin asserts that Joyce's "parodies reveal himself—Joyce the Jacobean divine, Joyce the Restoration diarist, Joyce the Augustan essayist," and so forth.[23] A recent monograph by Robert Janusko accepts Levin's basic assumption: "the men whose styles Joyce chose to imitate are the giants of English prose, the past bearers of the 'mystical estate' which has devolved on" Joyce, whose "parodies celebrate the members of this apostolic succession."[24] Those who assume that the narrative's various styles are versions of Joyce, "The Holy Writer," make Stephen's mistake of believing that authors are Allfathers who share their "mystical estate" in holy communion with their Reader-Sons.

But discourse in "Oxen" is more radically disparate than communal; meanings are disseminated, not sterilized, because the episode is "myriadminded" (9:769). To perceive its voices as unison is to be tone-deaf, like Stanley Sultan, who hears only one note in "Oxen." For Sultan, the chorus of Allfathers insists that "proliferent continuance" (14:15) or procreation is the moral imperative and, conversely, continence, contraception, masturbation, and fornication are wrong. Sultan ignores the parodic implications of the voices; even when he raises the possibility that tone might be significant, he is too often bound by his thesis to take the passage at anything other than face value. Looking at the masks he sees only the contours of Joyce's features beneath them. Though Sultan sometimes refers to the voices as "parodies," he scants the possibility that Joyce might not fully endorse their assertions; always they "reveal primarily" Joyce's own views, or make a virtually "direct statement."[25] Even if we construe the narrator of this episode as, in some sense, Joyce or some single "Arranger," it does not follow that he believes everything said in "Oxen," any more than in "Cyclops." Like Buck, Joyce is protean, performative, and antic, donning masks and playing parts, not for systematic exposition but for the elaboration of folly, as the author implied when he said that some lines in this episode were "quite unconvincing and meant to be so."[26]

[23]Harry Levin, *James Joyce: A Critical Introduction* (Norfolk, Conn.: New Directions, 1960), 106.

[24]Robert Janusko, *The Sources and Structures of James Joyce's "Oxen"* (Ann Arbor, Mich.: UMI Research Press, 1983), 56. Janusko also notes the "variety of viewpoints" in "Oxen" (55).

[25]Stanley Sultan, *The Argument of "Ulysses,"* 291.

[26]Cited by Alan M. Cohen, "Joyce's Notes at the End of 'Oxen of the Sun,'" *James Joyce Quarterly* 4 (1967): 198.

If I am right to read "Oxen" as a Buck-like medley, then Sultan has been fooled into assuming the "absolute value that constitutes the chapter's thematic burden" asserted in its opening lines.[27] "Proliferent continuance" (14:15) is unquestionably the subject of the episode, but it is far from its absolute value. "Oxen" opens with a primitive invocation, requesting fertility ("quickening and wombfruit") of the sun, "bright one, light one" (14:2, 3). Resonating with ritual authority, "Oxen" recalls another invocation to the sun opening another episode—Buck Mulligan's performance atop the *omphalos,* which echo should alert us not to defer too quickly to this authority.[28] In his new role as "Le Fécondateur" (14:778), Buck may be the gods' response to "send us . . . quickening and wombfruit"; beware of what you want—you may get it.

There follow three paragraphs in the "Sallustian-Tacitean" voice pronouncing the transcendental imperative, "proliferent continuance." That, at least, is how most commentators interpret the many lines of almost unbroken, unpunctuated, and unreadable appeals to authority: "Universally . . . mortals with sapience endowed . . . in doctrine erudite . . . deserving of veneration . . . by ancestors transmitted customs . . . as the best historians relate . . . " and so on (14:7–33). This is not divine injunction, but pompous nonsense, less like Miltonic sublime than vintage hokum. In other words, this passage is pure parody because it is double-voiced. In Bakhtin's useful definition of parody, "the author again speaks in someone else's discourse but . . . introduces into that discourse a semantic intention that is directly opposed to the original one. The second voice, once having made its home in the other's discourse, clashes hostilely with its primordial host and forces him to serve directly opposing aims. Discourse becomes an arena of battle between two voices."[29] Bakhtin's comment applies to *Ulysses* generally, in sug-

[27]Sultan, *The Argument of "Ulysses,"* 300. My critique of Sultan is similar to that made by Karen Lawrence in *The Odyssey of Style in "Ulysses,"* 137.

[28]Joyce also wrote to Budgen that "Oxen" is "linked back to each part subtly with some foregoing episode of the day. . . . " Besides the omphalos, numerous motifs connect "Telemachus" and "Oxen." Both episodes include many references to bodily parts, father-mother-child, water, cow-cattle-kine. Even Stephen's graphic memory of his mother's vomit is echoed by the "Pflapp!" of vomit at the end of "Oxen of the Sun" (14:1589).

[29]Mikhail Bakhtin, *Problems of Dostoevsky's Poetics,* ed. and trans. by Caryl Emerson (Minneapolis: University of Minnesota Press, 1984), 193.

gesting yet another way Joyce envisions "Doublends Jined" (*FW* 20:16). It is the receptivity of the text to so many voices and the shifting, relative authority of that second voice which is both ludic and elusive (to use two words with the same root). In *Tom Jones* or *The Dunciad,* the relationship between the competing heroic and satiric discourses is comparatively stable, so that conclusions about such "A"-level favorites as "Fielding's conception of prudence," while not without complications, are attainable. In *Ulysses,* no sooner do we feel comfortable with the uses and implications of "someone else's discourse"—the Lamplighter style of "Nausicaa," or the Satirist in "Cyclops"—than it yields to a new perspective. In "Oxen of the Sun," the process of narrative fission is accelerated, in a frenzied proliferation of styles, all potentially telling. Consequently, inferences about "Joyce's attitude toward procreation" are "dubious" (14:932) at best.

Moreover, the putative argument of "Oxen of the Sun" is too dogmatic for a novel that continually satirizes hectoring authority, including (perhaps particularly) an author's. Though I will later develop the opposite point, I would say that, as much as any narrative strategy, the disappearance of the artist defines *Ulysses* and distinguishes it from earlier fiction. Part of Oxymoronic Joyce, the part that imagined "Oxen of the Sun" as a theatre for his pluralism, illustrates Barthes's point that to write "is to reach that point where only language acts, 'performs,' and not 'me' . . . the author is never more than the instance writing, just as *I* is nothing more than the instance saying *I*."[30] Hence when the author-god descends, it is in comically shrunken forms, not as imposing but as parodic presence; even the image of the writer, god "paring his fingernails," cuts him down to size.

Though *Ulysses* is packed with religious references, "Oxen" has a notably high proportion of allusions to divinity. "Oxen" begins and ends with references to "Allmighty God" (14:166, 1589). A partial catalog of divine visitations in between includes: "Of that A. Horne is lord" (14:74), "Holy Ghost, Very God, Lord and Giver of Life" (14:226–27), "Loud on left Thor thundered" (14:408–9), "old Nobodaddy" (14:419), "Believe-on-Me" (14:459), "Giver of good

---

[30]Roland Barthes, "The Death of the Author," in *Image–Music–Text,* trans. Stephen Heath (New York: Hill and Wang, 1977), 143, 145.

things" (14:752), "Beneficent Disseminator of blessings to all Thy creatures" (14:766), "the Deity" (14:825), "the Supreme Being" (14:879), "One above, the Universal Husband" (14:1318–19), "God's air, the Allfather's air" (14:1407–8), *"Benedicat vos, omnipotens Deus, Pater, et Filius"* (14:1445–46). For my purposes, one of the episode's salient apostrophes is to "the Author of my days" (14:763). We even glimpse a metamorphosis of Poseidon, the sea-god, now a diminished thing: "pissedon green" (14:1456). Characters appear in the guise of gods, or with divine epithets: Mulligan as "Le Fécondateur" (14:778), Purefoy as "old Glory Allelujurum" (14:888), Stephen as "Bous Stephanoumenos, bull-ockbefriending bard . . . lord and giver of their life" (14:1115–16).[31] And of course, "Father, Word, and Holy Breath" (9:61) metamorphose into "The Holy Writer" (14:872).

Gods descend in droves in this episode because the various speakers invoke them to reinforce their positions. The episode is largely admonitory, exhortative, and judgmental; the opening voice urging "proliferent continuance" sets "the tone for a chapter which is frequently presented in the form of public addresses and documents."[32] In this, Joyce imitates one of his favorite writers, Laurence Sterne, whose *Tristram Shandy* parodies legal, ecclesiastical, and medical documents to much the same end: "L——d! said my mother, what is all this story about? A COCK and a BULL, said Yorick—And one of the best of its kind, I ever heard."[33] Like *Tristram Shandy,* "Oxen of the Sun" is full of Irish bull, and not only in its parody of Papal missives. When the speakers stop calling on God, in the nineteenth-century parodies, they appeal to other forms of authority: personal experience, memory, or sensation; the "mysteries of karmic law" (14:1169); or scientific sanction.

The variety of "gods" cited in "Oxen" expresses the multiplicity

---

[31]Joyce's multilingual wordplay in "Oxen" anticipates *Finnegans Wake.* "Bous Stephanoumenos" is "garlanded bull," or "schoolboy Greek: Ox- or bull-soul of Stephen" (Gifford 245). Similarly, Theodore Purefoy's name, as John Gordon notes, "combines Greek and Latin derivatives (to spell out gift-of-God Pure-faith). . . . " See John Gordon, "The Multiple Journies of 'Oxen of the Sun,'" *ELH* 46 (1979): 159. It was also Gordon who first spied the God in "pissedon green," 168.

[32]John Gordon, "The Multiple Journies," 162.

[33]Laurence Sterne, *Tristram Shandy,* 9:xxxiii.

and contrariety of *attitudes*. There is no "Universal" norm or ideal any more than Old Nobodaddy, Poseidon, and The Supreme Being are identical. "Oxen" is not a monolithic argument but, like *Ulysses* itself, a collage of competing perspectives without dogmatic authority: "a strife of tongues . . . this chaffering allincluding most farraginous chronicle" (14:952, 1412). The voices project their values onto the godhead—meeting themselves, as it were. For instance, "Dickens" imagines the "One above" as "the Universal Husband" (14:1318–19); so, too, is medieval piety different from eighteenth-century Deism. In "a language so encyclopaedic" (14:1203) we cannot expect a universal truth delivered from One Above to The Holy Writer: "proliferent continuance" is not an ethical or biological imperative, but an artistic, narrative credo.

One quality the voices do share is self-righteousness, as when "Junius" assails Bloom's masturbation or "Carlyle" attacks "copulation without population" (14:1422). The tendency in "Oxen" to judge and denounce dogmatically is typified by Junius: "But with what fitness, let it be asked . . . has this alien, whom the concession of a gracious prince has admitted to civil rights, constituted himself the lord paramount of our internal polity" (14:905–7). Let it be asked, indeed, but let it not be taken too seriously, since Junius speaks with little "fitness" for the facts of the novel. To call Bloom an "alien" is to ignore Bloom's Irish birth and recall the Citizen's bigotry. Junius regards Bloom as the medieval voice terms him, one "of Israel's folk" (14:72). Although generally regarded as Jewish, he is only barely and dubiously so, for he is not a practicing Jew, nor was his father; Bloom is not really anything in particular, and is only regarded as one of "Israel's folk" by prejudiced Dubliners derogating or dismissing him. The most we can say, I think, is that he has Jewish blood, affinities, and sympathies, and in "Cyclops" surprisingly identifies himself as such.[34]

Sometimes in "Oxen of the Sun" it is difficult to tell who is speaking, but realizing that *somebody*—someone subjective, not ultimately authoritative—is the source of everything stated is crucial. Joyce's one-time assistant Samuel Beckett somewhere spoofs this fundamental aspect of narrativity: "What does it matter who is

---

[34]In "Eumaeus," Bloom defines himself with characteristic ambivalence: "God, I mean Christ, was a jew too and all his family like me though in reality I'm not" (16:1084–85).

speaking, someone said."[35] We must always evaluate the evaluators, and never take anything on authority; no voice should be uncontested, none is sacrosanct. Joyce is not necessarily confiding in us through surrogates like Bunyan, Carlyle, or Junius; he regards his creation with less rigidity and more indulgence than his authors do. Joyce, in this, is like Bloom and Stephen, "both indurated by early domestic training and an inherited tenacity of heterodox resistance professed their disbelief in many orthodox religious, national, social and ethical doctrines" (17:22–25). In Joyce's comic gospel, not even the medical students, tediously trite, insensitive, and silly though they be, are damned for failing to be married fathers.[36]

Impersonating many styles and conflicting values with "lofty impersonal power" (*SL* 7) and comic equanimity, the text withholds ultimate judgment by mixing parody and pastiche. Some passages, such as the opening, or the Bunyan or Junius parodies, become battlegrounds for contending voices, while others are more accurately characterized not as parody but as pastiche. As Jameson notes, the two comic strategies are often confused: "Pastiche is, like parody, the imitation of a peculiar or unique style, the wearing of a stylistic mask, speech in a dead language: but it is a neutral practice of such mimicry, without parody's ulterior motive, without the satirical impulse, without laughter, without that still latent feeling that there exists something *normal* compared to which what is being imitated is rather comic."[37] An extended example of pastiche, and a passage that incidentally reassures the reader that some sense can be made of this bizarre episode, is the medieval voice, beginning "Before born babe bliss had" (14:60) and running through "woman's woe with wonder pondering" (14:186); though even here, with so much that characterizes the Leopold one knows and likes, one should not confuse medieval piety with the text's, much less the novelist's, "point of view." Every speaker, "Oxen" implies, has a

[35]Though it doesn't matter where it appears, it is quoted by Michel Foucault, in "What Is an Author?" In *The Critical Tradition: Classic Texts and Contemporary Trends,* ed. David H. Richter (New York: St. Martin's Press, 1989), 979.

[36]Joyce's early match was anomalous. As a matter of fact, Irish men tended to marry late, partly because of economic uncertainty.

[37]Fredric Jameson, "Postmodernism and Consumer Society," in *The Anti-Aesthetic: Essays on Postmodern Culture,* ed. Hal Foster (Port Townsend, Wash.: Bay Press, 1983), 114.

partially "legitimate prerogative" (14:919), but none has divine right. "Oxen" authors are, like Stephen in "Scylla and Charybdis," strong misreaders, telling their own stories, always meeting themselves. "Oxen of the Sun" is far more unstable in its authority and more comically self-reflexive than critics tend to acknowledge. The narrator of "Oxen" is a brilliant impersonator with a wide range and no particular point of view, rather like our old friend "Mercurial Malachi" (1:518), who also defies efforts to determine the seriousness and pertinence of any assertion. As so often in *Ulysses,* the text is playing as well as signifying, fooling while it is meaning. First encountered in "Cyclops" (12:1658), the phrase "Many a true word spoken in jest" is subsequently repeated twice (15:207, 18:775).

In "Oxen," "true words" are always spoken in jest, and authority and parody are hard to distinguish. The cumulative effect is disorienting, which accounts for the urge to simplify it, as when one commentator says that the parodies are not pointedly "critical . . . The exaggerations of past styles are always good-humoured . . . manifestly acts of homage."[38] *Ulysses* is rarely so deferential, nor is meaning in "Oxen" so static: every thesis has an antithesis, or "counteracting influence" (17:291), with results now jocoserious, now antic. As always, what we make of a moment, an episode, or the whole novel, depends in large measure on what we bring to it or seek from it. Parody in *Ulysses* is a crucial means of undermining authority, insisting that meanings are indeterminate, that values are mutable, and perspectives temporary. A version of the comic law is the term "parallax," a word introduced early in the novel and recalled in "Oxen" (14:1089); parallax suggests that what we see depends upon where we stand—hence, Joycean multiplicity. The novel's comic preference for "myriad metamorphoses" (14:1108) is figured in the "vein of mimicry" (14:736) of the antic narrator of "Oxen," whose many guises suggest that authorial identity itself is potentially, perhaps inevitably, protean, multiple, and provisional. That is why this book is so aptly characterized as the "Book of Many Turns."[39]

The splintering of "The Word" at the end of "Oxen" carries the

---

[38]C. H. Peake, *James Joyce: The Citizen and the Artist* (Stanford: Stanford University Press, 1977), 261–62.

[39]See Fritz Senn's splendid essay, "Book of Many Turns," in *Joyce's Dislocations,* 121–37.

momentum of parody to its manic conclusion, annihilating authority, and burlesquing the connection between divine and authorial presence. Here, parody is richly subversive, in the fashion of folly, where everything, especially the most sacred, is turned topsy-turvy. By now, in the contemporary Babel depicted at the end of "Oxen," the monolithic authority of yore is so thoroughly fragmented that we cannot definitively identify the speakers. No border is secure: Biblical, spiritual, and Apocalyptic blend with profane, vulgar, and slangy. Someone, possibly Stephen or the "narrator," if that individuation designates anything at this point, says, "Sinned against the light and even now that day is at hand when he shall come to judge the world by fire. Pflaap! *Ut implerentur scripturae*" (14:1575–77).

Such inventive and relentless parody of authority typifies *Ulysses*. "Sinned against the light" cites Scripture and reinforces the imagery of the episode introduced in the opening invocation; now though, universal darkness buries all. (The phrase also echoes Deasy's know-it-all know-nothingism). "Pflaap!" is the impact of drunken vomit on the concrete, literally bringing down to earth the high-falutin' aspiration. "*Ut implerentur scripturae*" is more Gospel, "that the Scripture might be fulfilled," John's description of the crucifixion.[40] The ultimate authority in western culture is brought down to a mundane level, in a bathetic plunge, so often apparent in this novel, from the sublime to the ridiculous. "Up like a rocket, down like a stick" (13:895).

The final voice in "Oxen," that of John Alexander Dowie, is one last parody of God-like authority and an absurd self-parody—the kind of moment that Stanislaus Joyce must have had in mind when he characterized this episode as "deliberately farcical" (Ellmann 578). "Shout salvation in King Jesus. You'll need to rise precious early, you sinner there, if you want to diddle the Almighty God" (14:1588–89). A masterful imitation of the prose masters culminates in a carnival pitch. The vulgar sell is also an exhortation to the reader whose patience might be waning: we are urged to keep up our spirits and not to expect this Almighty Author to deliver any-

---

[40]As Don Gifford points out, "The phrase, which in the Vulgate is in the indicative, is changed to the subjunctive in *Ulysses*; that is, that which the Gospels assert as objective fact is rendered hypothetical (it might be, but not necessarily will be, fulfilled)" (Gifford 449).

body, including the reader, without monumental effort, if then. The "utterance of the word" (14:1390), as always in *Ulysses,* is a "nickel dime bumshow" (14:1586). The Word may be "salvation" or it may be "Love"—or it may be "Pflaap!" Such are its "myriad metamorphoses" (14:1108). It is a "coughmixture with a punch in it for you, my friend . . . Just you try it on" (14:1590–91). "Oxen of the Sun" is an extreme instance of the difficulties posed by the entire novel in that everything is a jocoserious parody of authority or antic demolition, severely challenging the reader with devastating mockery of authorial privilege. Instead of joining a stately apostolic succession as our ultimate Allfather, Joyce dons the cap and bells, spoofs "Holy Breath" (9:61), and sends us back, laughing, to "the constant readers' room" (9:1115).

Seriocomic Farce

Gogarty's charge that *Ulysses* "smeared with farce the grandest story ever written in verse"[41] would have left Joyce nonplussed. Just as the author responded with sublime equanimity to accusations that his work was full of vulgarity, puns, and trivia, he would likely have accepted the characterization of farceur and asserted its "seriocomic" (15:447) value. As David Hayman argues so effectively, Joyce's writing shows "a growing reliance on the character types and dramatic techniques with the broadest and most primitive appeal: clowns and farce."[42] The episode most brazenly involved with farce is "Circe," to the extent that Joyce must have been experimenting with the limits of folly: how much confusion and how much implication could he wrest from this old and much-abused literary genre?

If comedy is the poor stepsister of literature, farce must be the scorned scullery girl, admitted to the palace of art, if at all, only by the back door. The phrase "mere farce" is virtually redundant; L. J. Potts defined farce as "comedy with the meaning left out."[43] Tradi-

---

[41]Oliver St. John Gogarty, *Intimations* (New York: Abelard Press, 1950), 67.

[42]David Hayman, "Forms of Folly in Joyce: A Study of Clowning in *Ulysses,*" 260. This essay is still the best single discussion of Joycean comedy.

[43]L. J. Potts, *Comedy* (London: Hutchinson University Library, 1949), 152.

tionally, farce depicts a world even more determined and reductive than that of satire, where by definition wives are unfaithful, husbands cuckolds, bachelors lechers, and every female an object of desire and source of corruption. All subtleties seem to be obliterated, along with any distinctions between reasonable and crazy behavior: everything is magnified to ludicrous proportions. It is not hard to see why so many serious artists and critics deplore farce: the knockabout pummelings of *A Comedy of Errors* and the incessant hammering in Three Stooges films have no real source nor tendentious effect, so that we are insulated from empathy and discouraged from analysis.

The word farce is derived from the French *farci* or *farcie* and the Latin *farsa,* for "stuffed," because it serves a heterogenous mixture of racy ingredients. The stuff of farce is usually dreaded fears and repressed longings, and its action liberates exaggerated disgust, fury, and degradation. Farce, noted John Dryden, "entertains us with what is monstruous and chimerical."[44] Though it is cruel, sometimes scabrous, we may be entertained because its characters remain marvelously invulnerable, always rebounding from brutality, even dying and reviving: as the old music hall songs would have it, "he's dead but he won't lie down." Farce, though not comedy generally, encourages Bergson's "momentary anaesthesia of the heart" precisely because it (but not comedy) releases both protagonists and audience from the strictures of reality, from living, in Lamb's neat phrase, "always in the precincts of the law-courts."[45]

Farce is the appropriate genre for dreaming, in that it breaks taboos and is relieved of ramifications: it merrily defies logic, common sense, decency, probability, and propriety. Bawdiness and ribaldry are *de rigeur*. Farcical figures, cavorting in drag or becoming willing cuckolds, act with scant motive and without consequence: farce has a dreamlike fluidity, in which nothing seems solid, stable, or reliable, not a marriage, not an identity. The characters are free to act fervidly, especially with hyperbolic capacity for sex and violence, but they often know or reveal that they are enacting a performance. Adding to the sense of unreality is the prominence of coincidence. However impassioned, the characters carry on oddly, not just with

[44]John Dryden, Preface to *An Evening's Love.*
[45]Charles Lamb, "On the Artificial Comedy of the Last Century," in *The Works of Charles Lamb* (Philadelphia: Parry and McMillan, 1859), 416.

extravagant buffoonery but as though entranced, stupefied, intoxicated; the place itself seems to disorient them, to upset normal balance as well as controls. Everything is accelerated—the director is constantly urging the actors to "keep it tight" or to remember "tempo, tempo"—especially the many entrances and exits. The sudden appearance or exit, so crucial to the farcical rhythm, also signifies the farcical attitude, objective, impersonal, inhumanly detached. The whirligig of events restricts the characters to caricatured action and expression instead of the individuation of a fully rendered figure. Protagonists can afford this truancy from feeling, for their pain is illusory and transient, and danger always evaporates. "It is altogether a speculative scene of things," said Lamb, "which has no reference whatever to the world that is."[46]

Even this brief overview suggests some of farce's appeal to Joyce and its applicability to "Circe." A repellant but perennially popular farcical viewpoint is vividly articulated in "Circe" by Virag, one of many featured characters whose presence complicates the case for a festive, "life-affirming" *Ulysses*. Perhaps Circe's most memorable scene, in which Bloom watches Blazes and Molly cavort, is the purest example of the episode's fundamental farcicality. What makes an interesting problem, rather than merely an apt category, is how Joyce simultaneously elaborated on and transcended the farcical. As one of Joyce's best critics observes, this episode, "where comic stereotypes are dominant, is the most serious of the book's chapters . . . [it] includes every imaginable form of foolery but . . . [it] may well be the most serious chapter in the book, a true rite of passage."[47] Consistent with his comic principles and project, Jocoserious Joyce found the way down to be the way up, exploiting more fully than any previous farceur the potential of this meanest comic form. "Circe" truly emerges, in Mrs. Breen's phrase, as a "seriocomic recitation" (15:447).

Circean figures enact the ridiculous; in this tendency they often appear more like clowns in a skit, fooling us, than characters in a situation, revealing "themselves." Not even the most outlandish behavior surprises anyone in "Circe." A Virag may appear out of nowhere, orate offensively and inscrutably, and make that remark-

[46]Lamb, "On the Artificial Comedy," 417.
[47]David Hayman, *"Ulysses": The Mechanics of Meaning,* 73, 102.

able exit, unscrewing his head and quacking off.[48] At times we seem to be in a music hall or burlesque house: at one point, minstrel singers pop up. To all this, people onstage are oblivious; nobody even notices Virag's outrageous performance, while characters regularly enter and exit without affecting the other performers. Sometimes they seem to know they are actors, as when Zoe calls for "more limelight" (15:2063). There is an automatic, virtuoso quality to much Circean language, as though characters are delivering speeches written for them. Virag's grotesque rantings, like many other utterances in "Circe," are set pieces.

A variation of farcical oratory is the Circean "star turn," a brief appearance, running up and down the scale of emotions, with exaggerated antics, such as Stephen's entrance as Cardinal Dedalus.[49] Our initial enjoyment is encouraged by the stage directions: "*Then, unable to suppress his merriment, he rocks to and fro, arms akimbo, and sings with broad rollicking humour*" (15:2669–70). Immediately, though, "Cardinal Dedalus" begins "*grimacing*" and exclaiming, "I'm suffering the agony of the damned," then "*doubleshuffles off comically*" (15:2678–83). Such a moment is both disorienting and explicable, for it is a funny spoof of what Mulligan calls Stephen's "cursed jesuit strain . . . injected the wrong way" (1:209). Hence a comic convention, and even a rough comic justice, is operating: overweening Stephen is forced (like Malvolio) to play the fool. Although Circean emotions are hyperbolic and volatile, they have recognizable sources and implications. Here we glean the fine line between Stephen's forced jollity and anguish, with a hint that his state may be overacted.

Reactions in "Circe" are so uniformly hyperbolic that they both reinforce and call into question what we have come to know about the characters. Bringing back everyone in a helter-skelter tumult, "Circe" presents them in another genre, as though everyone were now a figure of farce. When Bloom encounters Mrs. Breen, an old flame that has long since died out, he suddenly becomes the romantic hero carrying the blazing torch: "Think what it means. All you

[48]The noted Joycean Chico Marx wonders, "Why a duck?" See, by all means, *Duck Soup.*

[49]Now "Simon Stephen," he becomes his father, according to his aesthetic, and might be addressed "Father Father."

meant to me then. (*hoarsely*) Woman, it's breaking me!" (15:477–78). The stagey quality of emotions in "Circe" has a kind of Brechtian *Verfremdungseffekt,* underscoring yet undermining their larger-than-life, epical stature. Even at the height of his "agony," terrified by the resurrection of his mother, Stephen's words and gestures are operatic: "*Ah non, par exemple!* The intellectual imagination! With me all or not at all. *Non serviam!*" (15:4227–28) he declares in a Babel of three languages, before finding a fourth. Appropriately it is from Wagner, that master of grandiloquent staging: "*Nothung!*" (15:4242).

Dramatizing the Molly and Blazes sequence as farce is a wonderfully disrupting comic strategy, for it is outrageously silly and cryptically suggestive, sending us in quest of sources and ramifications (is Bloom "masochistic"? is he punishing himself for failure to perpetuate the male line?). But farcical sequences such as the cuckolding of Bloom, or the sadism of Bella/Bello, are rendered differently, or appear quite different in the context of *Ulysses,* than the motiveless, meaningless knockabout of "Punch and Judy." The problem with, or perhaps the point of, the farcical scenes in "Circe" is that we have already come to know and care for Bloom, so that such moments, if they make us laugh, also make us squirm. I think the same uneasiness is aroused by the spectacle of Stephen doubleshuffling in agony, posturing yet pained.

Such veering between jocose and serious, I have argued, is pre-eminently Joycean. Though "nebulous obscurity occupies space" (15:2167–68) in the End of the World sequence, everything appears vividly spotlighted, so much so that readers of "Circe," moved by its bright, clear, lucid dramatization, often ignore the farcical component and go to the opposite extreme, assuming that this episode provides privileged access into the motives, conflicts, aspirations, and fates of Bloom and Stephen—their "real" characters, their unconscious, essential selves. To try to make psychological sense of this bizarre episode is irresistible, because of its subterranean, often sexual nature and its compelling power. When Bloom confronts his father, grandfather, and son, or Stephen encounters the spectre of his mother, we seem to be in touch with some kind of bedrock truth. For all its raucous antics, then, "Circe" strikes most readers as "joking apart, and getting down to bedrock" (15:2204–5) or, once more, a "true word spoken in jest" (15:207). Yet Circean humor is so pervasive and disorienting, its ironies by now so multiple, that it ricochets wildly. Perhaps Fritz Senn best defines its principle of unity: "In 'Circe' all contradictions are staged."[50] While suggesting uncanny illumination of characters and relationships, "Circe"—with its comic preference for flux instead of form, folly instead of logic— punctures certainties, mocks identity, and plays havoc.

One way the episode both implies and attacks meaning is by making the novel itself the object of humorous contemplation. Familiar narrative elements are recycled more frequently than in any other episode, suggesting culmination in a massive burlesque or caricature.[51] I have mentioned earlier that mirroring and echoing are standard tactics of the jester, so that when the Abbot of Unreason appears at the Feast of Fools in Scott's *The Abbot,* he naturally, but for no good reason, carries a mirror. "Circe" is a huge funhouse, reflecting and reiterating material, often in slightly altered, strange forms. Central motifs reappear, displaced, parodied, shrunken: a particularly funny recurrence is when Bello is selling Bloom's body, and a bidder offers a florin—to which a voice retorts, "One and eightpence too much" (15:3098). Almost nothing escapes parody, and rereading reveals that almost nothing will: Mrs. Breen forecasts Molly's ultimate affirmation by ejaculating, "Yes, yes, yes, yes, yes, yes, yes" and fading forever (15:576). Such incessant recapitulation and parodic foreshadowing connects the episode to the rest of the novel—indeed, makes it feel climactic and prophetic, while it plays Looney Tunes.

Over this madcap "other world" presides our Master of the Revels, barely but happily in control, the "basilicogrammate" (15:2304) or Lord of Language, a notoriously unruly dominion. For "Circe" seems to be generating itself, or blooming from seeds (plum seeds?) casually dropped by the wayside. Heeding the burden of "Oxen of the Sun," "proliferent continuance" (14:15), "Circe" proliferates wildly. Not only can everybody return, but anything can come to life—a picture, a waterfall, a button, a cap. The life-force vivifies humble inanimate objects as well as the remains of the dear departed. Circean words reveal a preternatural resilience; they will not stay put or pass away, but rise revivified and free of speakers. Char-

[50]Senn, *Joyce's Dislocutions,* 132.

[51]John Paul Riquelme, *Teller and Tale in Joyce's Fiction,* has a useful appendix called "The Structure of Allusion in 'Circe,'" including "Correspondences to Other Parts of *Ulysses.*"

acters can no longer be identified by "their" language, even when seemingly peculiar to the speaker. Molly utters "Nebrakada! Femininum" (15:319), which is the charm for seduction that Stephen had read at the bookstall that afternoon. Or A VOICE says of Ben Dollard, "Hold that fellow with the bad breeches" (15:2616), which echoes Simon's comment in "Wandering Rocks" (10:905), spoken when neither Bloom nor Stephen was present. Or May Dedalus tells Stephen, "I pray for you in my other world" (15:4202), which echoes Martha's slip, "I do not like that other world" (5:245).

Words, like selves, have mysterious new attributes in the "other world" of "Circe." A word may now have a life of its own and even the power to create reality: names can conjure dead souls.[52] Bloom calls "Mamma!" (15:281) and she instantly appears. When Stephen confronts his mother, it is not a vision he wants, but the word: "Tell me the word, mother, if you know. The word known to all men" (15:4192–93).[53] Lists proliferate to include all sorts of nonsense. So Bloom reads solemnly from a scroll a mélange of Hebrew and Yiddish words, like "Hagadah . . . Kosher . . . Bar Mitzvah . . . Meshuggah [Yiddish for "crazy"] . . . " (15:1623–25). So, too, the parade celebrating Bloom's reign mixes many familiar details, such as "the pillar of the cloud" (15:1407; the definite article reminds us that we have seen it before) and John Howard Parnell "in a chessboard tabard" (15:1412–13), and a perfectly berserk medley of guilds and trades, running to ten lines of type. Homer's epic catalogs are transformed to catchbasins, like the great procession (15:4335–61). With the many figures large and small who reappear are "The Nameless One" (the narrator of "Cyclops"), "Whatdoyoucallhim" (4:214), Miss Dubedatandshedidbedad (8:889), Penrose, Aaron Figatner, some figures who don't even "figure" but merely receive passing reference, and others who seem to be thrown in to make the procession as arbitrary and capricious as possible.

The Circean epic catalogs suggest a master plan run amok, in accord with its foolish preference for the random, the adventitious,

---

[52]A development in a sense predicted in "Oxen of the Sun": "Yet a chance word will call them [the reference is to "evil memories"] forth suddenly and they will rise up to confront him in the most various circumstances, a vision or a dream . . . " (14:1348–50).

[53]As Ellmann speculated and Gabler's corrected text confirms, the word is "love" (though the debate that seemed to be closed continues). See Denis Donoghue's comments in *We Irish,* 118–19.

the accidental. In "Circe," the Unconscious (*whose* unconscious is never clear or consistent: the novel's, perhaps)[54] seems to be liberated and triumphant, so that we are in a world stripped of civilized norms: where superego was, id shall be. As Karen Lawrence notes, "The book's previously suppressed or 'censored' material now surfaces. The offstage and 'ob-scene' are now spotlighted."[55] Some of the gags are what Lenny Bruce called "whoopie cushion" jokes, like dirty words buried in songs,[56] or the plasterer's bucket or the hat trick—just the sort of jokes favored by Buck Mulligan. Such trivial antics help convey the illusion that the whole episode is a gigantic Antic, in which normal rules and controls are inadequate and everything is boiling over.

This comic urge to proliferate, to elaborate gratuitously, is especially marked in the "stage directions," so ludicrously detailed in their descriptions of attire.[57] "Circe" invites the imp of excess, a zealot maniacal enough to say it all, as when introducing first Ellen Bloom, then Molly: 293 words of stage direction introduce only 122 words of dialogue. The comic effects are contradictory, suggesting both authorial impotence, as though Pandora had opened the box, and authorial mastery: like the headlines in "Aeolus," the manic stage directions call attention to the conjuring artist's flagrant artifice and godlike power to cast his characters in multiple roles. For when events, even words, veer dizzily out of characters' control, we are most aware of the artist's implicit presence. As in a classic farce, the characters have been subordinated to the flagrant whims of a manifestly theatrical world, determined by a master of the revels who merrily juggles characters into hilarious, humiliating situations.

Out of several comic traditions and numerous comic conventions, including music hall and vaudeville, pantomime and sight gags, "Circe" gathers energy and takes form as a kind of carnival. In its

[54]One of the finest observations on "Circe" is that of Nabokov: "The book is itself dreaming and having visions." See Vladimir Nabokov, *Lectures on Literature,* ed. Fredson Bowers (New York: Harcourt Brace Jovanovich, 1980), 350.

[55]Karen Lawrence, *The Odyssey of Style in "Ulysses,"* 151.

[56]I thought you'd ask. An example is the chant "If you see Kay" (15:1893). I once heard a short lesson in "how to speak Irish" at a humor conference in Cork. Say the following words quickly: "Whale oil, beef hocked."

[57]"Are you strong on costume?" Joyce asked a correspondent. "I want to make 'Circe' a costume episode also" (*SL* 272).

blasphemous antics, programmatic reversals, and theatrical extrava-
gances, "Circe" is a saturnalian festival mocking authority and
celebrating folly. As a carnival, it features sharp satire, in which
nothing remains sacred, providing a playhouse for clowns and fools,
and spoofing tradition, wisdom, and revelation; instead of immutable, received truths, "Circe" affirms a perpetual series of vice versas.
Here Buck Mulligan appropriately appears, "in particoloured
jester's dress of puce and yellow and clown's cap with curling
bell" (15:4166–67). Seen in the carnival tradition, a number of
puzzling elements in "Circe" make more sense, or at least compre-
hensible nonsense, cooperating with the carnivalesque humor.
During Bloom's comically exaggerated exaltation, debasement, and
recovery, for instance, Bloom's boys sing of Saint Stephen's day
(15:1453), a holiday often set aside for a Feast of Fools. In that
celebration, a fool, sometimes wearing ass's ears, like Bloom in the
pillory (15:1884), was proclaimed bishop or king in a mock-ritual.
A typical "plot" of the loosely organized show would be the pro-
mulgation of sham laws and edicts, the clown-king's death, and his
resurrection. The fun featured masks and monstrous visages, clerics
dressed as women, devils and spirits from the dead, wanton scenes,
indecent gestures, and scurrilous verses. Like the festival, "Circe" is
histrionic, with lavish costumes, surprise appearances, and outrageous performances. Everyone who appears on the stage of
"Circe," with its "maypoles and festal arches" (15:1398), has the
"grotesque style" of carnival humor, characterized by Bakhtin as
"exaggeration, hyperbolism, excessiveness."[58] The heart of the festive play in "Circe" is degradation of anything high, romantic, abstract, or spiritual: up like a rocket, down like a stick.

The simultaneity of sacred and profane is a cherished tenet at the
Circean Carnival.[59] As Bloom puts the principle with mock-
solemnity, "You call it a festivity. I call it a sacrament" (15:1681),
and a moment later he specifies what he represents: "General amnesty, weekly carnival, with masked licence" (15:1690). So it is not
surprising that this episode of foolery, fireworks, and free play—

---

[58]Bakhtin, *Rabelais and His World,* 303.

[59]Joyce once spoke of Dublin as "still a medieval city. I know that when I
used to frequent the pubs around Christ Church I was always reminded of
those medieval taverns in which the sacred and the obscene jostle shoulders."
See Power, *Conversations with James Joyce,* 92.

"This is midsummer madness" (15:1768), remarks Bloom—strikes many readers as random, chaotic, a "private joke," Joyce's "fantasia on his own novel."[60] "Circe" is conceived as a "carnival with masked licence," a holiday for the text from such mundane obligations as verisimilitude, consistency, and plausibility. Splendidly theatrical, very amusing, and utterly discombobulating, "Circe" is a triumph of comic demolition, in which Folly becomes master of the revels, and, as always, presents a show rich in madcap meaning.

Circe's carnivalesque tendencies provide a way to view its abundant, humorous uses of scriptural, theological, and liturgical material. It is a measure of Joyce's canniness that religious readers like Harry T. Blamires, Father Robert Boyle, and Father William Noon find so much sustenance in "Circe," though Blamires in particular is so intent on discovering grounds for faith that he is nearly deaf to Joycean humor.[61] Yet even Blamires's solemn confusion of parody with prophecy is provoked by the text—for, like medieval carnival, "Circe" offers a comic gospel. Although simple release of tension was one of its implicit justifications, carnival "had always an essential, meaningful philosophical content. . . . Moments of death and revival, of change and renewal always led to a festive perception of the world . . . coupled with serious myths were comic and abusive ones; coupled with heroes were their parodies and doublets."[62]

Like the feast of fools, "Circe" enacts a purgation and revival. Stephen begins the proceedings chanting *"with joy the* introit *for paschal time"* (15:73–74), connecting the proceedings to the *risus paschalis* or "Easter laughter," another traditional time for jollity, including the Feast of Fools. Typically, Stephen plays out his monkish jest at some length, citing several lines of the joyous ritual to suggest cleansing, renewal, revivification through water (which

[60]Gordon, *James Joyce's Metamorphoses,* 108; Arnold Goldman, *The Joyce Paradox,* 98.

[61]Blamires rather resembles Bunyan's Christian, who "put his fingers in his ears, and ran on, crying Life! life! eternal life!"

[62]Bakhtin, *Rabelais and His World,* 8–9, 6. Other scholars who describe the Feast of Fools include Barbara Swain, *Fools and Folly during the Middle Ages and the Renaissance* (New York: Columbia University Press, 1932); C. L. Barber, *Shakespeare's Festive Comedy* (Princeton: Princeton University Press, 1959). For a detailed dramatization of the Feast of Fools, see Sir Walter Scott, *The Abbot,* Chapters 14 and 15. This popular novel can be found among the dead priest's effects, at the beginning of "Araby."

he deplored that morning). Before we become too excited by signs of impending grace, though, Lynch scorns Stephen's holy blarney with a snort, "Pornosophical philotheology" (15:109). Though "Circe" neither produces redemption nor affirms any theology, it implies a kind of regeneration, in a comic analog of the Christian pattern. As close to the music hall as to the Church, a favorite activity in this festive interlude is burlesque of the sacred, but the opposite is also true: "Circe" somehow endows vulgarity with a metaphoric spirituality. Like the parodist who loves what he impersonates, or the satirist who harbors clandestine affinity for his victim, the master of the Circean revels lovingly mocks liturgy, scripture, and authority; as a result, the story may be said to break down entirely into license, nonsense, and play, some of it puerile and ludicrous, yet to borrow some of the aura of the forms and values it spoofs. *Ulysses* is not a satiric demolition, but a mock-heroic restoration.

The implicit comparison between Bloom and Christ is hyper bolically elaborated upon, complete with revelations, miracles, calumny, passion, sacrifice, and resurrection. The point, as in the mock-heroic, is not simple comic incongruity, but the surprising identity between sacred and profane. Of course we must beware of flat-footed inferences: though Bloom is constantly imaged as Christ, he is always exposed as an actor, bearing a counterfeit revelation and redemption, just as he wears a "false badge" (15:728) and is attacked with "soft pantomime stones" (15:1902).[63] The Circean comedy plays with the spiritual correspondence by multiplying and reversing it, in accord with the comic laws, "proliferent continuance" (14:15) and "up like a rocket, down like a stick" (13:895). Although many other references connect Bloom with the Messiah, he is just as frequently characterized as Elijah, which leads in another direction, establishing Stephen and not Bloom as Christ. Simultaneously, Bloom is depicted, or imagines himself, as the Antichrist. Soon after muttering about washing off the sins of the world, he complains about a cramp and says, "Mark of the beast" (15:209), which signifies the anti-Christian ogre in *Revelations*. The festive pattern of "Circe" is the world upside down, and so the episode culminates in a black mass. If ADONAI appears at the Black Mass to

[63]That archetypal con man Groucho Marx always appeared with an obviously painted mustache and empty spectacles.

chant "Dooooooooooog," we can count on hearing a reverse echo: "Goooooooooood!" (15:4711–16). Reversal, topsy-turvy, and turnabout are perennial comic strategies, and in "Circe" they indicate the extent to which Joyce both depends upon and repudiates orthodox dogma.

Joyce's oxymoronic vision links contraries, suggested by portmanteau words like "jocoserious" (17:369) and "seriocomic" (15:447); as the cap tells us, "Extremes meet" (15:2098).[64] "The ultimate return" (15:2212) is Stephen's phrase for the musical theory declaring that the greatest harmonies are created by pitches at greatest possible disparities. "Circe" especially delights in fusing the sublime and the ridiculous, as in Elijah's message: "Join on right here. Book through to eternity junction, the nonstop run. Just one word more. Are you a god or a doggone clod? If the second advent came to Coney Island are we ready? Florry Christ, Stephen Christ, Zoe Christ, Bloom Christ, Kitty Christ, Lynch Christ, it's up to you to sense that cosmic force. . . . Joking apart and, getting down to bedrock, A. J. Christ Dowie and the harmonial philosophy, have you got that?" (15:2192–2206). Elijah commands the stage like Erasmus's Folly to deliver a burlesque gospel, demanding our attention—"not the kind you give to godly preachers, but rather the kind you give to pitchmen, low comedians, and jokesters" (Erasmus 10). He's a vulgar carnival huckster, a foolish mountebank, peddling redemption like snake-oil; it's all joking, especially when he claims to be "joking aside and getting down to bedrock," but Joyce teases and tantalizes us with the possible significance of such folderol. Though the "harmonial philosophy" of "Circe" remains dubious and elusive, its comic thrust is persistent. "Are you a god or a doggone clod?" recalls Mulligan's play with god/dog, reiterates extremes meeting, and suggests a pervasive carnival credo.

"Circe" is certainly "seriocomic" or "jocoserious," but not in the simple sense of accommodating duality and achieving a harmony.

[64]"Circe" also refers cryptically to *"Vice Versa"* (15:3010). Joycean doubling is a bit dizzying here: F. Anstey's *Vice Versa* was a popular farce featuring a father-son reversal. Young James Joyce performed in it one Whitsuntide; as R. B. Kershner speculates, it is probably the "play within the play" of *Portrait*. In *Ulysses* Bloom remembers playing in *Vice Versa,* dressed as a female. For an interesting account of *Vice Versa* and its Joycean resonances, see Kershner, *Joyce, Bakhtin, and Popular Literature: Chronicles of Disorder* (Chapel Hill: University of North Carolina Press, 1989), 180–185.

"Circe" eludes even such capacious contraries, because binary modes of perception are themselves an object of satiric annihilation; its parodic impulse is so insistent, its ironies so unstable, that it is often hard to determine just where the "serious" element is, what modicum of meaning we can rely on. For example, in one sense, Elijah calling everybody Christ is blasphemy; in another it is utterly orthodox, in the spirit of Paul and Augustine, who exhort us to live *in imitatio Christi.* Many utterances in "Circe" seem to comment ironically on the quest for meaning: "Wildgoose chase this" (15:635); "A pure mare's nest" [slang for "tangle of illusion," or the sense of making a great discovery when in fact it is all an illusion].

A prime example of Circe's preference for presenting both the pure mare's nest and bedrock truth is the Circean recognition scene. "Circe" parodies the classic recognition scenes that endow the hero with enhanced perception, ranging from a clearer perception of fundamental identity or relationship in comedies such as *Twelfth Night* or *Joseph Andrews,* to a broader, deeper conception of one's place in the world in Sophoclean or Shakespearean tragedy. Instead of seeing face to face, Circean characters continue to view through a glass darkly, as in the scene between Bloom and his father Rudolph. Like Isaac touching Jacob, Rudolph "feels the silent face" (15:260) of his son, asking "Are you not my dear son Leopold who left the house of his father and left the god of his fathers Abraham and Jacob?" (15:261–62). As usual in "Circe," the scene is very moving, and resonates with much that we know or wonder about Bloom, yet matters are slightly askew: no real Jew would omit Isaac from the triad of fathers any more than a Catholic could forget any of the three persons in the holy trinity.[65] Earlier (5:200–205) Bloom had remembered a recognition scene in Mosenthal's *Leah,* featuring an old Jew named Abraham, so that this Circean moment dimly recalls what we have already heard, yet transmutes it and makes it strange: since Rudolph himself "left the god of his fathers" by converting, his reproach is very puzzling.

Whenever some serious connection seems to be affirmed— between characters, or between a character and his archetype—it is qualified; "Circe" abides by Bloom's Masonic vow, "ever conceal, never reveal" (15:4952). Though Bello vows to make Bloom re-

---

[65]The tableau at the end of "Circe" figures the trinity of Bloom the father, Stephen the son, and a ghost.

member his degradation forever (15:2893–94), some sort of spell seems to keep "Circe" inviolate even from recollection, ever concealed and never revealed, for there is a remarkable glitch between this episode and the final three: Circean experience, including such extraordinary drama as the resurrections of Rudy and Mrs. Dedalus, is almost totally forgotten by both Bloom and Stephen. The closest either protagonist comes to recalling anything from "Circe" is a brief moment in "Ithaca" when Bloom refrains from saying that he had "frequented the university of life" (17:555–56) because of "fluctuating incertitude" as to whether he had already said it to Stephen or vice versa; in fact Bloom had said it to Beaufoy in the brothel (15:840). And when Bloom compiles his budget for this day, there is no mention of any expenses incurred in Nighttown; is Bloom neglecting, censoring, or unaware of his experience in Nighttown? Ironically, the episode in which memories are so crucial is hardly remembered.

Yet this mystery, the virtual absence of Circean material from subsequent reflections of Stephen and Bloom, follows a comic logic by which its events are out of bounds, separate, other, rather than ominous, contingent, or contagious. Though it is provocatively connected to the story we have been reading, "Circe" is a self-contained holiday interlude or play, on a different level of discourse, like the relation of saturnalian folly to the normal course of events. It is as though the participants agreed to play the game or enact the festival, the prerequisite of which is passionate involvement but no necessary implications to the revelry (which strikes me as a good definition of fantasy). Huizinga characterizes playgrounds as "forbidden spots, isolated, hedged round, hallowed, within which special rules obtain. All are temporary worlds within the ordinary world, dedicated to the performance of an act apart."[66]

Attempts to distinguish actual events from hallucination within this episode miss the point, which is to confound such normal categories of perception. Ordinary logic cannot explain what Cissy Caffrey is doing in Nighttown, nor why prostitutes suddenly begin speaking like philologists, for they inhabit a no-man's land between make-believe and once-upon-a-time. The action of farce typically takes place in such an isolated, closed, encapsulated world. In this

[66]J. Huizinga, *Homo Ludens: A Study of The Play-Element in Culture* (London: Routledge & Kegan Paul, 1949), 10.

and in other ways, a textbook definition of farce partially pertains to "Circe": "Since [it] does not share with higher comedy the responsibility of commentary upon social conduct it may pursue its laughter into a world of fantasy where the unpredictable, even the impossible, is commonplace."[67] What Joyce achieves in "Circe" is the continual sense of the unpredictable, even the impossible, with the possibility of commentary upon conduct. In this way the episode is a giant game played for deadly stakes.

Indeed, "Circe" might be regarded as Joyce's version of Homeric or Virgilian epic games, for the episode abounds in tricks, dancing, capering, parlor games, and play, as well as references to the circus, the bazaar, and amusements.[68] One perennial purpose of play is to simulate danger. As in a haunted house, hobgoblins and ghosts pop up regularly, but with limited power. Our foolish hero's Circean adventures exaggerate his capacity for recuperation, to stage "life's upsomdowns" (*FW* 49:24). The comic pattern is especially evident following his degradation. Bello, the voice of mortification and despair, cruelly declares to Bloom, "Your epitaph is written. You are down and out and don't you forget it . . . " (15:3199–200). In the comic world of "Circe," though, nobody stays down and out. Bloom, having endured the ordeal unto sacrificial death, miraculously recovers: he "*half rises,*" causing his trouser button to snap, which breaks the spell. When the Nymph moves to castrate him, he "*starts up, seizes her hand*" and declares himself "Cat o' nine lives!" (15:3439, 3463).

"Circe" is Bloomagains Wake. And not just Bloom's—Here Comes Everybody! "Circe" fantastically exaggerates the novel's jocoserious law, countering the pull "down and out": "U.p: up. U.p: up" (15:1609). This episode of mock resurrections has an apt invocation: Stephen enters chanting "*with joy the* introit *for paschal time*" (15:73–74). After a long day in which he has been frequently drunk and usually mirthless, he musters enough cheer to proclaim, "Damn death. Long live life!" (15:4474). Eventually Stephen is punched by Carr, "*totters, collapses, falls stunned*" (15:4748) and figuratively

---

[67]*Princeton Encyclopedia of Poetry and Poetics,* ed. Alex Preminger et al. (Princeton: Princeton University Press, 1974), 271.

[68]Cheryl Herr, *Joyce's Anatomy of Culture* (Urbana: University of Illinois Press, 1986), Chapter 5, shows connections between the music hall and "Circe."

rises again as Rudy and, some readers think, a reborn Stephen. A powerful comic credo of the episode is Bloom's mock-heroic declaration, "All is lost now! Do we yield? No!" (15:1527–28).[69] Bello may want Bloom to "die and be damned" (15:3204) but his power is checked. If it is true that anything conjured up in "Circe" will fade, it is equally true that no one is down and out forevermore. The farcical turns in "Circe" collectively suggest carnival renewal and revival: what this means for Bloom's life after "Circe" may remain indeterminate, but it can't be all bad. I agree with James H. Maddox that, most likely, *"Bloom plodges forward"* (15:1267).

"Circe" provides slim but discernible grounds for hope, because the oscillation between down and up is so insistent that movement in either direction now implicitly entails its opposite. Lots of things come up or ascend in "Circe," many of which, like the Mirus bazaar fireworks, *"go up from all sides with symbolical phallopyrotechnic designs"* (15:1494–95). Anything conjured up in "Circe" will fade, a pattern that is as reliable as its opposite, that nothing ever disappears entirely; for, more than any other, "Circe" is the chapter of "the ultimate return" (15:2112). Like the Feast of Fools, "Circe" makes hay with Judgment Day, and is chockablock full of returns and resurrections, broadly comic in two major senses. Returns dramatize that nothing is ever lost, that humankind somehow endures; this stress on nature's cycles, the survival and triumph of life, animates the traditional comic vision, from *The Odyssey* to *Ulysses.* Second, though, is a farcical twist: that virtually everyone and everything reappears means that anyone and anything might pop up. "Circe" is a giant jack-in-the-box.[70] The cumulative effect is to parody—to make fun of and to preserve—the idea of return and resurrection, because, moved by the comic force of "magnetic influence" (13:984–85), everybody wants to get into the act: Cissy Caffrey, Jacky and Tommy Caffrey, Ellen Bloom, The Soap, Gerty

[69]Cf. Satan in Milton's *Paradise Lost*: "What though the field be lost? / All is not lost . . . courage never to submit or yield" (I:105–8).

[70]A jack-in-the-box head of Father Dolan springs up (15:3668–69). And, as my student Robert Newman observed, when Jack Power appears with others "in the jurybox" (15:1139), we have a figurative jack-in-the-box. The jack-in-the-box is also Henri Bergson's first example of a comic "arrangement . . . which gives us, in a single combination, the illusion of life and the distinct impression of a mechanical arrangement." See Bergson's "Laughter," in *Comedy*, ed. Sypher, 105–10.

MacDowell, Mrs. Breen, Pat the Waiter, the Gulls to whom Bloom threw cake, and a cast of thousands more. Dramatic resurrections are made by Paddy Dignam, Virag, Rudolph, May Dedalus, and little Rudy. So many spooks arise that it seems less like Judgment Day than Halloween. Paddy makes his descent, baying, "Dignam's dead and gone below" (15:1258–59), which is the cue for Tom Rochford, hero of the sewer line in "Wandering Rocks," to perform another heroic rescue, or a parody of the harrowing of hell.

Joyce himself regarded "Circe" as the sequence that "approached reality closer in my opinion than anywhere else in the book except perhaps for moments in the last chapter."[71] The episode that is most tightly related to what precedes it, gets down to bedrock, and is densest with suggestivity, is at the same time an anti-episode, a jocose staging of antics. Clowning, hyperbole, hypertrophy, and nonsense all provide "Circe" with means of revealing yet disclaiming a privileged view of Bloom's and Stephen's essential desires and fears. As one critic observes, "Acting *out* (that is, expression of the unconscious) and *acting* out (that is, theatricality) are one and the same."[72] It draws amply upon carnival, the feast of fools, pantomime, music hall, vaudeville, the circus, burlesque, and farce, with their surprise appearances and abrupt exits, see-through costumes and mistaken identities, plentiful accusations and physical abuse, numerous deceptions, dirty jokes and sight gags. "Circe" is a self-contained space without cause or effect, yet pregnant with implication, where actions proceed according to the jocoserious principles: topsy-turvy, higgledy-piggledy, willy-nilly, handy-dandy, and "*Vice Versa*" (15:3010).

---

[71]Power, *Conversations with James Joyce,* 75.

[72]Lawrence, *The Odyssey of Style,* 159. I would make a similar point about some of the more outrageous material in Joyce's intimate letters to Nora.

4

Buck Mulligan's Revenge: Or, The Follies of "Indentity"

Who Is He If It's a Fair Question

It is remarkable how quickly and thoroughly critics of *Ulysses* have abandoned the idea of a self, as though Buck Mulligan, flaunting his Nietzschean skepticism, had, after all, had the last laugh.[1] Perhaps the second most prominent casualty of Deconstruction, after the late, unlamented Transcendental Signifier, is the "self" or "personal identity." The very words, nowadays ironized and too suspect to approach without quotation marks, are understood as "creations, fabrications, patchworks—interpretations. Functions not facts. Effects of language, not causes."[2] Personal identity generally no longer appears merely problematical, but chimerical. Robert Alter defines Joyce's "ultimate sense of being as a precarious structure erected on a ground of nothingness . . . Individual identity, all human projects, structures, cultures, are momentary configurations of seeming coherence, pulled apart in the perpetual centrifuge of history and physical existence."[3] Cheryl Herr says that Joycean character is "properly construed as a narrative event . . . Throughout *Ulysses*

---

[1]Nietzsche is the favorite philosopher of several Joycean characters besides Buck, including Mr. Duffy in "A Painful Case" and Richard Rowan in *Exiles*. For Nietzsche's acid rejection of personal identity, see *The Will to Power,* trans. Walter Kaufmann and R. J. Hollingdale (New York: Vintage, 1968), 267–68.

[2]Vincent B. Leitch, *Deconstructive Criticism: An Advanced Introduction* (New York: Columbia University Press, 1983), 58.

[3]Robert Alter, *Partial Magic: The Novel as a Self-Conscious Genre* (Berkeley: University of California Press, 1975), 132–33.

we are never in touch with a stable character named Bloom but are given access to cultural codings that change, sentence by sentence, thought by thought."[4] Colin MacCabe argues a similar position: Joyce's inclusiveness "ruins the particularities of the identitites. . . . Instead of the identities shining through and effacing the writing, the progressive adding of more and more identities achieves the opposite effect."[5] In another recent study, Sheldon Brivic connects Joyce's conception of identity to contemporary science: Joyce "realized that pure being and identical identity were unknowable, for identical things did not exist in nature. . . . The convention of simple identity was far from Joyce's conception of the mind, which he saw as a shifting interaction rather than a monad."[6] So, too, John Paul Riquelme regards "the book's styles as allotropic forms [that] reinforce the notion of identity as chameleonic."[7] Bonnie Kime Scott observes that character "has not been a fashionable construction recently on the forefront of Joyce studies, where narrative, discourse, and semiotics have been attended to while the unified, individual subject has been decentered."[8] The seminal critic enabling such recent interpretations is Fritz Senn, whose major project, perhaps, is to "alert the reader to the hazards of hasty identification. The chain of all this links back, trickily, to the text as a strandentwining cable of doubtful identities . . . Verbal options favor suggestive possibilities more than distinct identities."[9]

With increasing unanimity, Joyceans—including many who would not describe themselves as poststructuralists—perceive identity as misperception of difference or absence, a mere trope, a floating signifier, and a will-o'-the-wisp; the quest for its traces in *Ulysses*

[4]Cheryl Herr, *Joyce's Anatomy of Culture* (Urbana: University of Illinois Press, 1986), 154–55.

[5]Colin MacCabe, *James Joyce and the Revolution of the Word,* 98.

[6]Sheldon Brivic, *Joyce the Creator* (Madison: The University of Wisconsin Press, 1985), 61.

[7]John Paul Riquelme, *Teller and Tale in Joyce's Fiction,* 182.

[8]Bonnie Kime Scott, "Introduction to Character and Contemporary Theory," in *James Joyce: The Augmented Ninth. Proceedings of the Ninth International James Joyce Symposium, Frankfurt, 1984,* ed. Bernard Benstock (Syracuse: Syracuse University Press, 1988), 135.

[9]Fritz Senn, "Dogmad or Dubliboused?" in *Joyce's Dislocutions,* 106, 111. See also his wonderful essay "Book of Many Turns," 111–37 in the same book.

thus appears utterly quixotic.[10] It is my view that receptivity to such possibilities is crucial if we are to appreciate Joyce's comic constructions and demolitions, but that *systematic* denial of selfhood is too absolute and solemn, for *Ulysses* does not work or play in any programmatic way: we need not necessarily throw out the baby with the bath water. Even if we accept Saussure's theory that all experience is mediated, so that we have no immediate access to the "self," of the *existence* of the self we cannot be so sure. Our conclusions ought to be more tentative: though we cannot *know* the self, it does not follow that there cannot *be* a self. If the repudiation of singleness is high on every jester's agenda, the stubborn nature of personal identity is a perennial comic subject. While tragedies such as *The Iliad* dramatize what man is and must be, comedies such as *The Odyssey* show the resilience and elasticity of identity. Joyce was originally attracted to *The Odyssey* because its hero enacts so many roles, assumes so many guises, and makes so many turns. *Finnegans Wake* transmutes the word into "indentity," a neologism I construe as the simultaneous affirmation and denial of "identity," and that suggests the handy-dandy of *Ulysses,* playing with comic variations.

Identity is the essential comic theme and to an extent, I would argue, its prerequisite. The old switcheroo, disguise, and confusion are staples of countless comedies from Aristophanes and Terence, through Shakespeare, to Ionesco. Mixed-up identity is so traditional a theme that *The Importance of Being Earnest* makes it an extended joke, beginning with its title and culminating in its hero's climactic question, "Lady Bracknell, I hate to seem inquisitive, but would you kindly inform me who I am?" Even toddlers, if they are as clever and adorable as my little girls, will laugh at Pooh's befuddlement.

> "Bother!" said Pooh. "Isn't there anybody here at all?"
> "Nobody."
> Winnie-the-Pooh took his head out of the hole, and thought for
> a little, and he thought to himself, "There must be somebody

[10]An example of such an interpretation is Phillip F. Herring's analysis of the Man in the Macintosh: "It is generally assumed that he actually has an identity if one could only find it; my thesis is that he has none, that he is merely a teasing construct of words." See Herring, *Joyce's Uncertainty Principle* (Princeton: Princeton University Press, 1987), 106, and his chapter in the same book, "Indeterminacies of Identity," 103–60.

there, because somebody must have *said* 'Nobody.'" So he put his head back in the hole, and said:

"Hallo, Rabbit, isn't that you?"

"No," said Rabbit, in a different sort of voice this time.

"But isn't that Rabbit's voice?"

"I don't *think* so," said Rabbit. "It isn't *meant* to be."

"Oh!" said Pooh.

He took his head out of the hole, and had another think, and then he put it back, and said:

"Well, could you very kindly tell me where Rabbit is?"

"He has gone to see his friend Pooh Bear, who is a great friend of his."

"But this *is* Me!" said Bear, very much surprised.

"What sort of Me?"

"Pooh Bear."

"Are you sure?" said Rabbit, still more surprised.

"Quite, quite sure," said Pooh.

"Oh, well then, come in."

So Pooh pushed and pushed and pushed his way through the hole, and at last he got in.

"You were quite right," said Rabbit, looking at him all over. "It *is* you. Glad to see you."[11]

The vertigo is funny in "Pooh Goes Visiting and Gets Into a Tight Place" precisely because everyone can get off the merry-go-round and see that Pooh is Pooh and Rabbit remains Rabbit. One could make the same point about *Alice In Wonderland,* for in much comedy, the humor requires a shared assumption that personal identity is mutable but enduring, "everchanging . . . neverchanging" (17:2309–10). Polytropic Odysseus knows and demonstrates his identity, as do the temporarily puzzled characters in *A Comedy of Errors.* Indeed, the entanglements of Shakespearean comedies would be quite pointless, neither plangent nor amusing, if "self" were determined merely by role, costume, or situation, or imagined only as a provisional fictive construct. Viola's double entendres, foibles, and dilemmas require what *Twelfth Night* so throughly provides—a clear sense of her fundamental identity. Even the farci-

---

[11]A. A. Milne, *Winnie-the-Pooh* (London: Methuen Children's Books, 1973), 22–24. Why has no one noticed the striking connections between Joyce and Milne? "Pooh! Buck Mulligan said" (1:554).

cal mystification of those Ionesco figures in *The Bald Soprano* who meet on the train, make each other's acquaintance, and discover ridiculously slowly that they are married, depends on their having selves to lose.

Since comic writers regularly violate rules, it is nearly always foolhardy to generalize too confidently about what comedy "requires" or "does." Mindful that today's regulators are tomorrow's Malvolios, let me offer exceptions to my principle of enduring comic identity. *Finnegans Wake* and the fictions of Samuel Beckett might be said to deconstruct selfhood. In *Molloy*, for example, the self seems freed, or bereft, of its defining contingencies, so that, in Leo Bersani's fine phrase, we encounter not characters, but an "infinite geometry of relational play."[12] All reality appears provisional, suspect, including, or perhaps especially, those dubious and tenuous constructions we call selves: "Chameleon in spite of himself, there you have Molloy, viewed from a certain angle. . . . And even my sense of identity was wrapped in a namelessness often hard to penetrate, as we have just seen I think."[13] He can't remember his name, and the notion of narrative reliability and coherence is a joke. In discourse of "pure sounds, free of all meaning," where whatever is inscribed is erased, selfhood can only be contrived: "If I go on long enough calling that my life I'll end up believing it." The process of composing erodes identity: "But it is useless to drag out this chapter of my, how shall I say, my existence, for it has no sense, to my mind." Without prior grounding, and even before the arrival of Moran, all Molloy's utterances are self-parody: "That's a fairly good caricature of my state of mind at that instant." Moran more or less becomes Molloy, and the reader eventually recognizes himself as a "Moran," in quest of a "Molloy" who can never be apprehended. The text ends with the famous conclusion that it is midnight and it is raining, and that it is not midnight and not raining.[14] Molloy/Moran shares with the narrators of "Eumaeus" and *Finnegans Wake* the predilec-

---

[12]Leo Bersani, "Against *Ulysses*," *Raritan* 8 (1988): 20.

[13]Samuel Beckett, *Three Novels by Samuel Beckett: "Molloy," "Malone Dies," "The Unnamable"* (New York: Grove Press, 1965), 30. Subsequent passages from 31, 50, 53, 56, and 63.

[14]Cf. the zany footnote in *Watt*: "Haemophilia is, like enlargement of the prostate, an exclusively male disorder. But not in this work." Samuel Beckett, *Watt* (New York: Grove Press, 1959), 102.

tion for self-correction, self-contradiction, and irreducible inef-
fability: "I swear my gots how I'm not meself at all, no jolly
fear . . . " (*FW* 487:17–18); in such texts, compendia of the possible, self-representation can only be, in Molloy's phrase, "simple
supposition, committing me to nothing," for there is no *there*
there.[15] David Hayman nicely describes such flaunting of indeter-
minacy as "suspension of the suspension of disbelief,"[16] and Beckett
himself famously affirmed his dedication to "the expression that
there is nothing to express, *nothing from which to express,* no power
to express, no desire to express, together with the obligation to
express" (my emphasis).[17]

Ulysses, I argue, is not quite so radical, though it contains "Eumaeus" and other self-annihilating tendencies; it proposes a plethora
of suppositions, committing itself to nothing in particular on the
nature of personal identity, willing to make hay of either belief or
disbelief. It has both Beckett's "geometry of relational play" and the
"conservative ideology of the self" Bersani attributes to Joyce.[18] On
this subject, as on every other, we may select from an encyclopedic
range of entries, or prefer one voice from the medley. If we wish to
explore identity as a philosophic problem deserving precise scrutiny,
we will naturally incline toward Stephen Dedalus, whose "views are
most illuminating" (9:328) but, we must remember, never fully
authoritative, and often simply silly.

In "Scylla and Charybdis," Stephen provides a fairly straightfor-
ward and surprisingly traditional conception of personal identity. Its
essence emerges in comic form when he imagines a way to evade his
debt: "Wait, Five months. Molecules all change. I am other now.
Other I got pound" (9:205–6). Aware of his self-sophistry ("Buzz.
Buzz."), he considers the serious philosophical problem of how to
conceive continuity or identity through change: "But I, entelechy,
form of forms, am I by memory because under everchanging forms"
(9:207, 208–9). Always changing, moving toward his ultimate
form, he retains an essential selfhood by means of memory; Stephen
thus reaffirms both common sense and the arguments of Aristotle,
Augustine, and Locke. He then gives an example of memories that

[15]Beckett, *Three Novels,* 82.

[16]David Hayman, "Joyce → Beckett/Joyce," in *The Seventh of Joyce,* ed.
Bernard Benstock (Bloomington: Indiana University Press, 1982), 38.

[17]Samuel Beckett, "Three Dialogues," in *Proust and Three Dialogues with
Georges Duthuit* (London: Calder & Boyars, 1969), 103.

[18]Bersani, "Against *Ulysses,*" 20, 29.

define him: "I that sinned and prayed and fasted," and "A child Conmee saved from pandies" (9:210–11), scenes memorably dramatized in *A Portrait*. The paradox that we remain the same through change is summarized pithily: "I, I and I. I." (9:212). A gloss by James A. Snead is apposite: here Stephen "finds identity not unitary but myriad."[19] Exactly so: not "wholly a function of differences within a system,"[20] not quite infinite or ineffable, but myriad. In good jocoserious fashion, Stephen's conclusion is capped with a punning jest: "A. E. I. O. U." (9:213).

Stephen construes personal identity as same and different, like and unlike, requiring both wit and judgment to discern the potential parallels and antitheses. This oxymoronic notion of "indentity" extends beyond selfhood to Stephen's penchant for allusions and puns. "Scylla and Charybdis," as the literary episode, is more properly allusive than any other, chock full of bits of other texts; almost everything that Stephen says includes a word or phrase from a Shakespeare play. As an echo requires us to hear words twice, to remember where they originated and to wonder why they are repeated, so allusions do double service, retaining their original identity and becoming something new. In this sense, echoes and allusions are structurally comparable to puns, also abundant in "Scylla and Charybdis," in that they convey both an original and a transmuted meaning. Thus "A. E. I. O. U." lists the five vowels in alphabetical order, and provides the necessary conclusion to Stephen's syllogism: if I am an enduring self, and if that self owes A. E. a pound, then Q.E.D.: A. E. I. O. U.[21]

[19] James A. Snead, "Some Prefatory Remarks on Character in Joyce," in *James Joyce: The Augmented Ninth,* ed. Bernard Benstock, 139.

[20] This is Saussure's conception of identity, defined by Jonathan Culler in *Ferdinand de Saussure,* revised ed. (Ithaca: Cornell University Press, 1986), 38.

[21] The best puns seem natural, a twinning of two distinct discourses. For example, when Stephen is about to leave the library, he thinks, "My will: his will that fronts me" (9:1202), referring literally to the struggle between himself and Buck Mulligan, and metaphorically to his invention of "my will," his version of Shakespeare. When a term in a pun carries no particular primary meaning or association, the pun deteriorates into weak wit, also evident in this episode: "A shrew, John Eglinton said shrewdly" (9:232) or "Mr Secondbest Best said finely" (9:714–15). In such instances, the key word is reinvoked gratuitously, without stretching us between disparate yet relevant implications. (As I argued earlier, that Stephen is capable even of lame-witted wordplay indicates progression away from his morning rigidity and toward Mulligan-like verbal antics.)

Stephen maintains an essentially Romantic conception of the artist as the source and medium of creation.[22] Citing Shelley's famous image of the fading coal and recalling Aristotle, he concludes, "that which I was is that which I am and that which in possibility I may come to be" (9:382–83). In other words, the self retains its elemental form through growth and development, and this coherence will prevail through future change. "So in the future, the sister of the past, I may see myself as I sit here now but by reflection from that which then I shall be." (9:383–85). In such comments, Joyce endows Stephen with confidence that he will one day become the maker capable of integrating and viewing everything from a different, higher vantage point. It is of course an optimistic theory, supremely protective and assertive, one that a young artist, but perhaps not jocoserious "riddlemakers" (15:1435), may need to believe: "A man of genius makes no mistakes. His errors are volitional and are the portals of discovery" (9:228–29). Phrases like "a man of genius" and "portals of discovery," in their magnification of the artist and hint of infinite vistas, have an unmistakable nineteenth-century flavor. At the same time, in another Romantic tendency especially evident in Shelley and Byron, Stephen perceives the self as remarkably vulnerable, never able to transcend experience, so that the seduction of young Shakespeare had irreparable consequences: "No later undoing will undo the first undoing" (9:459). Perhaps the most Romantic aspect of Stephen's theory is the perpetually autobiographical nature of the artist's discourse: "That is why the speech . . . is always turned elsewhere, backward" (9:471–72), toward the original wound or grievance. The difference between a mere mortal and a great artist is of course the imaginative uses to which the writer puts the pain: "because loss is his gain, he passes on towards eternity in undiminished personality, untaught by the wisdom he has written or by the laws he has revealed" (9:476–78).

Stephen's premises about selfhood, that the self is always evolving and in flux but still "ineluctably preconditioned" (15:2120–21), are consistent with what Stanislaus Joyce specified as the organizing principle of *Portrait,* "the idea . . . that a man's character, like his body, develops from an embryo with constant traits" (S. Joyce 17).

---

[22]So fully delineated by M. H. Abrams in *The Mirror and the Lamp: Romantic Theory and the Critical Tradition.*

In several compelling but inconclusive ways, *Ulysses* also conveys Stephen's traditional notion of personal identity, though now the possibilities are comically multiplied and contradicted. Consider again the prominence and implications of allusion. Several references to *A Portrait of the Artist as a Young Man,* such as the pandying, proclaim that one artist wrote this book and a previous book in which the same character appears, and that the two books, like the protagonists they characterize, have a continuous identity. Other allusions, more puzzling, reinforce the way the "speech . . . is always turned elsewhere, backwards," for this text includes titbits not only from the previous fictions, but from the life of James Joyce. Such cryptic, inscrutable references encourage us to conceive this text, like Stephen's self, as both "I, I and I. I."—autonomous yet contingent, somehow both myriad and unitary. As if to verify Stephen's assumption that artistic creation has its origins in real experience, "Scylla and Charybdis" (like the whole book, but especially here) bears numerous marks of contingency: names of real people, authors, titles, places, and private references all suggest that the relationship between life and art is the theme of the episode, appropriately introduced in Lyster's opening remark: "as one sees in real life" (9:4).[23]

Some of the ways in which Joyce makes himself, his other texts, and his life (including some obscure and other perhaps irrecoverable details) prominent elements of *Ulysses,* though they bear on the question of personal identity, are unsettling because they defy the formalist notion of a text as an autonomous verbal construct, a phrase that formerly fell more trippingly off the tongue. Amid his Shakespeare lecture, for example, Stephen says, "A brother is as easily forgotten as an umbrella," and thinks, "Where is your brother? Apothecaries' hall. My whetstone" (9:975–77). Knowing that Stanislaus Joyce held a clerkship there may not satisfactorily account, in intrinsic terms, for this extraneous reference to a brother of whom we otherwise never hear in *Ulysses.* Similarly, Stephen thrice alludes obscurely to Cranly, challenging us to recognize biographical material that never made it into *A Portrait.* Such gratuitous

---

[23]Insistence on such traces of real life bothered Joyce's publishers, not to mention people forced to play roles in his books. The real Richard Best, in a proclamation of identity worthy of any fabulist, was constrained to protest, "I am not a character in a fiction. I am a living human being" (Ellmann 363–64).

violations of the fiction, or transgressions of the boundary between author and narrator, have always vexed even sympathetic readers. Edmund Wilson complained that once "we are aware of Joyce himself systematically embroidering on his text . . . the illusion of the dream is lost."[24] The confounding presence of "Joyce himself" also disturbs Robert M. Adams, who objects to the way Joyce "intrudes, frequently, as an autobiographical fact which is beyond fictional explanation." Joyce "is present," says Adams, "as an unexplained animus; he omits, arranges, and juxtaposes elements; and occasionally, to remind us of his power, he appears as an agent of confusion, bafflement, and deliberate frustration."[25]

Precisely the elements Wilson and Adams regret I regard as manifestations of author *ludens,* like the Gracehoper, "always jigging ajog, hoppy on akkant of his joyicity" (*FW* 414:22–23). I take "joyicity" to be a revelation of Joyce's comic presence and a proclamation that the author's joyous spirit will continue to hop up, like Tim Finnegan: "Bedad he revives, see how he rises!"

There have always been readers, including very thoughtful ones, who object to fiction that acknowledges that it is playing make-believe and asserts the reality of the author. Henry James deplored authorial intrusions breaking the illusion of verisimilitude, and ignored the possibility that intrusion might contribute to a comic enterprise quite different from the great tradition he himself exemplified. "Joyicity" gestures toward a reality outside of and preceding the fiction, winking at the reader, indicating that we can never fully recuperate or fathom what we are reading, because the boundaries between imagined discourse and history are comically porous; nothing, not personal identity, a text, or reality itself, is so simply one thing. The formulaic Arabic expression, that this happened and did not happen, recalls the "easily forgotten" Stanislaus's remark that his brother was always confessing, but in another language. Here, too, Joyce follows the example of Laurence Sterne, who did quick-change acts with his autobiographical personae: one of his fictive characters even delivers a sermon originally given by the

[24]Edmund Wilson, *Axel's Castle,* 235. Wilson is here referring to *Finnegans Wake,* but his point is that the later book "exaggerates the qualities we have noted in 'Ulysses'" (233).

[25]Adams, *Surface and Symbol,* 185. S. L. Goldberg also observed "a hidden character: *the author himself,*" distinct from the real James Joyce and his variety of personae, "but Joyce the artistic or poetic personality whose voice has completely passed into his work" (Goldberg, *The Classical Temper,* 35).

Reverend Sterne at the cathedral church at York. After his great success, the author alternately introduced himself as "Tristram Shandy," and vehemently denied the connection, depending on his circumstances and needs at the moment.

Works in the great comic tradition of Cervantes, Rabelais, Fielding, Sterne, Beckett, and Joyce constantly flout the "illusion of the dream," with variations on Puck's final recognition that he is only a "shadow." What Henry James considered a "betrayal of a sacred office"[26] exactly characterizes the Puckish comic enterprise of a writer such as Henry Fielding. Instead of the Jamesian pretense that this "history" of Tom Jones actually happened, Fielding stresses that he is telling a story—a rigorously controlled narrative, parceled into books and scenes. Fielding suavely reminds us, at every anxious moment, that he is there to manipulate all the strings. He pretends that strange "Accidents" are responsible for the characters' fates, but destiny is ultimately controlled by the author, as he expects us to realize very quickly. What looks like Accident is actually Comic Fortune, determined by Fielding's providential presence.

Of course, the distinctions between the Joycean and Fielding-esque "second selves" are every bit as crucial as their comic kinship. The most obvious difference is that Fielding sustains a stable, coherent, consistent narrative identity, while Joyce metamorphoses into many narrative guises, in accordance with his comic principle of proliferent continuance. The second major difference between Joyce and his comic predecessors is that he projects what Adams calls "the autobiographical fact" of his presence less often and less obviously. Yet Joyce implicitly and intermittently leaves traces of his ludic identity, a diminished but real presence, making comic turns in James's "sacred office," "whether it be thumbprint, mademark or just a poor trait of the artless," as he puns in *Finnegans Wake* (114:31–32). Joyicity thus illustrates a version of personal identity, affording us glimpses of its author, nowhere to be seen, everywhere present, like Shakespeare "a ghost, a shadow now" (9:479–80). Whatever happened to the actual James Augustine Joyce (1882–1939), this purveyor of joyicity is subject to the laws of folly, drawing all things down and up: in this sense the author becomes a series of parodic "selves," perpetually sacrificed and redeemed.

Joyce implies "his own" continuing presence even in Molly's apparently unmediated soliloquy, in some coy allusions that suggest

[26]Henry James, "The Art of Fiction," in *The Portable Henry James,* 394.

the author's implicit, if discreet, propinquity. Remembering some girlish exhibitionism, Molly is "sure that fellow opposite used to be there the whole time watching" (18:920–21), thus intuiting her fictiveness and recognizing her author. Another gesture toward the author is, "where do those old fellows get all the words they have omissions with his shortsighted eyes on me cocked sideways" (18:1170–71). And there is Molly's celebrated address to her maker, "O Jamesy let me up out of this" (18:1128–29). Despite the elaborate pretense of absence, so thorough that the sound of a train's whistle is almost intrusive, the textuality in "Penelope" is signified by signs that this narrative is a composition, not merely recorded consciousness. For instance, Molly mentions "Xmas" (18:453), a word nobody uses except as a shorthand for writing "Christmas." She, or someone, twice corrects her spelling with a slash through incorrect letters in "sympkathy" (18:730) and "newphew" (18:730). "Penelope" thus impersonates an "unmediated" speaker, but reveals an author continuing to play peek-a-boo, so that we continue unto the last to be surprised by joys.[27]

Such thumbprints upon the pages of *Ulysses* remind the reader that this work is an artifact, produced by an artificer, some "neverchanging everchanging" (17:233–34) self. In calling the implied author "Joyce" I do not imagine that James Joyce is somehow directly available in his text—but I do wish to suggest that some recognizable, coherent, continuous spirit enforces its presence in a comically shrunken yet persistent way. In playing bo-peep, *Ulysses* suggests that its author inhabits the text merely as another of its many voices. "It is not that the author cannot 'come back' into the Text . . . however, he can only do so as a 'guest,' so to speak" as Roland Barthes puts it, "his signature is no longer privileged and paternal, the locus of genuine truth, but rather ludic. He becomes a 'paper author': his life is no longer the origin of his fables, but a fable that runs concurrently with his work. There is a reversal"—one that, I'd argue, particularly appealed to Antic Joyce and helps account for the unaccountable autobiographical allusions, "and it is the work which affects the life, not the life which affects the work."[28]

---

[27]Paul de Man, in a phrase relevant here, notes "the fallacy of unmediated expression," in *Blindness and Insight: Essays in the Rhetoric of Contemporary Criticism* (New York: Oxford University Press, 1971), 17.

[28]Roland Barthes, "From Work to Text," in *Textual Strategies: Perspectives in Post-Structuralist Criticism,* ed. Josué V. Harari (Ithaca: Cornell University Press, 1979), 78–79.

We have intimations of authorial presence even when we are inside the consciousness of an individual character, as in "Scylla and
Charybdis," in which the point of view seems to be Stephen's, yet
the narration is much more flamboyantly inflected than in "Proteus," and far more playfully composed than Stephen would have
occasion to organize in the heat of performance. Some Master of
the Revels seems to preside, organizing and dramatizing events—
placing that *"Entr' acte"* (9:484) fortuitously near the middle of the
episode, just when Stephen has delivered himself of a major point.
As I have contended, Stephen has no way of knowing that the
episode is about halfway completed, nor that his words at this juncture foreshadow Bloom's passage between himself and Buck at the
end of the chapter. The arrangement of characters, the suggestion
that events are determined by some overseer, is remarkably thorough. Right before Bloom passes out between Stephen and Buck,
Stephen is conscious of "feeling one behind" (9:1197), just as he
thought "Behind. Perhaps there is someone" (3:502) at the conclusion of "Proteus," as an intuition of the proximity of "Mr Leopold
Bloom" (4:1). One could make a similar observation about the oft-
noticed reappearances of Gerard of Fetter lane: either Bloom and
Stephen share some inconceivably specific memory, or the material
belongs to the novel's persisting consciousness.

More striking still are the writer's antics in "Scylla and Charybdis." While Stephen is playing with Shakespearean themes and
language, the text is also capering. This Shakespearean chapter
seems to have spawned a court jester who usurps the role of play-
wright, staging a scene with speakers and stage directions (9:893–
934). Perhaps the most flagrant intrusion, drawing attention away
from the characters and toward the presentation of the narrative, is
the bizarre but rarely remarked-on typographical oddity, ending:

Punkt.

> Leftherhis
> Secondbest
> Leftherhis
> Bestabed
> Secabest
> Leftabed.

Woa! (9:700–707)

At this point we are evidently not auditors at a discussion, but readers of a text that has been arranged by an author and left to its fate. If this is Stephen's consciousness, no one has satisfactorily explained why or how. It is true that Stephen is manic throughout the episode, sometimes excitedly saying things that have mainly private reference, such as "Lizzie, grandpa's lump of love, and nuncle Richie" (9:1039). The more obvious explanation for such nonsense is that Antic Joyce is clowning around, as he will do more and more often after this *"Entr' acte,"* reminding his reader that behind all his roles there is a magisterial player, but one who cannot or will not impose his monolithic authorial presence: "he has hidden his own name, a fair name . . . in the plays, a super here, a clown there, as a painter of old Italy set his face in a dark corner of his canvas" (9:921–23).

To put the case in these terms is to recognize that in clowning, and in making cameo appearances or comic resurrections, Joyce belies Stephen's prescription for the author's disappearance. Yet even that famous Flaubertian credo reveals not pure absence but hints of continued presence, for Stephen never pronounces the death of the author: "the personality of the artist passes into the narration itself, flowing round and round the persons and the action like a vital sea." The author, "within or behind or beyond or above his handiwork" (*P* 215), is not quite "refined out of existence," but leaves discernible traces: *within, behind, beyond,* not banished, extirpated, or annihilated. Thus Stephen's aesthetic implies a godlike artist nowhere visible but everywhere present. As Joyce remarked in a letter, "it seems that in certain cases absence is the highest form of presence."[29] Or, as the teller of *Finnegans Wake* grunts, "Say . . . who in hallhagal wrote the durn thing anyhow?" (*FW* 107:36–108:1).

At his best, Joyce has things both ways. His masterful evocation of individual consciousness, and the fluent movement into and out of characters' perspectives, sustains the dimension of contingency, the illusion that life is happening, or could happen, just like this. Yet, simultaneously with this natural or realistic drama, countless details evince the dyer's hand. The novel's episodic organization and multiple correspondences never let us forget that we are reading discourse, massively determined, inflected, structured. Even veteran

[29]This is Ellmann's translation of Joyce's Italian (*L* 3:357).

readers can be surprised and delighted to discover how wittily Joyce carries out the systematic correspondences: when Bloom thinks, "Felt so off colour" (8:854–55), he idiomatically and appropriately characterizes his gloom in the episode without a designated color. The very phrase "retrospective sort of arrangement" (11:798) is an apt expression of joyicity, in that it is introduced naturally and casually, by the men in the hearse mocking a pompous friend's expression; it is typical that a phrase introduced in mockery becomes one of the text's phrases of self-definition. Similarly and effectively, when Father Cowley urges Simon to "play it in the original" (11:602), he is also giving voice to our nostalgic longing for the original narrative mode of the novel.

Anyone who has read Stephen's Shakespeare theory sympathetically would expect to find *Ulysses* full of autobiographical references, in-jokes, and self-reflexive commentary. There is considerable difference, though, between Stephen's theory and the novel's usual practice, for Stephen regards Shakespeare's works as haunted by spectres, obsessed with trauma and conflict from the author's life, while in *Ulysses* allusions to the author and his enterprise are more often ludic.[30] Joyce seems to have attained the state that Yeats evokes at the end of "Lapis Lazuli," in which the artist can contemplate all ephemeral things, including himself and his works, with comic detachment: "All things fall and are built again, / And those that build them are gay." This is what Santayana meant when, in the same year *Ulysses* was published, he concluded that "everything in nature is lyrical in its ideal essence, tragic in its fate, and comic in its existence."[31]

To this we should add, "and antic in its tendency." Certainly the nature of personal identity in *Ulysses* requires some such supplement, for Buck's comically destabilizing and fructifying influence begins to be felt powerfully in "Scylla and Charybdis" and dominantly in "Sirens." Among the games played by the maniacal narrator of that episode is hide-and-seek, confounding identity. We can no longer be quite sure of locating the characters—as in the opening scene, wherein Misses Kennedy and Douce, barmaids at the Or-

[30]Joyce probably liked the fact that "allusion" and "ludic" share a common root.

[31]George Santayana, "The Comic Mask," in *Comedy: Meaning and Form,* ed. Robert W. Corrigan (New York: Harper & Row, 1981), 56.

mond Hotel, pass time by deriding passersby. Their first target, "the fellow in the tall silk" (11:70), is Gerald Ward in the viceroy's parade, but he is associated by an interpolation with "a man" (11:85) identified as "Bloowho" (11:86).[32] Then the ladies turn their scorn to "that old fogey" (11:124) in the pharmacy, who is also connected or elided with our hero because, in the middle of their conversation, the narrator asks, "But Bloom?" (11:133). "Sirens" deliberately confuses matters, when Miss Kennedy asks, "Will you ever forget his goggle eye?" (11:146) by drawing attention to that feature of Bloom's so often remarked this day: "old sloppy eyes," "Cod's eye," and so on. Directly we return to Bloom's consciousness, also groping for names and identities: "Bloowhose dark eye read Aaron Figatner's name. Why do I always think Figather?" (11:149–50).

The comic epithet "Greaseabloom" (11:185, etc.), punning on "Greasy I" (11:176),[33] typifies the slippery nature of identity in "Sirens." In a conversation to which Bloom is not privy, Ben Dollard, Father Cowley, and Simon Dedalus recall the night Dollard turned to the Blooms to borrow some pants; two pages later, Bloom happens to remember the same episode, in language that calls attention to the coincidence. Molly was laughing at the ill fit that put "all his belongings on show" (11:557): "O, saints above, I'm drenched!" (11:557–58) is presumably Bloom's memory of Molly's delight— except that it echoes (again almost exactly) Miss Douce, before Bloom entered the bar (11:181). Like so many other refrains in this chapter of the "Echo" (11:634), this blends Molly and Miss Douce, or blurs the distinction of identity. "Character," as we initially and confidently conceived it in this novel, comically disintegrates in a number of bizarre developments, such as the displacement of a piece of Stephen's consciousness (the bit about Gerard) into Bloom's mind. By the time Bloom makes his exit from the Ormond bar, he is dubbed "Henry Lionel Leopold dear Henry Flower earnestly Mr Leopold Bloom" (11:1261–62), which suggests the chapter's—

[32]Shari Benstock and Bernard Benstock, in *Who's He When He's at Home: A James Joyce Directory* (Urbana: University of Illinois Press, 1980), 25, observe that "the 'Bloowhose' mentioned here is *not* the object of the barmaids' derision, despite the persistent misreading of the passage that occurs."

[33]"Greasy" in Irish pronunciation rhymes with "daisy" and thus reinforces Bloom's role as holy fool.

and, increasingly, the novel's—technique of accretion. Another source of comic discombobulation in "Sirens" is play with names in general and Bloom's name in particular. In the overture to "Sirens," our hero's very name is trumpeted and subjected to elaborate variations: "Blew. Blue Bloom is on the. . . . Bloo. Bloomed . . . So lonely blooming" (11:6, 19, 32). Reliable facts, even basic identity—"Is that a fact?" Simon Dedalus asks twice (11:279, 282)—yield to interpretations, renderings, renditions—perhaps like a piece of music.

Who is "Bloowho" (11:86)? Is he the character whom many readers claim to know and love better than any other in literature: "His moral nature is simple and lovable. Many have found him a dear man, a dear person" (15:1799–1800)?[34] Or merely a sound, an arbitrary signifier? The question "Who are you? Do you know him?" (15:4784), implicit throughout "Sirens," becomes explicit and raucous in "Circe." Deploring unity, stability, and coherence, "Circe" mounts a "seriocomic" (15:447) satire of personal identity, dramatizing the carnivalesque nature of selfhood. Like the episode itself, identity now appears to be a potpourri of acts: not a harmony, nor even a medley, merely a comic cacophony. Under any conventional notion of "self," "Circe" pulls out the rug or lays down a banana peel.

Bloom's is not the only identity to melt in "Circe." The Fan, like a long-lost love, asks Bloom, "Have you forgotten me?" Naturally confused and perpetually ambivalent, Bloom replies, "Nes. Yo" (15:2764–66). The Fan then poses the discombobulating questions raised by the whole chapter: "Is me her was you dreamed before? Was then she him you us since knew? Am all them and the same now me?" (15:2768–69). Well, who knows? Molly, for instance, scarcely resembles the Molly we "knew," as signaled by her appearance not as "Molly" but as Boylan's correspondent "Marion," in a farce recalling *Pierrot Le Fou*. The Marion who cavorts with Boylan, a performance calculated to punish her husband—"Let him look . . . And scourge himself!" (15:3778)—is not the "same" Molly who conceals her love letter and harbors mixed feelings about

---

[34]Surely the most endearing critical remark made by Harold Bloom is his characterization of Leopold Bloom as "the most lovable person in Western fiction." See Bloom's introduction in *James Joyce: Modern Critical Views*, ed. Harold Bloom (New York: Chelsea House, 1986), 3.

adultery; that she refers to Boylan as "Raoul, darling" (15:3770) indicates the extent to which she is a figure in Bloom's fantasy or a fabliaux tenuously connected to the rest of the story, for Molly has not yet seen *The Sweets of Sin.*

If "Sirens" is a wild echo-chamber, "Circe" is a hall of mirrors, where twins and doubles proliferate. The carnival logic seems to be that if the self is not a stable, continuous entity, it can find its image or double everywhere and anywhere, including incongruous places: THE SOAP sings, "We're a capital couple are Bloom and I" (15:338). On the Circean stage the Bohee brothers do a turn (15:412–26), as do Philip Drunk and Philip Sober. P. Drunk mentions "Reduplication of personality" (15:2523) and the feeling of being "here before" (15:2525). Besides the actual twins and doubles, we have numerous submerged references, like Jimmy Henry's announcement that the Court of Conscience is now open: "Free medical and legal advice, solution of doubles and other problems" (15:1630–31). Or Ben Dollard's question in Court, "When twins arrive?" (15:1669). The title of Bloom's "High School play *Vice Versa*" (15:3010–11), could be the subtitle of "Circe," in which so much is (as Bello says) "turn about" (15:3178). Stephen, who finds his double (one might say) in his opposite Bloom, ends the chapter on the ground, *"sighing, doubling himself together"* (15:4934).

An example of the carnivalesque confusion of Circean selfhood occurs when Martha appears, addressing her penpal as "Henry! Leopold! Lionel, thou lost one! Clear my name" (15:753–54). We are reminded that however intimate their correspondence may be, she does not even know his real name. Here she apparently discovers it—in one of the many recognition scenes in "Circe"—only to have it slip away from her into the opera with which she shares a name, bits of which we heard in "Sirens." Since "Martha" means both Bloom's correspondent and a character in an opera (in which the heroine is *disguised* as "Martha"), it is appropriate that she call Bloom by the name of the opera's hero, Lionel. And it is apt on two counts that Bloom be addressed as "thou lost one": that is the role he plays as her penpal, and he is certainly lost in Nighttown. Martha ends her apostrophe with a demand that Bloom clear her name.[35] Since all considerations of personal identity in "Circe" lead not

[35] Just as her letter moved quickly from compassion to egocentricity: "Are you not happy . . . tell me what you think of poor me" (5:246–48).

toward recognition but toward confusion, Bloom, trying to evade her, uses the well-worn excuse, "Mistaken identity" (15:760).

As in "Sirens," names in "Circe" are a very important source of comic confusion. Bloom's name is constantly pronounced, echoed, disguised, and parodied: "Bang Bang Bla Bak Blud Bugg Bloo" (15:189), "the new Bloomusalem" (15:1544), "a bloom of edelweiss" (15:1032), the "flower that bloometh" (15:2489–90), "gibbering, Booloohoom" (15:3044–45), "Bloombella" (15:4122), "Stop Bloom! Stopabloom!" (15:4363), and "Bloom, in gloom, looms down" (15:4888). Like Tennyson's Ulysses, our hero has become a name—and a word, or a phoneme. But a name in "Circe" is less likely to guarantee identity than to serve as a gag. Names seem as arbitrary as the hundreds of costumes characters don and discard. When The First Watch demands Bloom's "name and address" (15:718), he claims to have "forgotten for the moment" (15:720). He pretends to be the other Bloom, the dentist mentioned in "Wandering Rocks" (10:246–48), but the Watch finds the hidden card "identifying" him as "Henry Flower." Pressed, Bloom produces "the flower in question. It was given me by a man I don't know his name" (15:738–39). To fend off the Watch, Bloom improvises another role, that of confidante: "Bloom. The change of name. Virag" (15:740–41), yet another response to the simple query, "who are you?" Eventually, Bloom is sacrificed, receives elaborate funeral obsequies, and is no sooner gone than forgotten—only to return with a joke: "I felt it was expected of me. Force of habit" (15:3243). It's a good jocoserious jest, in that Bloom is true to comic form, his rolypoly resilience, while spoofing the episode's pattern and the reader's expectation of yet another comic resurrection.

Though Bloom is always on stage in "Circe," his identity appears more precarious than ever. Even while depicting his client as an utterly conventional character, J. J. O'Molloy defines Bloom as "Not all there, in fact" (15:955). Although he claims to know Bloom in some privileged sense—"When the angel's book comes to be opened . . . " (15:1001)—what he says is blarney, a whimsical rush of clichés and contradictions. Bloom himself is of course assumed to have only biased or inadmissible evidence: "The accused will now make a bogus statement" (15:896–97). Bloom can't even deliver a coherent self-defense—a self being a prerequisite for self-defense—only a "long unintelligible speech" (15:899).

Further elaboration on Bloom's elusiveness comes in the medical testimony by the doctors. Bloom becomes another personified oxymoron who belies Dixon's conclusion that "his moral nature is simple" (15:1799). While certain epithets, such as "the new womanly man" or "perversely idealistic" (15:1798–99, 1781), are apposite, much of the diagnosis is madcap *Alice in Wonderland* stuff, such as Mulligan's opinion that "ambidexterity is also latent" (15:1780). Contradictory himself, Bloom is here the cause of contradiction in other men. His mock-biblical genealogy includes wheezes such as "Weiss begat Schwarz" (15:1860) (white begat black), and the name of an American comic-strip character.

Earlier in the novel, Bloom's very mutability had a certain consistency, so that we might have described him as versatile, adaptable, a man of many turns. In "Circe," though, these tendencies run rampant (like the stage directions in "Circe") so that he is whatever he plays, whatever the skit requires, or whatever people call him—in effect, a *tabula rasa* on which anyone can write. THE CRIER declares, "Whereas Leopold Bloom of no fixed abode is a wellknown dynamitard, forger, bigamist, bawd and cuckold" (15:1158–59), a list that contains one metaphorically true charge, one widespread rumor, and four manifestly silly accusations. Elsewhere Bloom is called, aptly if hyperbolically, "the world's greatest reformer" (15:1459), "an anythingarian" (15:1712), "a dear man" (15:1800), and "more sinned against than sinning" (15:1783). More outrageously, though, he is also termed "Stage Irishman!" (15:1729), "the funniest man on earth" (15:1737), and "a very posthumous child" (15:1808–9). It is characteristic of "Circe" that the absurd designation "Stage Irishman" is momentarily accurate, for at one point Bloom becomes exactly that (15:1960–68). He is truly an anythingarian.

But no designation in "Circe" sticks. Playing with Mrs. Breen, Bloom reenacts an old parlor game, in which the word *teapot* is substituted for important words in the sentence. Bloom says more cogently than he realizes, "I'm teapot . . . " because in "Circe" he *is* almost anything or anybody (15:457). On the sands of the beach, his gesture of self definition, "I AM A . . . " (13:1258, 1264) was inconclusive, we now learn to our amusement, because he is a TEAPOT. "Circe" takes to a comic extreme the multiple correspondences and metempsychoses of the whole novel, so that Bloom, regarded intermittently as Odysseus, Moses, Elijah, Christ, and so on is now seen to "resemble many historical personages" (15:1845) simultaneously; Bloom is called everything under the sun, and only subjective preferences, or the theatrical requirements of the moment, magnify some descriptions over others.

"Circe" renders the "soultransfigured and . . . soultransfiguring" (15:1002–3) nature of things and dramatizes the comic contention that personal identity is partly a function of role, significantly defined by costume. On this stage, change of sex is as easy as a change of clothing for Bella/Bello or Bloom/Blooma. Costumes represent the multiplicity of roles, the possibilities of playacting and cross-dressing, which typifies comedy from *As You Like It* to *Tootsie,* from the medieval Feast of Fools to the Halloween parade in Greenwich Village. The Homeric archetypes are polytropic Odysseus, who does everything but cross-dress, and monolithic Achilles, who for nearly all of *The Iliad* is himself only in armor.[36] If Bloom is forced to play degrading roles such as butler to Molly and Blazes or horse to Bella/Bello, he is also free, in exhilaratingly comic ways, to play *many* roles. On this subject, Kenner has a brilliant comment: "To change one must only (only!) change one's role."[37] As Kenner's rueful parenthesis reminds us, the implications for Bloom's life are unclear, but "Circe" forecloses no possibilities. Ultimately, the loss of self in "Circe" is not particularly frightening: just as Circean monsters have the papier-mâché quality of carnival props, the episode's assault upon identity is less ominous than playful, more like *Alice in Wonderland* than *The Unnamable.* I have argued that "Circe" is strangely removed from the rest of the text and does not inevitably bear upon what precedes or succeeds it. Neither Bloom nor Stephen seems to remember anything that happened in "Circe." The entire episode has the aura and transience of a dream, and the rhythm and ramifications of farce: evidently Bloom is not troubled or even puzzled by the multiplication of Circean "Blooms," or by the fact that he is construed so differently and oddly by other Circean figures such as Dr. Dixon or J. J. O'Molloy.

[36]It is true that to avoid being drafted Achilles cross-dressed in Skyros and was caught out by Odysseus, an episode that Stephen remembers in the class of "things not known: what name Achilles bore when he lived among women" (9:350–51). In *The Iliad,* though, Achilles would not be caught dead in drag. The Shakespearean models of polytropic and monolithic identity are Falstaff, who can be anybody but himself, and Hotspur, who can only be one self: "wither I must, I must" (*1H4:* II.3.108).

[37]Kenner, "Circe" (Hart and Hayman 360).

The foolish narrator of "Eumaeus" takes very seriously the carnivalesque mockery in "Circe" of coherent, stable, unified identity. Characteristically, the Penman, eager to please, tries gamely to be worthy of his authorial role, by adopting what he considers to be a sophisticated skepticism. So, he extends the zany Circean logic by zealously questioning everything and everyone. And he goes overboard, frantically and obsessively stressing the limits of perception, as though *nothing* can ever be identified clearly. Through repeated parenthetical expressions, he reminds us, with gratuitous regularity, of the transience of things: "a *quondam* friend of his father's" (16:109), "in the meanwhile" (16:211), "at present" (16:51), "what was temporarily supposed to be called coffee" (16:360), "Mr Bloom was all at sea for a moment" (16:380), "for a brief duration only" (16:698), "on the moment . . . on the moment" (16:707, 711), "a fleeting glimpse" (16:723), "now broken down and fast breaking up" (16:943), "for the time being" (16:974–75), "The eyes were surprised at this observation because as he, the person who owned them pro tem. . . . " (16:1149–50), "at the moment" (16:1479–80), and "give us this day our daily press" (16:1237–38). Sometimes the emphasis on temporality in "Eumaeus" is ludicrously inapt, as in, "Stephen . . . paused at the, for a moment, the door" (16:1706–7). Of course he means that Stephen paused momentarily, but in the context of so many urgent references to passing time, it sounds as though the door is about to melt or metamorphose. In remarking that "Eumaeus" shows that "every fleeting insight is a transitory phase in a process," Fritz Senn seems to follow the Penman too scrupulously,[38] because the cumulative effect of so many incidental reminders of ephemerality is to characterize the Penman as a crackpot, the sort of demented soul who is constantly afraid of the sun freezing or of falling into a black hole.

In his inane fashion, our Penman insists upon qualifying virtually every assertion, with phrases such as "to be sure," "as such," "not to say," "not to put too fine a point on it" (16:60), or "not by any manner of means" (16:739). Because the characters at the shelter are so full of blarney, they do need to be called to account, but not so frantically. We hear the Penman add incessantly, "if report spoke true" (16:554), "in all human probability" (16:945–46), "if the whole thing wasn't a complete fabrication from start to finish"

---

[38]Fritz Senn, *Joyce's Dislocutions,* 110.

(16:151–52), "Skin-the-Goat, assuming he was he, evidently . . . "
(16:985), giving way to "as for the lessee or keeper [Skin-the-Goat],
who probably wasn't the other person at all" (16:1048), then "the
pseudo Skin-the-etcetera" (16:1070), "if he was reliably informed"
(16:1067–68). The Penman reflects and exaggerates Bloom's skepticism to a ridiculous extent; he can barely mention anything or
anyone without a condition. Even trying to say something as simple
as, "Bloom wanted to find a taxi, assuming there was one," comes
out as radical repudiation of personal identity: "both of them being
e.d.ed, particularly Stephen, always assuming that there was such a
thing to be found" (16:17–18).

Indeed, the Penman of "Eumaeus" seems to believe that we cannot count upon the enduring identity of anything, as though every
character and thing were maddeningly "equivocal" (16:1630). It is
understandable that a reader might conclude that "in this episode, at
least, Bloom is for the most part a locus of random identities, identities which circulate around or near him but do not inhere."[39] But
the narrator of "Eumaeus" has taken the Circean carnival and the
cacophony of "Sirens," two clowning spoofs of identity, as authoritative demonstrations; his monkey-see, monkey-do is just as silly. Like
Tristram Shandy, this narrator exposes his crackbrained folly by
insistently complicating everything: even the simplest things are
perceived as confusing, as though everything were a function of
narrative, or a verbal construct, "whatever you like to call it." This
last formulation is reiterated obsessively, because to this fool, as to
Tristram Shandy, the responsibility for narrating is comically
onerous; the possibilities seem infinite: "or whatever you like to call
them" (16:854), "if I can so call it" (16:891), "or whatever you like
to call it" (16:1871).

At least arguably, identity is less confounding than the confounded narrator of "Eumaeus" would make it. Although we are far
from Homer's stable, clear, and lucid universe, where the long-gone
man of many turns can prove his identity conclusively while his wife
weaves and unweaves her tapestry to preserve her constancy, where
the reiterated epithets suggest a persistent, apprehensible continuity
beneath the flux of experience, and where a helmet is always, bright-
ly and evidently, a helmet, *Ulysses* is not yet a self-consuming artifact. That awful coffee in the cabmen's shelter, for example, may be

[39]Gerald L. Bruns, "Eumaeus" (Hart and Hayman 379).

called "whatever you like to call it," but it remains defiantly static, petrified, solidified; beneath the Penman's whimsical variations, we recognize the "whatever you call it," and wish the narrator would wake up and smell it. The arbitrary designations, aspiring toward a writer's "exquisite variations" (16:1810) or a philosopher's "best authority" (16:756), do not in themselves annihilate identity, any more than D. B. Murphy's vignette about Simon Dedalus explodes our conception of Simon Dedalus. Not everything in Joyce's comic vision is a subjective construction: to some extent, a rose is a rose and blarney is blarney.

"Ithaca" presents another daring variation in the comedy of "indentity," by inventing an apparently authoritative narrator who (or which) opposes the notion of a self. The episode looks like a catechism and sounds like an encyclopedia; "Ithaca" seems as reliable as the rock of ages, especially between the flagrantly fatuous "Eumaeus" and the emphatically subjective "Penelope." It turns out to be more wandering rocks, however—another humorous assault upon authority and a thoroughly comic treatment of personal identity. Whether "Ithaca" wants us to believe anything is dubious, but if it does, its vision of identity is summarized by what Bloom sees when he gazes in the mirror: "The image of a solitary (ipsorelative) mutable (aliorelative) man" (17:1350). He is not defined by a stable hierarchy of relationships to family and community; he is solitary and mutable—a walking contradiction, ipsorelative, "a self-contained organization of cross-references," and aliorelative, "an externally referential organization" (Gifford 588).

The idea of "Bloom" is rendered in "Ithaca" as "mutable" beyond recognition. He is understood by analogies, "known" as Henry Flower, Virag, "Everyman or Noman" (17:2008). Bloom may be magnified by analogy to resemble Odysseus, Moses, or Elijah; conversely we may "reduce Bloom . . . by elimination of all positive values to a negligible negative irrational unreal quantity" (17:1933–35)—reduced to a quantity, not an essence. With so elusive a self, Bloom is indeed hard to find; appropriately, a reward "will be paid for information leading to his discovery" (17:2004–5).

But the narrator of "Ithaca" is only one more voice in the Joycean cacophony, and not necessarily the final authority on personal identity. This narrator is a hopeless pedant, using words like *ipsorelative* and *aliorelative,* and describing Bloom's simple role-playing as "quasisimultaneous volitional quasisensations of concealed identities" (17:781–82); he is as mesmerized by his abstractions, categories, and complications as the narrator of "Eumaeus" is trapped by his skepticism. Such an alazon, or tedious blowhard, should be taken with a grain of salt, if not hooted from the stage. The deconstruction of identity in "Ithaca" has both the pertinence and silliness of folly throughout the novel, with the same confusing and amusing mixture of possibilities. As a parable of identity, we are free to choose between two of little Leopold's activities. At age eleven he published a verse that ended, "*Then please place at the end / The name of yours truly, L. Bloom*" (17:400–401), which sweetly conveys the boy's naive trust in personal identity. Soon, though, he is playing anagrams with his name (17:406–9), suggesting that selfhood is not implicit but constructed.

"Ithaca" is paradigmatic, especially of the middle and late episodes of the novel, in presenting personal identity as a comic rhapsody. If *Ulysses* maintains any fundamental premise, it is the comic conviction that nothing is absolute, including relativism—a point that periodically escapes some contemporary critics, for whom systematic repudiation of identity is thoroughly serious business. With encyclopedic inclusiveness, Joyce devises tricks, lacunae, rabbits out of hats, red herrings, blind alleys, and wild goose chases—ludic variations that could conceivably continue indefinitely or infinitely. Yet Joycean identity is also established in the early episodes as sufficiently substantial to set up these narrative games, or, to formulate it another way, to withstand the test of mockery: the comedy depends upon an interplay between the basic fact and the confounding possibilities. One might conclude that *Ulysses* resembles *Tristram Shandy* most tellingly in its unreliable narrators' attempts to deny a personal identity that somehow endures, even prevails. With jocoserious detachment and amusement, resembling Sterne's gay abandon, Joyce's various narrative shenanigans question, but do not obliterate, personal identity—just as Tristram's insistence that character is infinitely elusive never destroys the fundamental simplicity of Walter or Toby. Occasionally Bloom surprises us, as in "Cyclops," when he defines himself with uncharacteristic clarity and emphasis. Reluctant to express Jewish affinity with his butcher, this son of a man who converted, who himself knows little about Judaism, in the obviously hostile environment of "Cyclops," boldly proclaims himself "a jew" (12:1808).[40] The "Bloom" of, say, "Hades," is relatively

---

[40]See Ira B. Nadel, *Joyce and the Jews: Culture and Texts* (Iowa City: University of Iowa Press, 1989).

timid, self-effacing, and deferential to his peers; but in "Cyclops" he moves so far toward the opposite pole that the apparently mock-heroic epithet "impervious to fear" (12:216) becomes suprisingly apt. Heretofore deferential and meek, he is suddenly brave, even reckless. In most ways, though, the Bloom of the later episodes remains the Bloom we have known. Even the hyperbolic theatrics of "Circe" exaggerate his basic tendencies toward charity, a pervasive compassion evident to a variety of narrators in "Oxen of the Sun" and antipathetic to the narrators and characters in "Cyclops."

Ulysses implies the persistence of identity through its remarkably powerful memory. Its narrators may be diverse, contradictory, and variously unreliable—lard-witted and tone-deaf like the narrator of "Eumaeus," malicious like the unnamed satirist in "Cyclops." Bloom may forget or suppress what he experienced in Nighttown—but the book as a whole has "the same consciousness" that Locke cites as the source of personal identity. Virtually nothing narrated is lost, and, as we have seen in "Circe," nearly everything returns, including apparently inconsequential titbits, asides, and throwaways. The novel is constantly recapitulating, displacing, and re-orienting materials. Often aware of itself as a literary artifact, *Ulysses* is like Stephen's "self," remembering that "that which I was is that which I am and that which in possibility I may come to be" (9:382–83). Like an artist, the text is "myriadminded" (9:769), absorbing everything, forgetting nothing. Even in its myriad guises, its multiple metamorphoses, the narrative thus maintains a relatively continuous identity, like the great writer who is "all in all" (9:1018–19). For all the discordant splitting and conflicting fragmentation, Joycean identity remains comic, humorously elusive yet fundamentally apprehensible—especially compared to a text such as Beckett's *Watt*: "it was in vain that Watt said, Pot, pot . . . For it was not a pot . . . It resembled a pot, but it was not a pot of which one could say, Pot, pot, and be comforted." For most readers of *Ulysses,* the novel's three major characters, viewed inside, outside, and from many angles, are remarkably, richly consistent. Molly, Stephen, and Bloom never forget the sources of their selfhood, which are surprisingly familiar and traditional: one's family, home (or exile), body, joys, sorrows, education, social norms, longing for love. Perhaps this is what Joyce meant when he insisted that though his techniques were complicated, his material was always simple.

Joycean identity, to the extent that we can generalize about a subject rendered so variously, is always open to reconstruction, but resists deconstruction, because it has two fundamentally comic, enduring elements: elasticity and contrariety. One last Joycean oxymoron, Stephen's lovely word "myriadislanded" (3:394), applies to the self that is both single and multiple. While Joycean comedy stresses that there is something inherently funny about being limited to a single body and consciousness and that a rigid, dogmatic, or simplistic conception of the self is ludicrous, it also shows that completely repudiating personal identity is profoundly ridiculous. Even the most rigorously skeptical philosophers sometimes seem to intuit the jocoserious nature of the self, as when the eminently lucid Locke, imagining complications to his empirical investigation of personal identity, begins to sound eerily like Tristram Shandy: "Had I the same consciousness that I saw the ark and Noah's flood, as that I saw an overflowing of the Thames last winter, or as that I write now, I could no more doubt that I that write this now, that saw the Thames overflowed last winter, and that viewed the flood at the general deluge, was the same *self,* place that self in what *substance* you please, than that I that write this am the same *myself* now whilst I write (whether I consist of all the same substance, material or immaterial, or no) that I was yesterday."[41] And David Hume, extending Locke's critique and failing to discover any logical grounds for belief in identity, at the end of his *Treatise of Human Nature,* Book 1, frankly concedes that his skeptical speculations are "manifest absurdities": "Most fortunately it happens, that since reason is incapable of dispelling these clouds, nature herself suffices to that purpose, and cures me of this philosophical melancholy and delirium, either by relaxing this bent of mind, or by some avocation, and lively impression of my senses, which obliterate all these chimeras. I dine, I play a game of back-gammon, I converse, and am merry with my friends; and when after three or four hours' amusement, I wou'd return to these speculation, they appear so cold, and strain'd, and ridiculous, that I cannot find in my heart to enter into them any farther."[42] Hume's redemption by Nature, the lifesaving instinct to eat, play, and be merry, has a marked comic emphasis,

[41]John Locke, *An Essay concerning Human Understanding,* ed. A. S. Pringle-Pattison (Oxford: Clarendon Press, 1924), 193–94.

[42]David Hume, *A Treatise of Human Nature,* ed. L. A. Selby-Bigge (Oxford: Clarendon Press, 1967), 268.

strikingly apt for adversaries of identity and students of folly: "If I must be a fool, as all those who reason or believe any thing *certainly* are, my follies shall at least be natural and agreeable."[43]

Folly Am I Writing?

Perhaps inadvertently, Stephen conveys a vision of reading and writing as folly—for the fate of an author, as he renders it, is apotheosis and degradation. Though he imagines writers such as Shakespeare passing on "towards eternity in undiminished personality" (9: 476–77), Stephen's Shakespeare is a comic caricature, a hapless victim, seduced, manipulated, and betrayed by Anne Hathaway: "Father, Word, and Holy Breath. Allfather, the heavenly man" (9:61–62) melted down to "sacrificial butter" (9:64). Since the author is in this sense "made not begotten" (3:45), to recall Stephen's striking conception of filiation, any author's "indentity" (*FW* 49:36) is mutable, multiple, and provisional, not eternal, undiminished, or authoritative. In *Finnegans Wake,* the idea of author as Allfather is mocked in a comic lament: "If you were only there to explain the meaning, best of men" (*FW* 28:10–11).

To write, it seems, is not only to be consecrated as "The Holy Writer" (14:872) or god of one's creation, but to be desecrated, like Philip Beaufoy, whose *Titbits* story Bloom admires and besmirches. Beaufoy's end as comic butt is metaphorically shared with his betters, including Shakespeare, which helps explain that enigmatic vision in the Circean mirror: "*(Stephen and Bloom gaze in the mirror. The face of William Shakespeare, beardless, appears there, rigid in facial paralysis, crowned by the reflection of the reindeer antlered hatrack in the hall.)*" (15:3821–24). Lo, the mighty Bard, stripped of his lion's mane, trapped in Stephen's caricature; Shakespeare's words indicate how far he has fallen: "*(in dignified ventriloquy)* 'Tis the loud laugh bespeaks the vacant mind. *(to Bloom)* Thou thoughtest as how thou wastest invisible. Gaze. *(He crows with a black capon's laugh)* Iagogo! How my Oldfellow chokit his Thursdaymornun. Iagogogo!" (15:3826–29).[44] Dependent like Stephen (and

---

[43]Ibid., 270.

[44]Harry Blamires finds in this passage "a characteristic power and intensity," while William York Tindall, another proponent of life-affirming comedy in the novel, merely notes that "the artist seems cuckold as well as deceiver." Do we

everyone else) on "borrowed words,"[45] literature's greatest voice is reduced to demeaning "ventriloquy," quoting Goldsmith—the anachronism underscoring the indignity. "Thou thoughtest as how thou wastest invisible," a feeble imitation of Elizabethan English ("wastest"!), exposes Bloom's desire not to be seen in the red-light district, but I don't know how a capon would crow, nor why Shakespeare does so now, especially after saying what he did about "the loud laugh." Iago may be mentioned because Bloom has been watching Marion and Blazes make the beast with two backs; "chokit" suggests, dimly, what Othello did to Desdemona. But Oldfellow (Father?) is obscure, as is Thursdaymornun—unless it is somehow pointed toward Stephen's birthday.[46] For a recognition scene it is highly disorienting, and leaves Bloom as lost as we are; his reaction to the speech is, "When will I hear the joke?" (15:3831). Are we not invited to conclude that the joke is on Shakespeare and the notion of authorial perpetuity and power? If such is Shakespeare's fate, so, too, is it Joyce's own, and every author's, viewed always through a glass darkly, never face to face. "This is my awethorrorty" (*FW* 516:18–19).

The "awethorrorty" of the "Holy Writer"—like every other idealized concept in this "mocking mirror" (2:159), *Ulysses*—is parodied, uncrowned, degraded. Near the end of "Scylla and Charybdis," we glimpse "the constant readers' room. In the readers' book Cashel Boyle O'Connor Fitzmaurice Tisdall Farrell parafes his polysyllables" (9:1115–16). Farrell is that preeminently jocoserious figure, an author, comically, futilely, affixing his signature to guarantee

---

detect in their reticence some puzzlement? See Harry Blamires, *The Bloomsday Book,* 199, and William York Tindall, *A Reader's Guide to James Joyce* (New York: Farrar, Straus & Giroux, 1959), 212.

[45]Implicit in Joyce's instruction to his translator Valery Larbaud that "the fewer quotation marks the better. . . . S.D.'s mind is full *like everyone else's* of borrowed words" (*L* 1:263, my emphasis) is the premise that discourse is, as Stephen says of Shakespeare, "always turned elsewhere, backwards" (9:472). Stephen, though striving to be univocal, shares with Shakespeare, Joyce, and everyone else the penchant for "borrowed words." Buck, that flamboyant "original," opens the novel by quoting the Celebrant's opening phrase of the Mass, which is itself a phrase from *Psalms* 43:4. The question, it appears, is not whether one will ever be original, but what attitude one takes toward indebtedness.

[46]Gabler's revised text changes "Thursdaymomum" to "Thursdaymornun," which eliminates the promising connection with Stephen's "Mum."

his authorship. *Ulysses* is the epitomal "readers' book" because it so provocatively and richly illustrates Barthes's definition of a text: "not a line of words releasing a single 'theological' meaning (the 'message' of the Author-God) but a multi-dimensional space in which a variety of writings . . . blend and clash."[47] In such a text, the author's identity proliferates continually, so that he bears many names, like Cashel Boyle O'Connor Fitzmaurice Tisdall Farrell—or no name, appearing with "*the featureless face of the Nameless One*" (15:1144). *Ulysses* is persistently self-reflexive, not only because it abounds in autobiographical allusions and jests, or, as recent critics have stressed, because it constantly reveals its own origins and composition and suggests means of interpretation, but because so many of its figures are funhouse versions of authors. Writing, or more sublimely, to be an author, is of course Stephen's calling and Bloom's daydream; in addition, numerous figures besides Farrell have a touch of the artist and are associated with authorship: Deasy flourishing classical allusions and wishing "to be printed and read" (2:398), J. J. O'Molloy spewing florid rhetoric and bearing the author's initials, Mulligan reciting his parodies and travesties, Joe Hynes casually collecting and garbling information for Paddy Dignam's obituary, Gerty constantly sensing that "there was a story behind it" (13:337), and many others.

D. B. Murphy, for example, may be understood as a parodic projection of the author,[48] and thus a purveyor of folly. On Murphy's chest is tattooed an anchor, "the figure 16 and a young man's sideface looking frowningly rather" (16:675–76). Like Stephen, who cites the mole on his chest as evidence of his enduring identity (9:378–80), Murphy reveals hints of his kinship with Joyce, writing his sixteenth episode about two characters separated by sixteen years, who meet on June 16. The frowning youth with the Greek name is the Stephen whom Joyce has left behind and to whom he has returned—the self, changed but continuous, that Stephen foresees in the mole passage from "Scylla and Charybdis": "So in the future . . . I may see myself as I sit here now but by reflection from

---

[47]Roland Barthes, "The Death of the Author," in *Image–Music–Text,* 146.

[48]This seems to be a favorite point of recent critics. See James H. Maddox, *Joyce's "Ulysses" and The Assault upon Character,* 160, John Gordon, *James Joyce's Metamorphoses,* 114, and Brook Thomas, *A Book of Many Happy Returns,* 136.

that which then I shall be." What Stephen in "Scylla" can not yet envision is the ironic detachment with which he will see himself, nor the comic proliferation of selves by which Joyce can enter so many clowns and fools—though that too is prophesied: "He has hidden his own name, a fair name . . . in the plays, a super here, a clown there" (9:921–22). Murphy is one of those clowns, "the old stager" (16:930) with lots of tricks and fables. Of course, Murphy is no more likely than the Man in the Macintosh to unlock any ultimate mystery. Instead he hands us a postcard addressed to someone else, or to one of his aliases, on which "there was no message evidently" (16:490). Like everybody in "Eumaeus," his identity is "equivocal" (16:1630), but the preponderance of "the usual blarney" (16:1635) is no cause to banish Murphy, for it is no sin for a "doughty narrator" (16:570) to labor in his vocation.

Another doughty narrator and clowning performer whose appearance furthers the cause of folly is the inscrutable, obnoxious Virag. Virag's title is "basilicogrammate" (15:2304), pig-Greek for "royal literate" or "lord of language," suggesting a special relationship with the author; indeed, he enters holding a roll of parchment, which he invokes with mystical mumbo jumbo and regards as a sacred text: "This book tells you how to act with all descriptive particulars" (15:2393–94). Two quills project over his ears, so that he looks like both an ass and a writer;[49] accordingly he performs music hall patter and proclaims that law of folly, "From the sublime to the ridiculous is but a step" (15:2401–2). Half-clown, half-prophet, Virag, like Murphy, is a satiric caricature of an author, and a forerunner of Shem the Penman, who is treated with such savage hilarity in *Finnegans Wake*.

To be an author is to be a fool, in part because writing entails the need to be read and understood, unless the author wishes to "wastest invisible."[50] If it is true that the number of fools is infinite, what greater folly than to be dependent on foolish readers? Perhaps an author's fondest delusion, perpetuated by Stephen in his Shakespeare lecture, is the hope of perfect communion, or "consubstan-

[49]Cf. "the sufferant pen of our jocosus inkerman militant of the reed behind the ear" (*FW* 433:8–9).

[50]What originally struck me as a deliberately inept Elizabethan version of the past tense of the verb "to be" is also a canny pun on "waste," suggesting folly's premium on excess, throwaways, and bodily waste.

tiality" between writer and reader, "the son of his soul" (9:171).[51] In a lucid, playful interval, even Stephen spoofs the possibility of such ideal union: "When one reads these strange pages of one long gone one feels that one is at one with one who once . . . " (3:144– 46). Oneness, unity, wholeness, integrity, identity are folly's great adversaries and, in comic works, its victims. As at a circus, where the spectator may be dragged off by the clowns, a comic text such as *Ulysses* draws the reader willy-nilly into its topsy-turvy world, for to read this book, as to write it, is to play the fool. Readers of *Ulysses* are regularly fooled, and if we deny that we are fools, we make ourselves the easiest target. In this much at least, united in folly with the author, readers are "at one with one who once . . . "

Sometimes Stephen seems to be on the cusp of a comic revelation, the correlation between writing and folly, as when, checking Sargent's sums at Deasy's school, he meditates cryptically: "Across the page the symbols moved in grave morrice, in the mummery of their letters, wearing quaint caps of squares and cubes . . . Imps of fancy of the Moors. Gone too from the world, Averroes and Moses Maimonides, dark men in mien and movement, flashing in their mocking mirrors the obscure soul of the world, a darkness shining in brightness which brightness could not comprehend" (2:155– 60). Evidently Stephen senses an affinity between himself and these "dark men" whose compositions are "mocking mirrors." If the Biblical allusion captures Stephen's self-aggrandizement and grandiose conception of writing, it also suggests the handy-dandy of a comic gospel: what the world ordinarily perceives as darkness may be the brightness it cannot yet comprehend. Yet there is a further implication, a Joycean boomerang: whatever its grave intent, any writing, even transcribing algebraic signs, becomes "mummery"[52] or playacting, its symbols "imps of fancy." (Imps are notorious for disobeying orders.) Stephen is trembling on the verge of this jocoserious recognition, a way of seeing himself and his world that might become Joyce's habitual cross-eyed vision, the perception that sublime and ridiculous are of a piece.

An apparent connection between Stephen as author and Bloom as

[51]Cf. the Arian heresy, "the consubstantiality of the Son with the Father" (1:658). Truly Stephen has, as Harry Levin remarks, lost his faith but kept his categories.

[52]Buck had called Stephen a "lovely mummer" (1:97).

reader is also a teasing allegory of the author-reader relationship. After composing his poem in "Proteus," Stephen wonders, "Who ever anywhere will read these written words?" (3:414–15). Hundreds of pages later, Bloom walks the same beach and picks up a scrap of paper. "Never know what you find" (13:1249), he muses. In his role as holy fool, he echoes the New Testament: "Bread cast on the waters" (13:1251). This small coincidence seems to be another comic indicator, justifying a rough faith that individuals might unite, and things that fall may rise. Earlier in the book, I have speculated that we might justly entertain expectations of substantial intercourse between Stephen and Bloom: the 1920 Linati scheme in fact designates the "Nostos" episodes as "the fusion of Bloom and Stephen,"[53] with no hint that such a union might be parodied into oblivion.

So a reassuring and perfectly plausible answer to Stephen's question, "Who ever anywhere will read these written words?" (3: 414–15) is "Bloom." Arguably some revelation is at hand. After all, the richly elaborated-upon correspondences between the two of them sometimes move beyond empirical likelihoods into quasi-mystical possibilities. As a rule of thumb (and a source of infinite pleasure for Joyceans), almost nothing in *Ulysses* is truly lost; in this sense at least, Joyce's world resembles a traditional comic novel or a Shakespearean romance, in which uncles return from Australia[54] and abandoned babies are reunited with their parents. But *Ulysses* is not *David Copperfield* or *Joseph Andrews,* and the frustrated or inadequate force of confluence is one of its comic patterns. Regrettably, I think the more likely answer to Stephen's question is, "Noman." Notice, too, that when Bloom picks up that piece of paper, whatever it is, he "brought it near his eyes and peered. Letter? No. Can't read. Better go" (13:1247). The process of writing and reading is often stymied, part of Joyce's more skeptical comedy of communication in this blooming, buzzing confusion. Sometimes we merely "suppose there's some connection" (13:1014). The trick is all the more sly because only a careful reader, keenly watching details in quest of Joycean patterns and implications—"Fool someone else, not me" (15:3477)—would be fooled. "See the wheeze?" (7:591).

[53]Michael Groden cites this in *"Ulysses" in Progress,* 35.

[54]David Lodge manages a delightful variation on this venerable comic convention in *Nice Work.*

In a jocoserious world, a throwaway can always be a potential revelation or means of connection. One of Joyce's great followers, Donald Barthelme, regards collage as "the central principle of all art in the twentieth century." The preponderance of stuff in *Ulysses* makes it what Barthelme would call an "anxious object, which does not know whether it's a work of art or a pile of junk."[55] Should one regard Bloom's momentary misreading of the throwaway, "Bloo . . . Me? No. Blood of the Lamb" (8:8–9), as an inspired misprision? Reading, as we see from Bloom's little moment as the "blood of the lamb," is inherently comical, always tempting us to magnify the minuscule—except that in *Ulysses,* the trivial and the momentous are often the same. Bloom casually discards the throwaway, but "it's always flowing in a stream . . . which in the stream of life we trace. Because life is a stream" (8:94–95). A text differs from life because a narrative such as *Ulysses* encourages us to trace more carefully; in life, we would be very unlikely to see that scrap a second time, and the writing on the paper would be less likely to have such resonance—for the throwaway heralds in the person of Dr. John Alexander Dowie the coming of Elijah, the prophet foreshadowed by Malachi in the last book of the Old Testament. Its various manifestations can be construed as meaningless juxtaposition, comic incongruity, satiric deterioration, or prophetic omen.

It is typical of Joyce the "Archjoker" (12:559) to draw his reader into the web of folly, especially in ways that provide misleading hope. The remarkable coincidence in the bookstalls, cited earlier, is another example of a trap cunningly set for fools like us—that is, readers concerned enough to ferret out minute connections and educated enough to recognize somewhat arcane sources. That Bloom apparently picks up a volume of Aristotle, and Stephen the Pentateuch, seems to be a striking instance of what I've called "magnetic influence," foreshadowing more complete entry into each other's consciousness. But, as Daniel R. Schwarz notes, each has only

---

[55]The concept of an "anxious object" is Harold Rosenberg's, and is cited by Barthelme in Joe David Bellamy, *The New Fiction* (Urbana: University of Illinois Press, 1974), 51–52. Joyce as a maker of collage is like Old Monks, the printer: "Queer lot of stuff he must have put through his hands in his time: obituary notices, pubs' ads, speeches, divorce suits, found drowned" (7:197–99).

discovered "an apocryphal version of the other's focus [giving] . . . a false sign that Stephen and Bloom are on a converging course,"[56] for Bloom is actually perusing a compendium of medical horror stories, *Aristotle's Masterpiece Completed,* while Stephen is thumbing through some specious handbook blending Jewish mysticism, folklore, and superstition. I agree with Schwarz that "by debunking the substance of the particular parallax, Joyce shows the reader the danger to his or her sense-making of being overly eager for parallels,"[57] though I'd add that the book Stephen peruses reflects quite satisfactorily Bloom's blurred "focus." What Bloom knows about Judaism wouldn't stuff a gnat.

These supposed connections fool us into hoping for and expecting more from the protagonists and their impending union. Once we are disabused, the signs may signify exactly the opposite: a fortuitous connection now appears gratuitous, and foreshadows the inability of Bloom and Stephen to become "Blephen Stoom" (17:549). Comically incomplete communion between reader and text, mirroring the frustration of the characters, is often characteristic of comedy. To a disconcerting degree, the reader of comedy is always on shaky ground. He is there, after all, to be fooled, like a member of the congregation addressed by the Imam in an old fable of folly. "Do you know what I have come to tell you?" asks the priest. "No," answers the congregation. "No more do I," replies the priest, and he leaves. The next week he asks, "Do you know what I have come to tell you?" "Yes," respond the people. "Then you do not need me to tell you," he says, and leaves. The third week he repeats his question, and the people are confused. Some say yes, others no. "Then those of you who know tell those who do not," says the Imam, and he leaves.

Like this holy fool, the comic writer catches us in folly wherever we are. Humor depends upon the reversal of expectations, including the anticipation of folly, so that the biggest fool is he who denies that he is a fool. Still we are bound to be puzzled and chagrined by clowning gestures like that of Robert Burton in *The Anatomy of Melancholy:* "Say at a word, are they fools? I refer it to you, though you be likewise fools and madmen yourselves, and I as mad to ask

[56]Schwarz, *Reading Joyce's "Ulysses,"* 160.
[57]Ibid., 161.

the question."[58] The paradox that comedy requires a reader wise enough to play the fool is obvious in books such as *Tristram Shandy,* which would not be funny unless a lot of us blandly accepted fictive conventions, such as the proper location of an acknowledgement or consecutive pagination. Yet even relatively conservative, stable comic works such as *Tom Jones* require a reader willing to be fooled, by the omissions and false leads regarding Tom's origins, for example. Those who resist Fielding's blandishments, manipulations, and condescension are summarily lumped with critics and other cretins. As a result, Fielding's reader may wish to be part of the game yet feel wary or edgy, like the child playing tickle-monster with Daddy.

Readers of comedy, like members of the Imam's congregation, are likely to feel such wariness and harbor ambivalence about the position in which they are placed.[59] Virginia Woolf was not merely revealing her humorlessness when she criticized *Ulysses* on the grounds that "a first-rate writer . . . respects writing too much to be tricky."[60] Joyce has been blessed and cursed with some brilliantly resisting readers, who object to what I regard as fundamental comic strategies. Robert M. Adams, in his still-indispensable study, demonstrates the impossibility of systematically separating "the surfaces from the symbols," the stuff of Dublin life "from the things which represent abstract concepts of special import to the patterning of the novel." Assiduous reading and extensive research convince Adams that "the meaningless is deeply interwoven with the meaningful in the texture" of *Ulysses.* There is no "standard of relevance . . . [we are] at the whim of a symbol-monger," and risk "the distraction (not to say humiliation) of appreciating flyspecks and pursuing the accidents of our own astigmatism."[61]

Adams very sensibly resists being fooled—a fate I consider synonymous with reading *Ulysses,* where one reader's cocoa is another reader's godfood, and my lightning bolts may be your lightning bugs. He is surely right that Joyce often relinquishes authoritative

[58]Robert Burton, *The Anatomy of Melancholy,* ed. Floyd Dell and Paul Jordan-Smith (New York: Tudor, 1927), 59.

[59]The adversarial quality of the comedian's encounter with the audience is reflected in the colloquial expression for a successful performance, "I knocked 'em dead," and conversely for a dismal response, as in George Burns's tag line, "I died in Altoona."

[60]Virginia Woolf, *A Writer's Diary,* 56.

[61]Adams, *Surface and Symbol,* xvii, 245, 85.

control of implications. Most of Joyce's note-sheets for *Ulysses,* he says, "consist of small free-association patterns . . . and phrases and words which were ultimately scattered freely through the book . . . [to enable it] to grow and seek its attachments as it would." Joyce "allowed the book to grow, in large part, by a process of accretion and cross-patching, which involved a huge ragbag of miscellaneous words and phrases . . . [with] no distinct tendency for the novel as a whole."[62] Exactly: Joyce's "spatchcocked" (9:991)[63] composition and "proliferent continuance" (14:15) are comic techniques by which Rabelais, Sterne, and Joyce "keep it up" (11:871, etc.) and unsettle the hash. So deep-rooted is Adams's objection to Joycean flotsam and jetsam, such as the "miscellaneous, heterogenous character" of lists,[64] that he repeats the legendary story[65] of the nearly blind Joyce dictating to Beckett, when their labors were interrupted by a knock at the door. Joyce's "Come in" was duly recorded by the intent Beckett, and at the end of the day when the manuscript was read back, the author decided to leave the gratuitous phrase as a monument to chance. To my knowledge, no one has ever found that extraneous phrase in *Finnegans Wake,* though the anecdote deserves to endure for dramatizing Joyce's comic conviction (or faith in folly). Bloom is a figure of the fooling writer when, answering Martha Clifford, he pretends for Richie Goulding's sake to be composing an advertisement.

Joycean readers become fools because it is impossible to avoid over-reading and misreading. Since the novel proves to be "a goldseam of inexhaustible ore" (17:1753), we are always digging for gold—or fool's gold. Throughout the early episodes, we can not assume that any throwaway is incidental. In *Ulysses,* pieces fit together wonderfully, constantly; repeated readings persuade every reader that countless connections lie hidden, so that we must always remember Stephen's question, "does it mean something perhaps" (3:497). In a book so massively, magnificently determined, it is

[62]Ibid., 146, 40.

[63]"Spatchcocked" is one of my favorite small examples of Joycean self-reflexivity. It appears in "Scylla and Charybdis," where it sounds authentically Elizabethan, but it is actually a relatively recent coinage, meaning "to insert, interpolate, or sandwich. . . . To add to, or modify by interpolation" (*OED*), which nicely defines an element of joyicity.

[64]Adams, *Surface and Symbol,* 40.

[65]Ibid., 246; also told by Ellmann, 649.

natural and necessary to read "Sherlockholmesing" (16:831). "There might be other answers lying there," Bloom thinks. "Like to answer them all" (8:323). Of course wondering if and what something means isn't the same as determining the answer, or even knowing whether we are asking the right questions, for many Joycean signs are delivered not by an "Author-God" but by an avowed trickster, who once said that he would rather play the rednosed comedian than the bluejawed tragedian (Ellmann 696). The burlesque of narrative reliability, implicit in *Ulysses,* becomes explicit in *Finnegans Wake*: "Thus the unfacts, did we possess them, are too imprecisely few to warrant our certitude, the evidencegivers by legpoll too untrustworthily irreperible . . . " (*FW* 57:16–18).

When *Ulysses* isn't fooling us, it is likely to be setting us up—as, for example, with that piece of paper or the plumes of smoke, which were noticed early on by both Stephen (1:575) and Bloom (4:238, 271), and were spotted numerous times throughout the day. They recall scriptural and classical signs of hope: homesick Odysseus imagines smoke wafting from Ithaca, and O'Molloy mentions "the pillar of the cloud by day" (7:865–66) followed by the wandering Israelites.[66] By "Lestrygonians," when "a puffball of smoke plumed up" (8:44), its reappearances in *Ulysses* seem significant. An anagogic interpretation is first offered, appropriately, by Stephen, that assiduous reader of all signatures, when he characterizes the star that supposedly rose at Shakespeare's birth as "a star by night . . . A pillar of the cloud by day" (9:944). When Stephen perceives "two plumes of smoke ascended, pluming . . . " (9:1219) and thinks of lines from *Cymbeline,* the smoke seems to be a genuine celestial phenomenon, signifying the impending "Blooming" of Stephen or his union with Bloom.

The second half of *Ulysses* continually returns to the plume of smoke, but whether as a providential sign or an ironic trace remains unclear. When "Long John Fanning blew a plume of smoke from his lips" (10:1013), we might recall Freud's reminder that sometimes a banana is just a banana, for the very material that once provided some ground for hope, a hint that Stephen and Bloom exist under a watchful eye, is now "by legpoll too untrustworthily

[66]Joyce used the image in this sense, citing an aria from *Madama Butterfly,* in a letter to Nora (*SL* 173).

irreperible." Indeed, the next time the smoke is mentioned (by Bloom at the end of "Nausicaa"), it is absent: "Liverpool boat long gone. Not even the smoke" (13:1274–75). By this point in *Ulysses,* I'd argue, its symbolic implications have dissipated. In "Circe," "the pillar of the cloud appears" (15:1407), rendered farcical in a characteristically berserk Circean procession, along with bird fanciers, masseurs, and plumbing contractors. By the time the Erin's King sails, its *"broadening plume of coalsmoke"* (15:3383) is merely a distant, dingy remnant of its original form, for which Bello provides the sarcastic epitaph: "*(laughs loudly)* Holy smoke!" (15:2866). Though in "Ithaca," the "reapparition of a matutinal cloud (perceived by both from two different points of observation, Sandycove and Dublin) at first no bigger than a woman's hand" (17:40–42) links the protagonists, it is also "Ithaca" that demonstrates that *any* two things can be compared and connected. Even when an Ithacan "celestial sign" is explicitly designated and "observed" (17:1210), it conceals as much as it reveals, leaving us, like Martha Clifford, imploring the author to "please tell me what is the meaning" (8:328). Accordingly, the last appearance of "a pillar of cloud by day" (17:1999) is part of an extended joke in response to the Ithacan question, "Under what guidance, following what signs?" (17:1991). The assault upon "awethorrorty" and the jocoserious dissemination of possibilities teaches us to distrust "guidance," and to consider all "signs" as manifestations of innumerable possibilities devised by the Ithacan encyclopedist or other readers.

Though the plumes and pillars of smoke are vivid examples of a jocoserious "legpoll," first raising, then parodying, optimistic expectations, many other motifs illustrate the pattern, including the homerule sun rising, the advertisement proclaiming the coming of Elijah, and the victory of *Throwaway.* Like the monarchs who consulted the oracle at Delphi, fixed on their fates and deceived by ambiguity, Joycean characters (and readers) who incessantly scan the skies or cast lots, confident that they can correctly decipher the signs, are often mistaken. The comically imperceptive Bantam Lyons might be taken as Joyce's spoof of a reader, constantly on the watch for clues, signs, harbingers—yet the object lesson cuts the opposite way, because Joycean bricolage may indeed contain signs: *Throwaway* wins the Gold Cup. The reader assigning values to a plume of smoke or a throwaway may become foolish Bantom Lyons, but the reader ignoring apparent ephemera may miss an essential pattern or a hot tip. The very fecundity of *Ulysses* implies that some providential design still prevails.

Every time we return to this "constant readers'" (9:1115) book, we are puzzled by some mysterious little crumb, and wonder if it means something perhaps. One never knows whether the crumbs are "the daily bread of experience" or "the radiant body of everliving life" (*P* 221). While Stephen Dedalus imagined himself "a priest of eternal imagination" (*P* 221), the older author saw himself more like Shakespeare's clowning rogue Autolycus, that "snapper-up of unregarded trifles." "Chance," said Joyce, "furnishes me with what I need" (Ellmann 661). Always attracted to coincidence, he avidly searched for the kind of patterns that Jung termed "synchronicity." Superstitious enough to publish his books on birthdays, fascinated by the possibility that chance might reveal fate, Joyce bequeathes to Bloom such speculations. Having thought about Parnell, Bloom spies the great man's brother: "Now that's a coincidence" (8:502–3). Just then, Bloom spots A. E., mentioned by Lizzie Twigg in her letter, with a young woman. "Now that's really a coincidence: second time. Coming events cast their shadows before" (8:525–26). The Aristotelian distinction between "substantial or accidental," accepted by young Joyce in his meditations on comedy,[67] becomes another dichotomy rejected by *Ulysses*.

Any commentary illustrates ways in which readers of *Ulysses* are fooled into either ignoring the significant or exaggerating the trivial: what Tindall famously makes of cocoa, for instance, resembles Kinbote's commentary in *Pale Fire*. Still, it is understandable that we take signs for wonders. Before Bloom urinates in the yard, a "visible luminous sign" (17:1171) attracts his gaze, and he brings to Stephen's attention this "visible splendid sign" (17:1178). When an encyclopedist begins using such terms, are we not encouraged to seek anagogic meanings? The "celestial sign" (17:1210) of the zodiac observed simultaneously by both certainly seems to comment favorably on their conjunction. Whether Tindall's interpretation of

---

[67]"Aesthetics," in *CW* 144. The Yale manuscript adds the phrase "general or fortuitous." Susanne K. Langer says, "Destiny in the guise of Fortune is the fabric of comedy." See "The Argument of Comedy," in Langer, *Feeling and Form,* 331.

the cocoa, or an astrological reading of the heavens, is substantial or accidental, crucial or absurd, seems undecidable.

In the book of folly, something that we might call the Wetherup Principle usually obtains. Wetherup, it may be recalled, appears as a passing reference in the newspaper office, yet is commemorated in the headline "WHAT WETHERUP SAID" (7:337). Whoever concocts those headlines has foolishly moved Wetherup from the margin to the center, illustrating the tendency to generalize and summarize misleadingly or inadequately, or to discover omens in throwaways. There, remarks the fool, but for the grace of God go I.

This encyclopedia of humor comprises competing strains of skepticism, mockery, cheerfulness, and hope, so that whatever attitude Wetherup or a critic strikes can be only partially valid. *Ulysses* begins with, and in the person of Buck Mulligan gives powerful voice to, the first two elements—which in "Sirens" become dominant, only to be surprisingly subsumed at the end. Yet, despite Buck's flamboyant leveling, the first several episodes carefully cultivate hope for the protagonists. Hence the pattern of the novel parodies *Paradise Lost* in more than its comic treatment of fall and recovery; where Milton's reader reenacts the fall by succumbing to the blandishments of sin, Joyce's reader is fooled into naive optimism. The second half of *Ulysses* is a massive critique of hope and a series of pratfalls for the optimist, which is why the figure of an author is so often a "*sinister figure*" (15:212) like Virag. Elaborating on the "affirmative" aspects of *Ulysses* too exclusively, as is often done quite vaguely, and always placing too much emphasis on Molly's final word, is misleading. The comedy of *Ulysses* contains, yet is in continuing tension with, its satiric impulses, so that both "Gracehoper[s]" (*FW* 414:21) and "tragic jester[s]" (*FW* 171:15) will always find succor. As with all other Joycean dichotomies, they are apparent contraries meeting in unstable equilibrium.

Frequently Joyce has his cake and eats it too, which is why he cherishes oxymora such as jocoserious and seriocomic. On the one hand, Joyce remains adamantly neutral, content to let his characters and readers struggle to impose theories or interpretations upon his creation; he is only paring his fingernails while we are busily, foolishly misreading signs and contriving meanings. On the other hand, it seems equally arguable that the beginning of the book quite systematically nourishes optimism later to be discounted or rendered dubious. *Ulysses* giveth with one hand and taketh away with the other, constantly teasing and tempting readers. Antic Joyce is a fabulous mountebank, like Mercurial Malachi, who provides a name for a game very popular among readers of *Ulysses*: "—*Eureka!* Buck Mulligan cried. *Eureka!*" (9:1053). The purpose of *Eureka* is to discover a minute hint or network of connections revealing the novel's ultimate meaning. We readers are incessantly playing *Eureka,* for reading *Ulysses,* like writing it, is a kind of heroic folly, teasing us with hints of connections that may or may not exist. Sorting Shakespeare, Bloom discovers the painfully comic truth that "in spite of careful and repeated reading of certain classical passages, aided by a glossary, he had derived imperfect conviction from the text, the answers not bearing in all points" (17:389–91).

Bloom is, in many ways, a model reader, constantly reading or remembering things that he has read. He rereads almost everything—newspapers, letters, even advertisements—with that Bloomian blend of appreciation and skepticism: "Kind of stuff you read: in the track of the sun," he muses. "Sunburst on the titlepage. He smiled, pleasing himself. . . . Ikey touch that: homerule sun rising up in the northeast" (4:99–104). Enthroned at stool, he is the jocoserious "royal reader" (13:1066–67), taking pleasure, paying attention, reviewing, "yielding but resisting" (4:506–7)—in that sublimely oxymoronic description of both reading and excreting.

Yielding but resisting, instead of *always meeting oneself.* To Stephen, for whom the stakes are much higher, the process of reading must yield pure union, in which "the royal reader" achieves atonement or "consubstantiality" with "the holy author." Bloom as reader is energetically there, but subordinate, identifying with the writer without consecrating him. Almost naturally, Bloom is inspired to imagine his own sketch and to mark a comic communion with the author by using "Matcham's Masterpiece" as toilet paper. As reader, Bloom seeks merger yet remains distinct, like the constituent elements in an oxymoron. In reading, Bloom sympathizes, identifies, yet allows otherness, difference, that "indentity of undiscernibles" (*FW* 49:36–50:01).

No writer has ever perceived more vividly than Joyce the inevitable connections between reading, writing, and folly, nor so adamantly maintained the potential value of folly. Alternately speaking of himself with self-aggrandizement and self-mockery, Joyce grandly described his work as comparable to "the mystery of the mass" (S.

Joyce 103–4) designed "to keep the professors busy for centuries arguing over what I meant," or addressed to the ideal reader suffering from ideal insomnia, but would self-deprecatingly deny that his books require intensive analysis: "No, no, it's meant to make you laugh" (Ellmann 521, 703). Even in his fame, when he might well have been forgiven for playing the sage, he preferred to play the clown, with quips anticipating Woody Allen.[68] Posing for a portrait, he instructed the artist, "Never mind my soul. Just be sure you have my tie right." Ultimately he came to see himself as "the foolish author of a wise book" (Ellmann 566, 471).[69]

Joyce discovered his image everywhere, both because he was megalomaniacal and because he carried that favorite fool's prop, the mirror. The foolish standing of the author in his text, now merely one of many voices, "no longer privileged and paternal, the locus of genuine truth, but rather ludic" (in the Barthes phrase cited earlier) is illustrated by Joyce's penchant for leaving a "poor trait of the artless" (*FW* 114:32) and for ridiculing himself or his autobiographical surrogates, or both. As the writer's vocation is both holy and farcical, self-mockery becomes a condition, if not a definition of artistry—and a significant degree of Joyce's imaginative energy goes into making himself "a motley to the view."[70] When Bloom thinks of Molly urinating, "Chamber music. Could make a kind of pun on that" (11:979–80), Joyce sarcastically recalls the title of his poems. Bloom's masturbation mocks Stephen's epiphany on the beach in *Portrait*. Nearly everything in "Circe" reiterates or reflects material from previous episodes, in a loony farce. The figure of Shem in *Finnegans Wake* savagely satirizes the life of James Joyce, writing "over every square inch of the only foolscap available, his own body . . . reflecting from his own individual person life unlivable, transaccidentated through the slow fires of consciousness into a dividual chaos, perilous, potent, common to allflesh, human only, mortal" (*FW* 185:35–86:6). *Ulysses* itself becomes that "usylessly unreadable Blue Book of Eccles" (*FW* 179:26–27), because folly is the way of allflesh—including the author and readers of this chaffering chronicle.

[68]E.g., "No, I don't believe in the afterlife, but I am taking a change of underwear."

[69]The later remark refers specifically to *Finnegans Wake*.

[70]Cf. Shakespeare's Sonnet 110: "Alas, 'tis true I have gone here and there / And made myself a motley to the view. . . . "

Bibliography

Adams, Robert M. *James Joyce: Common Sense and Beyond.* New York: Random House, 1966.

——. *Surface and Symbol: The Consistency of James Joyce's "Ulysses."* 1962. New York: Oxford University Press, 1967.

——. "Hades." In *James Joyce's "Ulysses": Critical Essays.* Ed. Clive Hart and David Hayman, 91–114. Berkeley: University of California Press, 1974.

Alter, Robert. *Henry Fielding and the Nature of the Novel.* Cambridge: Harvard University Press, 1968.

——. *Partial Magic: The Novel as a Self-Conscious Genre.* Berkeley: University of California Press, 1975.

Attridge, Derek, and Daniel Ferrer, eds. *Post-Structuralist Joyce.* Cambridge: Cambridge University Press, 1984.

Auden, W. H. *The Dyer's Hand and Other Essays.* 1953. New York: Random House, 1962.

Auerbach, Erich. *Mimesis: The Representation of Reality in Western Literature.* Trans. Willard Trask. 1953. Garden City, N.Y.: Doubleday Anchor, 1957.

Baker, Stuart E. *Georges Feydeau and the Aesthetics of Farce.* Ann Arbor, Mich.: UMI Research Press, 1981.

Bakhtin, Mikhail. *Rabelais and His World.* Trans. Hélène Iswolsky. 1968. Bloomington: Indiana University Press, 1984.

——. *The Dialogic Imagination: Four Essays.* Ed. Michael Holquist. Trans. Caryl Emerson and Michael Holquist. 1981. Austin: University of Texas Press, 1985.

——. *Problems of Dostoevsky's Politics.* Ed. and trans. Caryl Emerson. Minneapolis: University of Minnesota Press, 1984.

Barber, C. L. *Shakespeare's Festive Comedy: A Study of Dramatic Form and*

215

its Relation to Social Custom. Princeton: Princeton University Press, 1959.

Barthes, Roland. *S/Z.* Trans. Richard Miller. New York: Hill and Wang, 1974.

——. *The Pleasure of the Text.* Trans. Richard Miller. New York: Hill and Wang, 1975.

——. *Image–Music–Text.* Trans. Stephen Heath. New York: Hill and Wang, 1977.

——. "From Work to Text." In *Textual Strategies: Perspectives in Post-Structuralist Criticism.* Ed. Josué V. Harari. Ithaca: Cornell University Press, 1979.

Baudelaire, Charles. *The Essence of Laughter and Other Essays, Journals, and Letters.* Ed. Peter Quennell. New York: Meridian Books, 1956.

Beckett, Samuel. *More Pricks Than Kicks.* 1934. New York: Grove Press, 1970.

——. *Watt.* 1953. New York: Grove Press, 1959.

——. *Three Novels by Samuel Beckett: "Molloy," "Malone Dies," "The Unnamable."* 1955. New York: Grove Press, 1965.

Beja, Maurice, ed., with Phillip Herring, Maurice Harmon, and David Norris. *James Joyce: The Centennial Symposium.* Urbana: University of Illinois Press, 1986.

——, and Shari Benstock, eds. *Coping with Joyce: Essays from the Copenhagen Symposium.* Columbus: Ohio State University Press, 1989.

Bellamy, Joe David. *New Fiction: Interviews with Innovative American Writers.* Urbana: University of Illinois Press, 1974.

Benstock, Bernard. "L. Boom as Dreamer of *Finnegans Wake.*" *PMLA* 82 (1967): 91–97.

——. "Telemachus." In *James Joyce's "Ulysses": Critical Essays.* Ed. Clive Hart and David Hayman, 1–16. Berkeley: University of California Press, 1974.

——. *James Joyce.* New York: Frederick Ungar, 1985.

——, ed. *The Seventh of Joyce.* Bloomington: Indiana University Press, 1982.

——, ed. *James Joyce: The Augmented Ninth. Proceedings of the Ninth International James Joyce Symposium, Frankfurt, 1984.* Syracuse: Syracuse University Press, 1988.

Benstock, Shari, and Bernard Benstock. *Who's He When He's at Home: A James Joyce Directory.* Urbana: University of Illinois Press, 1980.

Bentley, Eric. "The Psychology of Farce," in *"Let's Get a Divorce" and Other Plays.* New York: Hill and Wang, 1958.

——. *The Life of the Drama.* New York: Atheneum, 1964.

Bergson, Henri. "Laughter." In *Comedy.* Ed. Wylie Sypher. Garden City, N.Y.: Doubleday Anchor, 1956.

Bermel, Albert. *Farce: A History from Aristophanes to Woody Allen.* New York: Simon and Schuster, 1982.

Bersani, Leo. "Against *Ulysses.*" *Raritan* 8 (1988): 1–32.

Blamires, Harry T. *The Bloomsday Book: A Guide through Joyce's "Ulysses."* 1966. London: Methuen, 1983.

Blistein, Elmer M. *Comedy in Action.* Durham, N.C.: Duke University Press, 1964.

Bloom, Harold, ed. *James Joyce: Modern Critical Views.* New York: Chelsea House, 1986.

Bogel, Fredric V. *Literature and Insubstantiality in Later Eighteenth-Century England.* Princeton: Princeton University Press, 1984.

Booth, Wayne C. *The Rhetoric of Fiction.* Chicago: University of Chicago Press, 1961.

Bowen, Zack. *"Ulysses" as a Comic Novel.* Syracuse: Syracuse University Press, 1989.

——, and James F. Carens, eds. *A Companion to Joyce Studies.* Westport, Conn.: Greenwood Press, 1984.

Briggs, Austin. "Chaplin and Joyce." Paper delivered at James Joyce Conference, June 1989.

Brivic, Sheldon. *Joyce the Creator.* Madison: University of Wisconsin Press, 1985.

Brower, Reuben Arthur. *Alexander Pope: The Poetry of Allusion.* Oxford: Clarendon Press, 1959.

Bruns, Gerald L. "Eumaeus." In *James Joyce's "Ulysses": Critical Essays.* Ed. Clive Hart and David Hayman, 363–83. Berkeley: University of California Press, 1974.

Budgen, Frank. "James Joyce." In *James Joyce: Two Decades of Criticism.* Ed. Seon Givens. New York: Vanguard Press, 1948.

——. *James Joyce and the Making of "Ulysses."* 1934. Bloomington: Indiana University Press, 1960.

Burgess, Anthony. *Re Joyce.* 1965. New York: Ballantine Books, 1966.

Burton, Robert. *The Anatomy of Melancholy.* Ed. Floyd Dell and Paul Jordan-Smith. New York: Tudor, 1927.

Busby, Olive Mary. *Studies in the Development of the Fool in Elizabethan Drama.* London: Oxford University Press, 1923.

Byron, Lord. *Don Juan.* Ed. Leslie A. Marchand. Boston: Houghton Mifflin, 1958.

Caillois, Roger. *Man, Play, and Games.* Trans. Meyer Barash. London: Thames and Hudson, 1962.

Caputi, Anthony. *Buffo: The Genius of Vulgar Comedy.* Detroit: Wayne State University Press, 1978.

Card, James van Dyck. *An Anatomy of "Penelope."* Cranbury, N.J.: Associated University Presses, 1984.

Cervantes, *The Adventures of Don Quixote*. Trans. J. M. Cohen. Baltimore: Penguin Books, 1950.

Chambers, E. K. *The Medieval Stage*. London: Oxford University Press, 1903.

Charney, Maurice. *Comedy High and Low: An Introduction to the Experience of Comedy*. New York: Oxford University Press, 1978.

Cixous, Hélène. *The Exile of James Joyce*. Trans. Sally A. J. Purcell. New York: David Lewis, 1972.

Cohn, Alan M. "Joyce's Notes on the End of 'Oxen of the Sun.' " *James Joyce Quarterly* 4 (1967): 194–201.

Cook, Albert. *The Dark Voyage and the Golden Mean: A Philosophy of Comedy*. Cambridge: Harvard University Press, 1949.

Cope, Jackson I. "Sirens." In *James Joyce's "Ulysses": Critical Essays*. Ed. Clive Hart and David Hayman, 217–42. Berkeley: University of California Press, 1974.

Cornford, F. M. *The Origin of Attic Comedy*. Cambridge: Cambridge University Press, 1914.

Corrigan, Robert W., ed. *Comedy: Meaning and Form*. 1965. New York: Harper & Row, 1981.

Cox, Harvey. *The Feast of Fools: A Theological Essay on Festivity and Fantasy*. Cambridge: Harvard University Press, 1969.

Crews, Frederick. *The Pooh Perplex: A Freshman Casebook*. New York: E. P. Dutton, 1963.

Culler, Jonathan. *Ferdinand de Saussure*. Rev. ed. Ithaca: Cornell University Press, 1986.

——, ed. *On Puns: The Foundation of Letters*. New York: Basil Blackwell, 1988.

Danby, John F. "The Fool and Handy Dandy." In *Shakespeare's Doctrine of Nature: A Study of King Lear*. London: Faber & Faber, 1949.

Davis, Jessica Milner. *Farce*. London: Methuen, 1978.

de Almeida, Hermione. *Byron and Joyce through Homer: "Don Juan" and "Ulysses."* New York: Columbia University Press, 1981.

de Lauretis, Teresa. *Feminist Studies/Critical Studies*. Bloomington: Indiana University Press, 1986.

de Man, Paul. *Blindness and Insight: Essays in the Rhetoric of Contemporary Criticism*. New York: Oxford University Press, 1971.

Derrida, Jacques. "From Restricted to General Economy." In *Writing and Difference*. Trans. Alan Bass. Chicago: University of Chicago Press, 1978.

——. "Structure, Sign, and Play in the Discourse of the Human Sciences." In *Writing and Difference*.

Despot, Adriane L. "Some Principles of Clowning." *Massachusetts Review* 22 (1981): 661–78.

Donoghue, Denis. "Joyce and the Finite Order." *Sewanee Review* 68 (1960): 256–73.

——. *We Irish: Essays on Irish Literature and Society.* New York: Alfred A. Knopf, 1986.

Dowling, William C. *Language and Logos in Boswell's "Life of Johnson."* Princeton: Princeton University Press, 1981.

——. *Jameson, Althusser, Marx: An Introduction to "The Political Unconscious."* Ithaca: Cornell University Press, 1984.

Draper, J. W. "Falstaff, 'A Fool and Jester.'" *Modern Language Quarterly* 7 (1946): 453–62.

Ehrlich, Heyward, ed. *Light Rays: James Joyce and Modernism.* New York: New Horizon Press Publishers, 1984.

Elliott, Robert C. *The Power of Satire: Magic, Ritual, Art.* Princeton: Princeton University Press, 1960.

Ellmann, Richard. *James Joyce.* Oxford: Oxford University Press, 1959. Rev. 1982.

——. *Ulysses on the Liffey.* 2d ed., 1972. New York: Oxford University Press, 1973.

——. *The Consciousness of Joyce.* New York: Oxford University Press, 1977.

Empson, William. *The Structure of Complex Words.* New York: New Directions, 1951.

Enck, John J., Elizabeth T. Forter, and Alvin Whitley, eds. *The Comic in Theory and Practice.* Englewood Cliffs, N.J.: Prentice-Hall, 1960.

Epstein, E. L., ed. *A Star-Chamber Quiry: A James Joyce Centennial Volume 1882–1982.* New York: Methuen, 1982.

Erasmus, Desiderius. *The Praise of Folly.* Trans. Clarence H. Miller. New Haven: Yale University Press, 1979.

Ferry, Anne Davidson. *Milton and the Miltonic Dryden.* Cambridge: Harvard University Press, 1968.

Fielding, Henry. *Tom Jones.* Ed. Sheridan Baker. New York: W. W. Norton, 1973.

Foucault, Michel. "What Is an Author?" In *The Critical Tradition: Classic Texts and Contemporary Trends.* Ed. David H. Richter. New York: St. Martin's Press, 1989.

French, Marilyn. *The Book as World: James Joyce's "Ulysses."* Cambridge: Harvard University Press, 1976.

Freud, Sigmund. *Jokes and Their Relation to the Unconscious.* Ed. and trans. James Strachey, 1960. New York: W. W. Norton, 1963.

Frye, Northrop. *The Anatomy of Criticism: Four Essays.* Princeton: Princeton University Press, 1957.

Galligan, Edward L. *The Comic Vision in Literature.* Athens: University of Georgia Press, 1984.

Gifford, Don. *Joyce Annotated: Notes for "Dubliners" and "A Portrait of the Artist as a Young Man."* 1967. Berkeley: University of California Press, 1982.

——, and Robert J. Seidman. *"Ulysses" Annotated: Notes for James Joyce's "Ulysses."* Berkeley: University of California Press, 1988.

Gilbert, Stuart. *James Joyce's "Ulysses": A Study.* 2d ed., rev. New York: Vintage Books, 1952.

Gilliatt, Penelope. *Unholy Fools. Wits, Comics, Disturbers of the Peace: Film & Theatre.* New York: Viking Press, 1973.

Givens, Seon, ed. *James Joyce: Two Decades of Criticism.* New York: Vanguard Press, 1948.

Gogarty, Oliver St. John. *Intimations.* New York: Abelard Press, 1950.

Goldberg, S. L. *The Classical Temper: A Study of James Joyce's "Ulysses."* New York: Barnes & Noble, 1961.

Goldman, Arnold. *The Joyce Paradox: Form and Freedom in his Fiction.* London: Routledge & Kegan Paul, 1966.

Goldsmith, Robert H. *Wise Fools in Shakespeare.* Liverpool: Liverpool University Press, 1958.

Gordon, John. "The Multiple Journies of 'Oxen of the Sun,'" *ELH* 46 (1979): 158–72.

——. *James Joyce's Metamorphoses.* Totowa, N.J.: Barnes & Noble, 1981.

Groden, Michael. *"Ulysses" in Progress.* Princeton: Princeton University Press, 1977.

Gurewitch, Morton. *Comedy: The Irrational Vision.* Ithaca: Cornell University Press, 1975.

Harari, Josué V., ed. *Textual Strategies: Perspectives in Post-Structuralist Criticism.* Ithaca: Cornell University Press, 1979.

Hart, Clive. *James Joyce's "Ulysses."* Sydney, Australia: Sydney University Press, 1968.

——. "Wandering Rocks." In *James Joyce's "Ulysses": Critical Essays.* Ed. Clive Hart and David Hayman, 181–216. Berkeley: University of California Press, 1974.

——, and David Hayman, eds. *James Joyce's "Ulysses": Critical Essays.* Berkeley: University of California Press, 1974.

Hayman, David. "Forms of Folly in Joyce: A Study of Clowning in *Ulysses*." *ELH* 34 (1967): 260–83.

——. "Cyclops." In *James Joyce's "Ulysses": Critical Essays.* Ed. Clive Hart and David Hayman, 243–75. Berkeley: University of California Press, 1974.

——. "Joyce → Beckett/Joyce." In *The Seventh of Joyce.* Ed. Bernard Benstock. Bloomington: Indiana University Press, 1982.

——. *"Ulysses": The Mechanics of Meaning,* rev. ed. Madison: University of Wisconsin Press, 1982.

Heilman, Robert Bechtold. *The Ways of the World: Comedy and Society.* Seattle: University of Washington Press, 1978.

Herr, Cheryl. *Joyce's Anatomy of Culture.* Urbana: University of Illinois Press, 1986.

Herring, Phillip F. "The Bedsteadfastness of Molly Bloom." *Modern Fiction Studies* 15 (1969): 49–61.

——. *Joyce's Uncertainty Principle.* Princeton: Princeton University Press, 1987.

——, ed. *Joyce's Notes and Early Drafts for "Ulysses": Selections from the Buffalo Collection.* Charlottesville: University Press of Virginia, 1977.

Highet, Gilbert. *The Anatomy of Satire.* Princeton: Princeton University Press, 1962.

Homer. *The Odyssey.* Trans. Robert Fitzgerald. Garden City, N.Y.: Doubleday, 1961.

Hotson, Leslie. *Shakespeare's Motley.* London: Rupert Hart-Davis, 1952.

Huizinga, J. *Homo Ludens: A Study of the Play-Element in Culture.* London: Routledge & Kegan Paul, 1949.

Hume, David. *A Treatise of Human Nature.* Ed. L. A. Selby-Bigge, 1888. Oxford: Clarendon Press, 1967.

James, Henry. *The Portable Henry James.* Ed. Morton Dauwen Zabel. New York: Viking Press, 1951.

James, William. *The Principles of Psychology.* Chicago: Encyclopedia Britannica, 1952.

Jameson, Fredric. "Postmodernism and Consumer Society." In *The Anti-Aesthetic: Essays on Postmodern Culture.* Ed. Hal Foster. Port Townsend, Wash.: Bay Press, 1983.

Janusko, Robert. *The Sources and Structure of James Joyce's "Oxen."* Ann Arbor, Mich.: UMI Research Press, 1983.

Jenkins, Ron. "Vita: Dan Rice," *Harvard Magazine* (May–June 1981): 51.

Joyce, Stanislaus. *My Brother's Keeper: James Joyce's Early Years.* Ed. Richard Ellmann, 1958. New York: Viking Press, 1969.

Jung, C. G. *Four Archetypes: Mother/Rebirth/Spirit/Trickster.* Trans. R. F. C. Hull, 1959. Princeton: Princeton University Press, 1970.

Kain, Richard M. *Fabulous Voyager: A Study of James Joyce's "Ulysses."* New York: Viking Press, 1959.

Kaiser, Walter. *Praisers of Folly: Erasmus, Rabelais, Shakespeare.* Cambridge: Harvard University Press, 1963.

Kenner, Hugh. *Dublin's Joyce.* 1956. Boston: Beacon Press, 1962.

——. *The Stoic Comedians: Flaubert, Joyce, and Beckett.* Boston: Beacon Press, 1962.

——. "Circe." In *James Joyce's "Ulysses": Critical Essays.* Ed. Clive Hart and David Hayman, 341–62. Berkeley: University of California Press, 1974.

——. *Joyce's Voices.* Berkeley: University of California Press, 1978.

——. *"Ulysses."* London: George Allen and Unwin, 1980.

Kernan, Alvin B. *The Cankered Muse: Satire of the English Renaissance.* New Haven: Yale University Press, 1959.

——. *The Plot of Satire.* New Haven: Yale University Press, 1965.

Kerr, Walter. *Tragedy and Comedy.* New York: Simon and Schuster, 1967.

Kershner, R. B. *Joyce, Bakhtin, and Popular Literature: Chronicles of Disorder.* Chapel Hill: University of North Carolina Press, 1989.

Krause, David. *The Profane Book of Irish Comedy.* Ithaca: Cornell University Press, 1982.

Lacan, Jacques. *The Language of the Self: The Function of Language in Psychoanalysis.* Trans. Anthony Wilden. New York: Dell, 1975.

Lamb, Charles. "On the Artificial Comedy of the Last Century." In *The Works of Charles Lamb.* Philadelphia: Parry and McMillan, 1859.

Lang, Candace D. *Irony/Humor: Critical Paradigms.* Baltimore: Johns Hopkins University Press, 1988.

Langer, Susanne K. *Feeling and Form: A Theory of Art.* New York: Charles Scribner's Sons, 1953.

Lanham, Richard A. *"Tristram Shandy": The Games of Pleasure.* Berkeley: University of California Press, 1973.

Lauter, Paul, ed. *Theories of Comedy.* Garden City, N.Y.: Doubleday Anchor, 1964.

Lawrence, Karen. *The Odyssey of Style in "Ulysses."* Princeton: Princeton University Press, 1981.

Leavis, F. R. *The Great Tradition: George Eliot, Henry James, Joseph Conrad.* London: Chatto and Windus, 1955.

Leitch, Vincent B. *Deconstructive Criticism: An Advanced Introduction.* New York: Columbia University Press, 1983.

Levin, Harry. *James Joyce: A Critical Introduction.* 1941. Norfolk, Conn.: New Directions, 1960.

——. *Playboys and Killjoys: An Essay on the Theory and Practice of Comedy.* New York: Oxford University Press, 1987.

Lewis, C. S. *A Preface to "Paradise Lost."* New York: Oxford University Press, 1961.

Litz, A. Walton. *The Art of James Joyce: Method and Design in "Ulysses" and "Finnegans Wake."* London: Oxford University Press, 1964.

Locke, John. *An Essay concerning Human Understanding.* Ed. A. S. Pringle-Pattison. Oxford: Clarendon Press, 1924.

Lynch, William F. *Christ and Apollo: The Dimensions of the Literary Imagination.* New York: Sheed and Ward, 1960.

MacCabe, Colin. *James Joyce and the Revolution of the Word.* New York: Barnes & Noble, 1979.

——, ed. *James Joyce: New Perspectives.* Bloomington: Indiana University Press, 1982.

Mack, Maynard. "*Joseph Andrews* and *Pamela*." In *Fielding: A Collection of Critical Essays*. Ed. Ronald Paulson. Englewood Cliffs, N.J.: Prentice-Hall, 1962.

Maddox, Brenda. *Nora: The Real Life of Molly Bloom*. Boston: Houghton Mifflin, 1988.

Maddox, James H., Jr. *Joyce's "Ulysses" and the Assault upon Character*. New Brunswick, N.J.: Rutgers University Press, 1978.

——. "Mockery in *Ulysses*." In *Joyce's "Ulysses": The Larger Perspective*. Ed. Robert D. Newman and Weldon Thornton. Newark: University of Delaware Press, 1987.

Magalaner, Marvin, and Richard M. Kain, eds. *Joyce: The Man, the Work, the Reputation*. 1956; New York: Collier Books, 1962.

Mast, Gerald. *The Comic Mind: Comedy and the Movies*. Indianapolis: Bobbs-Merrill: 1973.

Mercanton, Jaques. "The Hours of James Joyce." Trans. Lloyd C. Parks. *Kenyon Review* 24 (1962): 700–732.

Mercier, Vivian. *The Irish Comic Tradition*. London: Oxford University Press, 1962.

Meredith, George. "An Essay on Comedy." In *Comedy*. Ed. Wylie Sypher. Garden City, N.Y.: Doubleday Anchor, 1956.

Milne, A. A. *Winnie-the-Pooh*. 1926. London: Methuen Children's Books, 1973.

Morse, J. Mitchell. *The Sympathetic Alien: James Joyce and Catholicism*. New York: New York University Press, 1959.

Nabokov, Vladimir. *Lectures on Literature*. Ed. Fredson Bowers. New York: Harcourt Brace Jovanovich, 1980.

Nadel, Ira B. *Joyce and the Jews: Culture and Texts*. Iowa City: University of Iowa Press, 1989.

Newman, Robert David. "*The Play's the Thing*": Circe *as Play-Time in* "*Ulysses*." Unpublished undergraduate thesis, Williams College, 1988.

Newman, Robert D., and Weldon Thornton, eds. *Joyce's "Ulysses": The Larger Perspective*. Newark: University of Delaware Press, 1987.

Nietzsche, Friedrich. *Thus Spoke Zarathustra*. Trans. R. J. Hollingdale. 1961. Baltimore: Penguin Books, 1964.

Noon, William T., S. J. *Joyce and Aquinas*. New Haven: Yale University Press, 1957.

Olsen, Elder. *The Theory of Comedy*. Bloomington: Indiana University Press, 1968.

Opie, Iona, and Peter Opie. *The Lore and Language of Schoolchildren*. Oxford: Clarendon Press, 1959.

Peake, C. H. *James Joyce: The Citizen and the Artist*. Stanford: Stanford University Press, 1977.

Plato. *Cratylus*. In *Great Books of the Western World: Plato*. Trans. Benjamin Jowett. Chicago: Encyclopedia Britannica, 1952.

Polhemus, Robert M. *Comic Faith: The Great Tradition from Austen to Joyce*. Chicago: University of Chicago Press, 1980.

Pope, Alexander. *Poetry and Prose of Alexander Pope*. Ed. Aubrey Williams. Boston: Houghton Mifflin, 1969.

Potts, L. J. *Comedy*. London: Hutchinson University Library, 1949.

Power, Arthur. *Conversations with James Joyce*. Ed. Clive Hart, 1974. Chicago: University of Chicago Press, 1982.

Rabelais, François. *Gargantua and Pantagruel*. Trans. Sir Thomas Urquhart and Peter Motteux. Chicago: Encyclopedia Britannica, 1952.

Raleigh, John Henry. *The Chronicle of Leopold and Molly Bloom: "Ulysses" as Narrative*. Berkeley: University of California Press, 1977.

Redfern, Walter. *Puns*. Oxford: Blackwell, 1984.

Restuccia, Frances. "Molly in Furs." *Novel* 18 (1985): 101–16.

——. *Joyce and the Law of the Father*. New Haven: Yale University Press, 1989.

——, and John Limon. "Wordplay: God and Pun in *Ulysses*." *James Joyce Quarterly* 21 (1984): 275–78.

Rice, Thomas Jackson. *James Joyce: A Guide to Research*. New York: Garland, 1982.

Riquelme, John Paul. *Teller and Tale in Joyce's Fiction: Oscillating Perspectives*. Baltimore: Johns Hopkins University Press, 1983.

Russo, Mary. "Female Grotesques: Carnival and Theory." In *Feminist Studies/Critical Studies*. Ed. Teresa de Lauretis. Bloomington: Indiana University Press, 1986.

Sabin, Margery. *The Dialect of the Tribe: Speech and Community in Modern Fiction*. New York: Oxford University Press, 1987.

Salomon, Roger. *Desperate Storytelling: Post-Romantic Elaborations of the Mock-Heroic Mode*. Athens: University of Georgia, 1987.

Santayana, George. "The Comic Mask." In *Comedy: Meaning and Form*. Ed. Robert W. Corrigan, 1965. New York: Harper & Row, 1981.

Schlossman, Beryl. *Joyce's Catholic Comedy of Language*. Madison: University of Wisconsin Press, 1985.

Schwarz, Daniel R. *Reading Joyce's "Ulysses."* New York: St. Martin's Press, 1987.

Scott, Bonnie Kime. "Introduction to Character and Contemporary Theory." In *James Joyce: The Augmented Ninth*. Proceedings of the Ninth International James Joyce Symposium, Frankfurt, 1984. Ed. Bernard Benstock. Syracuse: Syracuse University Press, 1988.

Seidel, Michael. *Epic Geography: James Joyce's "Ulysses."* Princeton: Princeton University Press, 1976.

——. *Satiric Inheritance: Rabelais to Swift*. Princeton: Princeton University Press, 1979.

——, and Edward Mendelson, eds. *Homer to Brecht: The European Epic and Dramatic Traditions*. New Haven: Yale University Press, 1977.

Senn, Fritz. *Joyce's Dislocutions: Essays on Reading as Translation.* Ed. John Paul Riquelme. Baltimore: Johns Hopkins University Press, 1984.

——, ed. *New Light on Joyce from the Dublin Symposium.* Bloomington: Indiana University Press, 1972.

Shakespeare, William. *The Complete Works of Shakespeare.* Rev. ed. Ed. Hardin Craig and David Bevington. Glenview, Ill.: Scott, Foresman, 1973.

Slights, William W. E. "The Incarnations of Comedy." *University of Toronto Quarterly* 51 (1981): 13–27.

Smith, Barbara Herrnstein. *Poetic Closure: A Study of How Poems End.* Chicago: University of Chicago Press, 1968.

Snead, James A. "Some Prefatory Remarks on Character in Joyce." In *James Joyce: The Augmented Ninth. Proceedings of the Ninth International James Joyce Symposium, Frankfurt, 1984.* Ed. Bernard Benstock. Syracuse: Syracuse University Press, 1988.

Staley, Thomas F., ed. *"Ulysses": Fifty Years.* Bloomington: Indiana University Press, 1974.

——. *An Annotated Critical Bibliography of James Joyce.* Brighton: Harvester Wheatsheaf, 1989.

Stanford, W. B. *The Ulysses Theme: A Study in the Adaptability of a Traditional Hero.* Oxford: Blackwell, 1954.

Staples, Hugh B., ed. *The Ireland of Sir Jonah Barrington: Selections from His Personal Sketches.* Seattle: University of Washington Press, 1967.

Steppe, Wolfhard and Hans Walter Gabler. *A Handlist to James Joyce's "Ulysses": A Complete Alphabetical Index to the Critical Reading Text.* New York: Garland, 1985.

Sterne, Laurence. *Tristram Shandy.* Ed. Howard Anderson. New York: W. W. Norton, 1980.

Stonehill, Brian. *The Self-Conscious Novel: Artifice in Fiction from Joyce to Pynchon.* Philadelphia: University of Pennsylvania Press, 1988.

Sultan, Stanley. *The Argument of "Ulysses."* Columbus: Ohio State University Press, 1964.

Swift, Jonathan. *"Gulliver's Travels" and Other Writings.* Ed. Louis Landa. Boston: Houghton Mifflin, 1960.

Sypher, Wylie, ed. *Comedy.* Garden City, N.Y.: Doubleday Anchor, 1956.

Taylor, Mark C. *Erring: A Postmodern Anthology.* Chicago: University of Chicago Press, 1987.

Theoharis, Theoharis Constantine. *Joyce's "Ulysses": An Anatomy of the Soul.* Chapel Hill: University of North Carolina Press, 1988.

Thickstun, William R. *Visionary Closure in the Modern Novel.* Houndmills, Eng.: Macmillan, 1988.

Thomas, Brook. *James Joyce's "Ulysses": A Book of Many Happy Returns.* Baton Rouge: Louisiana State University Press, 1982.

Thompson, Ewa. *Understanding Russia: The Holy Fool in Russian Culture.* London: University Press of America, 1987.

Tindall, William York. *A Reader's Guide to James Joyce.* New York: Farrar, Straus & Giroux, 1959.

Torrance, Robert. *The Comic Hero.* Cambridge: Harvard University Press, 1978.

van Doren, Carl, and Mark van Doren. *American and British Literature Since 1890.* Chautauqua, N.Y.: Chautauqua Press, 1926.

Weber, Samuel. "It." *Glyph: Johns Hopkins Textual Studies No. 4.* Baltimore: Johns Hopkins University Press, 1978.

Weinstein, Philip M. *The Semantics of Desire: Changing Models of Identity from Dickens to Joyce.* Princeton: Princeton University Press, 1984.

Welsford, Enid. *The Fool: His Social and Literary History.* London: Faber & Faber, 1935.

Whitman, Cedric H. *Aristophanes and the Comic Hero.* Cambridge: Harvard University Press, 1964.

Willeford, William. *The Fool and His Sceptre: A Study in Clowns and Jesters and Their Audience.* Evanston, Ill.: Northwestern University Press, 1969.

Williams, Paul V. A., ed. *The Fool and the Trickster: Studies in Honor of Enid Welsford.* Totowa, N.J.: Rowman and Littlefield, 1979.

Wilson, Edmund. *Axel's Castle: A Study in the Imaginative Literature of 1870–1930.* New York: Charles Scribner's Sons, 1931.

Wimsatt, W. K., ed. *The Idea of Comedy: Essays in Prose and Verse.* Englewood Cliffs, N.J.: Prentice-Hall, 1969.

Index